ASSIGNMENT: OSWALD

ASSIGNMENT: OSWALD

JAMES P. HOSTY, JR.
WITH THOMAS HOSTY

ARCADE PUBLISHING ★ NEW YORK

FIRST EDITION

Library of Congress Cataloging-in-Publication Data

Hosty, James P.
    Assignment: Oswald / by James P. Hosty, Jr. with Thomas C. Hosty.
      p.   cm.
    Includes index.
    ISBN 1-55970-311-3
    1. Kennedy, John F. (John Fitzgerald), 1917–1963—Assassination.
  2. Oswald, Lee Harvey.   I. Hosty, Thomas C. II. Title.
  E842.9.H67 1995
  364.1'524—dc20   95-14109

Published in the United States by Arcade Publishing, Inc., New York
Distributed by Little, Brown and Company

10 9 8 7 6 5 4 3 2 1

Designed by API

BP

PRINTED IN THE UNITED STATES OF AMERICA

To my wife, Janet,
without whom I could never have made it.

And to my children, grandchildren, and their children.
This book is for them.

Acknowledgments

Through the years many people have offered me their support and encouraged me to write this book. I wish I could thank them all, but at the risk of omitting some I would like to thank the following:

First, Bill Reese, a good friend who helped me focus on the events surrounding the assassination and put it all down on paper. Bill and I drank quite a few cups of coffee together a few years back, sorting through the vast amounts of information and organizing it into written form.

When my wife, Janet, and I began researching and compiling material and photographs for the book, we inevitably had to turn to the National Archives. We were very impressed by the Archives staff, especially Steve Tilley and Roland Bordley, whose help was precious.

My literary agent, Charles Schollenberger, one of my most enthusiastic supporters, provided valuable assistance in the early stages of the project. My publisher and editor, Dick Seaver, helped clarify and shape the massive material into a meaningful whole.

In September 1993, my son Tom, a lawyer, began to work with me on my original draft manuscript. Over the next year and a half we structured the work, checked and rechecked facts against my memory, trying to recreate, accurately and honestly, the dramatic and tragic times in which I was so intimately, and painfully, involved. For most of this work I was home in Florida while Tom was in Kansas City, Kansas. It was a logistical challenge, but we got it done.

I also thank my other children for all of their support and encouragement over the years to write this book.

Finally, I wish to acknowledge my greatest supporter and confidante, my wife, Janet. I did not travel this journey alone. Janet was with me every step of the way. I know that I would never have survived the ordeal following the assassination without her.

James P. Hosty, Jr.

Part I:

The Cover-up

1

Monday, November 18, 1963

TIME: 8:15 A.M.

"Okay, let's have some quiet and get started."

Gordon Shanklin, the Special Agent in Charge (SAC) of the Dallas–Fort Worth FBI office, had called an impromptu meeting of the forty or so agents present in the squad room. I closed a file I was reviewing at my desk and gave my attention to Shanklin.

"As you probably all read over the weekend in the *Dallas Morning News,* President Kennedy and Vice President Johnson will be coming to Dallas this Friday," Shanklin said. "Frankly, this is news to me, and I confess it ticks me off to learn it first in the press. I just called headquarters and was told the *Morning News* story was the first they knew of Kennedy's visit to Dallas, too. It seems everyone was told except the FBI. I have to assume the FBI liaison with the White House isn't what it used to be.

"At any rate, I called this meeting to remind you all of a few things. As you probably know, the Secret Service wants no help from the FBI in protecting the president or his party. Vince Drain here" — Shanklin nodded toward Drain, who was sitting across from me at another desk — "has already made contact with the Dallas Secret Service office, but was politely rebuffed. He was told in so many words they needed no help from us.

"Because of all this, we're going to do everything by the book, which means if any of you know of any threats of any kind to the president or vice president, refer them to the Secret Service. I want you all to err on the side of caution. If you have any doubt about whether to report a piece of information to the Secret Service, go ahead and report it. Let's be on the safe side. . . . Okay, that's it. Let's get back to work."

Like Shanklin, I had read the *Morning News* article on Saturday morning. Kennedy was making a swing through Texas this week — to Houston, San Antonio, Fort Worth, Dallas, and Austin — to shore up political support in this key state; the next presidential election was less than a year away. Despite getting trounced in Dallas in 1960 by a 2-to-1 margin by Vice President Richard Nixon, Kennedy, with Johnson's help and influence, had been able to win Texas and its twenty-four electoral votes. But that was three years ago. Since then, Dallas had become more openly and vocally anti-Kennedy. Kennedy supporters like me were careful not to voice our pro-Kennedy opinions in this city, for fear of being verbally attacked and ridiculed.

In the 1920s, when the Ku Klux Klan played a dominant role in the city, Dallas had been known as the "Hate Capital" of the country. Back then the Klan's national leader, the Imperial Wizard Hiram Wesley Evans, had come from Dallas. These days it was apparent to me that a large and obnoxious segment of the Dallas population was seemingly cut from the same cloth as its 1920s predecessors. Because of this strong radical right wing, Dallas was considered enemy territory for Kennedy.

My caseload in the four-man counter-intelligence squad in the Dallas office was dominated by right-wingers. I spent much of my time tracking the movements and actions of both Klan members and members of former U.S. Army General Edwin Walker's radical militia group, known as the Minutemen. Convinced there was a Communist hiding under every bush, the Minutemen had been quietly and discreetly arming themselves with an impressive arsenal of weapons. In the eyes of the Minutemen, Kennedy was at best a dupe of the Communists, at worst a Communist collaborator.

Among the agents this morning, everyone was discussing this right-wing element in Dallas and the fact that in all likelihood a threat to the president would come from that direction. We were all painfully aware of United Nations Ambassador Adlai Stevenson's visit to Dallas just two weeks before, on October 31. During his visit, right-wingers had heckled and jeered him following his speech to a local group. One woman actually took her placard, which had a venomous anti-Stevenson epithet scrawled on it, and hit him over the head. We in

4

the Dallas FBI were worried that Kennedy might be subjected to a similar display of hate from the right wing. He and his party knew they might be in for a less than friendly reception, and I understood that several of his key advisors had warned him not to come. As a Kennedy supporter, I had to admire the man's guts.

Tuesday, November 19, 1963

TIME: 7:00 P.M.

After finishing supper with my family, I sat down to read the evening newspaper, the *Dallas Times Herald*. There under the bold headline, KENNEDY VIRTUALLY INVITES CUBAN COUP, the story began: "President Kennedy all but invited the Cuban people to overthrow Fidel Castro's Communist regime and promised prompt U.S. aid if they do. Kennedy's encouragement of a Cuban coup was contained in a major foreign policy speech before the Inter-American Press Association Monday in Miami Beach, Florida. The President said it would be a happy day if the Castro government is ousted."

I was struck less by Kennedy's provocative comments than the fact that the *Times Herald* had run this wire story in the first place. Printing this article was a radical departure from the newspaper's editorial policy of portraying Kennedy as weak when dealing with Communists. I later brought this up with a *Times Herald* reporter, Norman Phillips, and he told me that the *Times Herald* editors had decided after the Stevenson attack that the right-wing element in Dallas was getting out of control. The editors therefore decided to start being more even-handed when reporting news about Kennedy.

The newspaper also reported that on Friday, when Kennedy visited Dallas, he would speak at a luncheon to be held at the Dallas Trade Mart just off the Stemmons Freeway, also known as I-35E. The article also included a general description of the route Kennedy would take through downtown Dallas.

Thursday, November 21, 1963

TIME: 9:00 P.M.

Reading the *Times Herald* that evening, I noted a front-page diagram of the parade route Kennedy would take at noon the next day through downtown Dallas. I examined it casually, only interested in where I could position myself so that I could catch a glimpse of the president. At no time during my examination of the diagram was I interested in determining whether or not any of my case subjects might be located along the motorcade route. It had been beaten into me, by both the Secret Service and the FBI, that this was not of my concern.

My only obligation for the security of the president's trip was to report to the Secret Service anyone who had made a threat against the president or the vice president. In fact, just the day before, I had hand-delivered a report on one possible threat. I had picked up information from a source that a local Klan member had remarked that his group would have a "little reception" for Kennedy when he visited Dallas. I wrote up this information in a one-page report, including a physical description of the Klan member, and attached his photograph to the report. I walked the few blocks over to the Secret Service's office in the U.S. Courthouse and handed the report to one of their agents. I later learned that the Secret Service briefly interviewed the man, but took no action to detain him or monitor his whereabouts on Friday during the president's visit.

Friday, November 22, 1963
TIME: 7:30 A.M.

Four other FBI agents lived in the same general neighborhood in Dallas as I did, and we had a car pool arrangement. As usual, we left the car in the parking lot two blocks from our office and headed down the street toward the back entrance to the Santa Fe Building. As we were walking, I spotted a flyer on the sidewalk with Kennedy's picture on it. I picked it up; the flyer had two photos of Kennedy's face in mug shot fashion, one full face, one profile. It said: "John F. Kennedy, Wanted for Treason," for caving in to the Communists.

I showed it to the other four agents, and we all felt that, however tasteless, this was just another typical product of the Dallas radical right. I carried it into the office with me, and after I had signed in, showed it to my supervisor, Ken Howe.

"Ken, look at this flyer. Can you believe this stuff?"

"Yeah, Nat Pinkston found another one on the street," Howe replied.

"Well, I'm going to run this over to the Secret Service, just to be on the safe side," I said. After I picked up Pinkston's copy, I headed over to the U.S. Courthouse.

When I walked into the Secret Service office I was amazed at how quiet it was. Kennedy had arrived in Fort Worth late last night and was speaking at a breakfast there this morning. He was due to arrive in Dallas in just a few hours. Despite this, the Secret Service didn't appear to be at all fazed by the visit. It was just business as usual, I guess. I asked to speak to one of the four agents permanently stationed in the Dallas office. Agent Mike Howard stepped out front to deal with me.

"I'm Jim Hosty with the Dallas FBI," I said, pulling out my FBI credentials. Howard looked familiar to me, but we had never been formally introduced.

"What can I do for you, Jim?" Howard asked.

"When I was walking into the office this morning I found this 'Wanted for Treason' flyer. I thought you guys might want a copy, just in case," I said.

"We've received several copies of this already," Howard said. "Don't worry, Jim, it's no problem, we're on top of it." He made me feel I was imposing.

As he turned to leave I said, "I monitor a lot of subversive right-wingers over at the FBI. Is there anything you and the Secret Service want to know?"

"No." He shook his head. "Listen, Jim, we've got everything under control, okay?" With that he turned and walked away.

That exchange between Howard and me captured the essence of the relationship between the Secret Service and the FBI. The Secret Service, jealous of its mandate to protect the president, regarded the FBI as a threat to its jurisdiction. Only a few months before, the Secret Service had helped kill a bill before Congress that would have given secondary jurisdiction to the FBI, with the Secret Service retaining primary jurisdiction. The Secret Service had been adamant that it did not want the FBI to have *any* involvement in the president's security. With that bill dead in Congress, that was exactly how things stood on November 22.

Even though the Secret Service had roughly 300 agents nationwide, compared to the FBI's over 7,000, it wanted no assistance in protecting the president other than information indicating direct threats to his safety. Clearly, the Secret Service felt that if the FBI was given any chance, it would try bureaucratically to swallow up the Secret Service.

I hurried back to my office, not wanting to be late for the weekly Friday morning meeting between all the agents and Shanklin. I arrived at the squad room just in time. As I sat down, Shanklin was calling the meeting to order.

"Okay men, before I begin our meeting, I just want to remind all of you to report to the Secret Service any information you may have indicating any threats to the president or his party."

I made one last mental review of my caseload: nothing more to report. None of my case subjects gave any indication that they were a threat to the president or his party, which included Governor Connally. I sat back and listened to Shanklin review the other business.

After the meeting broke up, I picked up some papers concerning a case I would be working on that morning and headed for the door. On the way, I checked my mail slot and found a case transfer order. The form order, with a fill-in-the-blank format, indicated that as of this date a routine counter-espionage case on one Lee Oswald was now officially mine again. Earlier in the summer, the case had been transferred out of my hands to the New Orleans FBI office, when it was determined that Oswald was living there. Now it had been confirmed that he was living in Dallas, and the case had been transferred back to me. With the transfer order was a New Orleans mug shot, dated August 9, 1963. There were no reports attached to the transfer order, much to my annoyance. I made a mental note to contact New Orleans about the oversight, since I needed whatever background they had collected.

I put the Oswald transfer back in my mail slot and walked out the door. I was on my way to meet Agent Ed Coyle of the Army intelligence unit and Agent Jack Ellsworth of the Bureau of Alcohol, Tobacco, and Firearms (ATF) at Ellsworth's office on a case we were all involved in, concerning the theft of Army weapons, which we had learned were to be fenced to a subversive right-wing group.

TIME: 11:45 A.M.

Having wrapped up our meeting, Coyle and I were about to leave Ellsworth's office when Coyle commented that he was hoping to see the presidential motorcade as it passed through downtown. "You know," said Coyle, "it's a damn shame, but by federal law the Army can't provide any assistance to the Secret Service."

"I think the FBI should have a more active role, too," I said, "but as you guys know, the Secret Service wouldn't have it."

"That's nothing," Ellsworth said. "The ATF is part of the Treasury Department, just like the Secret Service, but they want absolutely no help from us either."

"Dallas being the right-wing hotbed it is," I said, "I sure hope the Secret Service knows what it's doing."

Both Coyle and Ellsworth nodded in agreement.

Coyle and I left Ellsworth's office and walked the few blocks to Main and Field streets, where Coyle's office was located. We both hoped to catch a glimpse of the president, who was due to pass down Main Street any minute.

Coyle and I nudged our way to the front row, standing right at the curb. As it was the noon hour, thousands of downtown workers were spilling out into the streets on their lunch hour. Coyle and I waited patiently as more and more people crowded along the motorcade route. I noticed very few police and no barricades along the street.

At about 12:20, I spotted the motorcade as it moved down Main Street at about 10 miles per hour. I noticed several cars in the motorcade and saw one large convertible with several men in coats and ties standing on the running boards. They had to be Secret Service agents. Surrounding the motorcade were several police motorcycle escorts. Clearly this convertible's passengers were being closely guarded, so I assumed the president was in that car.

As the guarded convertible approached, Coyle and I both strained to see its passengers. Then it passed right in front of us, just fifteen feet away. Then Coyle pounded his fist into my shoulder. "There he is! There's Kennedy!" Coyle yelled, pointing frantically at a convertible that had already passed us, just in front of the closely guarded one. I swung my attention to where he was pointing, but all I could see was the back of the president's head. He was waving to the crowd. His wife, Jackie, was seated next to him, wearing a bright pink outfit.

I was disappointed not to have seen the president better, but I was more shocked to see how poorly protected he was. He was in an open convertible with no Secret Service agents or police anywhere near him. Why the hell had they stationed the Secret Service on the vehicle behind him? Well, I guess it was none of my business, I remember thinking.

After the motorcade had passed, I asked Coyle if he wanted to join me for lunch.

"No thanks," he said. "I brought a sack lunch today."

"Okay. Talk to you later," I said, and walked back up the street to Murphy and Main, where one of my favorite restaurants, the Oriental Café, was located.

Since it was Friday and I was Catholic, I ordered a cheese sandwich and coffee. I was also trying to lose a little weight, per FBI policy.

As I sat at the counter waiting for my sandwich, I sipped my coffee and thought again how strange it was that the Secret Service had positioned its agents on the car *behind* the president's. Later, the president's chief of staff, Kenny O'Donnell, said that when the president began his motorcade trip through downtown Dallas, he and his staff had a choice: the president could have had various security measures put in place, including a bubble top and Secret Service agents riding on his convertible's running boards, or he could have had minimum measures to make his appearance in the motorcade as open and visible as possible for this politically motivated swing through Dallas. In the end, O'Donnell said, they chose politics over security.

2

Friday, November 22, 1963

TIME: 12:30 P.M.

BOOM . . . . . *click-click* . . . . *BOOM* . . . . . *click-click* . . . . *BOOM* . . . . *click-click*

TIME: 12:38 P.M.

"They've shot the president!"

The cheese sandwich in my mouth turned to sawdust. I pushed back from the counter where I was eating lunch, and swallowed hard. I choked out, "What did you say?"

"Oh, my God, they've shot the president!" the waitress said. She was sobbing and her body was shaking.

Without thinking, I took out my wallet, put a couple of dollars on the diner counter, and pushed my way out the front door onto the sidewalk at the intersection of Murphy and Main. Down the street, Joe Loeffler, one of two supervisors in my field office, came barreling out of the Unique Restaurant and started sprinting across the street to the office. Loeffler, a strange, anguished look on his face, saw me and yelled across the street, "Hosty, go back and get in a car. Turn your radio on and stand by for orders!"

I started running to the garage where the Bureau cars were parked. I had to cut my way through the lunch-hour minglers, sprinting as fast as I could in my wing-tips and brown suit, standard dress for an FBI field agent. I made it back to my assigned Bureau car, a blue '60 Plymouth, parked in the garage down the street from the Bureau's office. My chest heaving, my face dripping sweat, I fumbled to unlock the car door, slammed my bulky six-foot frame inside, and flipped on the radio. The airwaves were jammed with agents trying to make reports. One agent reported, "There are confirmed reports that the president has been shot, possibly one shot to the head."

Holy Christ! This couldn't be true. It couldn't be. My mind was racing, but I couldn't get my thoughts in order. I strained to listen to the other reports on the radio. Then one thought suddenly pushed its way to the front of my mind: Janet.

My wife was at the Dallas Trade Mart, where President Kennedy had been scheduled to deliver a luncheon address. She was one of the volunteer hostesses who was to serve the president and his party. Just last night we had received a report at the FBI field office that a radical right-wing group named the Indignant White Citizens Council was going to demonstrate at the Trade Mart while the president was there. The report said that violence was possible. Anger was now starting to boil within me. I was squeezing the steering wheel. I was dead sure one of those radicals had pulled a gun and shot at the president. To hell with orders. I had to see Janet: she might be caught up in the gunfire. Besides, the Dallas police at the Trade Mart probably would need all the help they could get.

I started the engine, slammed the car in gear, and yanked the wheel, pulling out into the flow of traffic. With traffic crawling along, I thought, This isn't going to cut. I grabbed the "cherry," the rotating red light beacon and, reaching out my car window, stuck it on my roof with its suction cup. I flipped on the cherry, hit the switch to my siren, and started weaving through traffic. My head was starting to throb and I was praying that everything would be all right, that both Janet and the president would be all right.

Wheeling into the parking lot at the Trade Mart, I nearly collided with an outbound car. As I jolted to a stop, I looked around and saw people streaming out of the Trade Mart building. Yet the place was surprisingly calm, almost eerie. No one was talking; a few people were quietly sobbing to themselves. That's strange, I thought; if Kennedy had been shot here, this place would be a madhouse. My initial conviction had to be wrong.

No matter. I climbed out of my car and started to push my way into the Trade Mart, yelling, "Coming through! FBI! Coming through!"

I kept thinking to myself, I have to find Janet, I have to make sure everything is all right. A woman wearing a navy blue apron who looked like one of the volunteer hostesses brushed by me. I put my hand on her elbow and asked her if she knew Janet Hosty. She told me to go back to the right corner, toward the doors to the kitchen where most of the hostesses were. I looked, and pushed and shoved my way to the corner she was talking about. My tension melted. There at a long table, standing with several other aproned women, was my wife.

I rushed up to her and grabbed both her arms. "Are you all right?"

"Yes, yes," she answered. "Oh, Jim, I just can't believe it. Who would do this? *Who?*"

I wasn't really listening to Janet. Relief was still rolling over me, wave after wave. My world was intact. Everything was going to be all right.

"Listen, can you get home all right?" I asked.

"Yes, I drove the car today."

"Okay, I have to go." I held her and looked into her eyes for a beat. Her normally soft hazel eyes were starting to brim with tears, and her usual sunny disposition had been replaced with fear-ridden anxiety. At that instant, I realized that I wasn't going to be seeing Janet for a while. I put my hand on her cheek, and kissed her. Then I turned and left.

On the way out I looked around for a couple of Dallas police officers I knew would be here, but couldn't spot them. When I got back into the car, I idled the engine and listened again to the radio. Kyle Clark, the Assistant Special Agent in Charge (ASAC) of the Dallas field office, was on. He was saying that Kennedy was at Parkland Hospital and was critically injured. Clark wanted four agents at Parkland immediately; once there, they were to stand by for further orders. I grabbed my radio mike. "This is 7392. I'm less than a mile from the hospital. I will respond to Parkland immediately and stand by for further orders."

Whipping the car around, I flipped the switches to the siren and the cherry. In less than two minutes I was at Parkland. What I saw was mass chaos: police cruisers everywhere, mobs of people swirling around the entrance to the emergency room. I whooped my siren a couple of times to clear people out of my way, and pulled up as close as I could to the emergency room door, which was about thirty yards away. I saw the president's bloody limousine and my heart sank even further. An agent reported on the radio, "There are several reports that shots were fired at Dealey Plaza, from a building on Elm Street, the Texas School Book Depository."

I decided to report my location. "This is 7392. I'm standing by at Parkland. What do I do next?"

"7392! Get back to the office, and get here fast!" It was Ken Howe, my immediate supervisor, and I could feel an edge to his voice. Not good. Something is going on. I could feel my head starting to throb again. My heart was beating madly. Sweat was drenching my shirt. I said to myself, Stay calm. Stay calm and focused.

I flipped on the siren and cherry again and was off. As I sped back to the office on the expressway, I passed Dealey Plaza and noticed a commotion down on Elm and Houston. There was a fire truck with its hook and ladder extended to the roof of a seven-story building on Elm Street. Police were surrounding the building. I said to myself, So that's where the bastard shot from, the roof of that building.

As I sped on, Bob Barrett, another agent, came on the radio to report that a police officer had been shot and killed in the Oak Cliff area, and he was on his way to check it out. Now that's odd, I thought. A cop is shot in broad daylight in a nice, quiet neighborhood. There has to be a connection between Kennedy and this officer's shooting. I screeched to a halt at the rear entrance to the FBI field office, and bolted from the car, through the door, and into the first elevator.

TIME: 1:25 P.M.

I hurried into the squad room on the eleventh floor and scanned the room for Howe. His eyes locked on mine. "Hosty! Come here," he said. He was holding a sheaf of papers; it looked like a Bureau teletype report. Though Howe was in his fifties, he didn't have a single gray hair, which made him look considerably younger than his years. While I had trouble keeping my weight down, Howe was a trim and fit six-foot man.

"What's up?" I asked.

"This teletype just came in from Washington," Howe said. "Headquarters is assuming that right-wingers are responsible for the attack on the president. They want all offices to identify, locate, and bring in all right-wing extremists, and they want it done right now. Hosty, you're the only agent in this office who monitors these damn right-wingers, so get moving on this, and for God's sake let's find this guy."

Normally rock-steady, Howe was now visibly close to the edge. I could understand: my head was pounding, and my heart was beating so damn hard it felt as if someone were clamping my chest, making it hard for me to breathe. My hands were clenching and unclenching. I couldn't believe this whole thing. The President of the United States gunned down less than six blocks from where I was eating lunch. And now FBI headquarters was asking me to help find the president's assassin, whom they assumed was from the right-wing groups I'd been monitoring.

Just then one of the other agents announced that Vince Drain, one of our agents at Parkland, was calling to report that the president had just died from the gunshot wounds to his head.

No one in the squad room spoke. It was as if we were all frozen, or turned to stone. Then, slowly, a few secretaries started to sob quietly. I had to fight back my own tears. I felt like screaming, running the hell out of this building. What in God's name was going on? As an Irish-American, Catholic Democrat, I felt a kinship to Kennedy. It was as if a relative had just been viciously murdered. I struggled — God did I struggle — to fight back the tears.

I took a deep breath, and with all the strength I could summon, pushed myself back into my work. The right-wing extremists — I had to get cracking as Howe had ordered.

In my head, I knew all the extremists under my watch. From memory, I culled a list of people to bring in for questioning, then checked our files to verify my mental list.

I called the Dallas police station, intelligence unit, and asked to speak to Detective Sergeant H. M. Hart, my counterpart, and the second in command at the intelligence unit there.

"Sergeant, Jim Hosty here. I'm compiling a list of radical right-wingers and I was wondering if the police had any of these folks under surveillance today."

"No," Hart replied. "And we haven't picked any up today, either. All of us in the intelligence unit were down at the Trade Mart monitoring the Indignant White Citizens Council."

"Let me read my list to you. I've got about fifty right-wingers here. Tell me if you guys know the whereabouts of any of them." I proceeded to tick off the names on my relatively long list.

When I finished, Hart said, "No, I don't think we know the exact whereabouts of any of those guys at this moment. We did provide the Secret Service with several of those names, but they did nothing about them. But, Jim, our unit is compiling a list of right-wingers right now, too."

"Well, I tell you what," I followed up, "would your unit be willing to coordinate lists and leads with us so that we don't duplicate efforts?"

"I don't see why not."

15

"I'll send someone over with a copy of our list so you can compare it with yours." With that, we said good-bye and hung up.

TIME: 2:15 P.M.

A hand clutched my elbow. I spun; Howe was in my face. "They've just arrested a guy named Lee Oswald, and they're booking him for the killing of the policeman over in Oak Cliff. Officer's name was Tippit."

It took me only a second or two to shift from the extreme right wing to Lee Oswald. Lee Oswald was a Communist who had defected to the Soviet Union and returned three years later with a Russian wife, Marina. I had an active file on both Oswalds, who were both considered espionage risks. I had learned on November 1 that Oswald worked at one of the Texas school book depository buildings in Dallas. I remembered thinking Tippit's and Kennedy's killings were related, and then it hit me like a load of bricks.

"That's him! Ken, that must be him. Oswald has to be the one who shot Kennedy!" Oswald was the son of a bitch who shot the president. We had a bead on the assassin.

"Listen," Howe said. "Do you have the Oswald file?"

"No, I don't. It should be in the active file cabinet."

Howe and I rushed over to the cabinet. The file was gone, which meant that the mail clerk probably had it for incoming mail purposes. We hurried to his office and started frantically looking for it. Loeffler, the only other supervisor in the office, joined us in the search, found the file, and handed it to me and Howe. Paper-clipped to the top we found a one-page communiqué from the Washington, D.C., field office. While Howe pulled out his reading glasses, I began reading the communiqué, which summarized a letter written by Oswald to the Soviet Embassy in Washington. The letter had been intercepted by the FBI, then read and copied by an intelligence agent before it was sent along to the Russians.

According to the communiqué, Oswald had written that he had been in Mexico City and had spoken with "Comrade Kostine." I had read something about this Mexico City meeting in October, but had been forbidden by FBI policy from questioning Oswald about it, as it would tip off Oswald, and presumably the Soviets, to our intelligence sources and methods in Mexico.

Howe now told me to take this communiqué immediately to Gordon Shanklin, the Dallas SAC. "Shanklin is on the telephone with headquarters," Howe said. I bundled everything up and hustled over to Shanklin's office.

Shanklin was standing behind his desk, still on the phone. With his glasses and thin hair, Shanklin looked like a fidgety, rumpled professor. He was a chain-smoker who was known to buy cartons of cigarettes by the grocery bag. As usual, cigarette ashes dotted his vest. In his fifties, Shanklin was so nervous it seemed at times as if he was afraid of his own shadow. But we agents completely understood his nervousness: for a SAC to survive with J. Edgar Hoover as his boss, he always had to be looking over his shoulder, always wary of Hoover's constantly changing whims and moods. I pitied all SACs, especially Shanklin, who was really a damn good man.

I waved the communiqué in Shanklin's face. If Oswald was in fact Kennedy's killer, then this letter had all the ingredients for a potentially explosive international situation.

Still on the phone, Shanklin read the communiqué. Then, with no visible reaction, he said, "Alan, I got Jim Hosty here. He's the agent who was working our file on Oswald. He's got the file here with him now."

Shanklin was quiet for a few minutes, listening to the person on the other end. Then Shanklin put his hand over the phone and said, "I got Belmont on the phone. He wants you, Hosty, to get down to the police department and take part in the interrogation of Oswald. Also, Belmont wants you to cooperate fully with the police and give them any information we have on Oswald. Get going. Now." Since Alan Belmont was the third in command of the Bureau, this was a significant order.

I left Shanklin's office, and as I headed for the door to leave I heard Howe on another phone with Agent Dick Harrison, who was at the police station: "Harrison, tell Assistant Police Chief Stevenson that Hosty is on his way, that he's our agent on the Oswald file. He's going to help in the interrogation of Oswald."

I felt my heart beating wildly again.

TIME: 3:00 P.M.

I slipped my car down the ramp to the police garage and found a slot to park. It was frantic there, people running around yelling, dozens of cars flying in and out of the garage. Heaving my burly body out of the car, I headed straight for the elevator. Car doors slammed to my right. Lieutenant Jack Revill and another officer, Detective Jackie Bryant had just emerged from their car and were walking briskly toward the elevator as well.

Revill was a trim, dark-complected, handsome young lieutenant on the fast track at the police department. He was college educated, part of the new breed of professional cop. He had just finished a successful tour of duty in the narcotics unit and had recently been given a prestigious assignment heading the intelligence unit. This unit primarily focused on organized crime but also monitored some political radicals, such as the Klan. Though Revill was a competent officer, I had noticed a glaring weakness on his part when it came to the non-organized crime aspects of intelligence work. He had no training in investigating Communists or radical right-wingers, and many times his naïveté showed. Revill was also a ruthless career climber with great ambitions. If necessary, he would step on anyone to advance his career. Revill was clearly gunning to be a police chief somewhere, and it was apparent that he would probably make it before too long.

Revill waved, signaling me to wait for him. Since I was in the intelligence unit of the Bureau, Revill and I frequently worked together.

At the elevator, we hesitated for a moment while several men with ABC News logos on their jackets tried to maneuver a huge, studio-size television camera through the elevator doors. The men were sweating, straining, cursing. Revill waved his arm in disgust at the two men and headed for the door to the stairwell. Bryant and I followed. There was pandemonium even in the stairwell. Over the mad din, Revill told me his news.

"Hosty, we got a hot lead. We've accounted for all the employees but one at the school book depository where the shots came from. The only employee not accounted for is a guy named Lee." I could barely catch what he was saying, but I could not help thinking, a bit smugly, For chrissake, Revill, you're way behind. Oswald's already been arrested for killing one of your fellow officers, and is strongly suspected of killing Kennedy, too. He's upstairs in this very station, and you don't even know it.

Revill and I never really got along, and disagreed often. Now I just couldn't contain myself, so, in a fit of utter frustration with Revill and everything in the world generally, I blurted, "Jack, the Lee you're talking about is Lee Oswald. He killed Tippit. He's a Communist and he probably killed Kennedy, too. He's under arrest right now upstairs!"

Revill jerked his head in my direction and shouted, "What the hell did you say? A Communist killed Kennedy! I can't believe that!"

Revill was an avid John Bircher–type conservative, and he absolutely detested Kennedy. So to tell him that a Communist had killed the man he regarded as a Communist sympathizer must have felt like a dull blow to the head.

Revill also knew that I was a lifelong Democrat, and that I had voted for Kennedy. Revill and I had had many arguments over politics, which frequently ended in shouting matches. I was constantly having to argue that Kennedy was really pro-American. In fact, just the day before, Revill and I had discussed the president's forthcoming trip to Dallas and the security detail. The Secret Service wanted to utilize numerous Dallas police officers to help with security, and Revill wanted no part of it. "I don't want to guard that son of a bitch. I think I might call in sick," he had said.

Revill's disbelief that a left-winger could have killed a Democratic president was shared by many, including me. It would have made sense if a right-winger had tried to kill Kennedy, which had been our mindset in Dallas all week.

Still climbing the stairs, Revill snorted, "Well, if you know that Oswald killed Kennedy, why the hell didn't you tell us? Why didn't you tell us Oswald was in town and was a known Communist?"

"Jack, I couldn't tell you. You know Bureau policy, the need-to-know rule," I said. I was referring to the Bureau's long-standing policy on espionage cases, that only those who "need to know" particular information are told. For better or worse, the Bureau did not consider local police part of the need-to-know group, and this drove Revill crazy.

At last we reached the third floor. As I stepped through the stairwell door, I was overwhelmed by the sights and sounds. There in the detective bureau, crammed into the narrow hallways, were dozens and dozens of reporters, camera crews, and unidentified onlookers. The networks had hauled their studios onto this floor. Huge studio television cameras were in place in the hallway, and television reporters were broadcasting live in front of them. The press was all over the place, and photographers were flashing their cameras incessantly. The place was in an uproar; people had to shout into each other's ears to be heard. Despite the desperate gravity of the situation, police security of the building was obviously extremely lax.

I looked around and spied James Bookhout, an FBI agent who worked as our liaison with Captain Will Fritz, the police's chief homicide investigator. Bookhout was standing in a doorway, on some sort of pedestal, so that he stood out above the crowd. When I saw that he was waving for me to join him, I started pushing my way through the mob. Bookhout was screaming at the press to clear out of my way. I squeezed past several reporters and Bookhout pushed me into a room and shut the door. We were standing in the small outer office to Fritz's private, glass-walled office. I told him that FBI agent Wally Heitman, who also worked counter-intelligence cases, was coming to join us, but Bookhout shook his head and said, "Let's go in. We can't wait." With that Bookhout opened the door to Fritz's office and led me inside. There, seated in front of me, was Lee Harvey Oswald.

TIME: 3:15 P.M.

Bookhout gently shut the door, and all of a sudden the room was quieter. Everyone in Fritz's office stopped speaking and turned to look at me. I saw Fritz, two other police detectives, and Oswald all seated in the office. I looked over at a desk against the wall, saw a pad of police affidavit forms, and grabbed it.

I took out my pen, looked at my wristwatch, and then wrote down the exact time: 3:15 P.M. I turned to Captain Fritz, who was seated behind his desk, and nodded to him. Then I turned to eye Oswald. My first impression of him was that he was a young punk. He was sitting there with a wise-ass smirk, the kind you wanted to slap off his face as his deep blue eyes, glaring and beady, confronted you eyeball-to-eyeball. He was skinny and small, and even though he was only twenty-four years old, he was already losing his hair — his hairline had deeply receded. He was clean-shaven, but his hair was mussed. He was wearing a wrinkled white T-shirt and brand-new shiner, still red and slightly swollen, above his right eyebrow. His hands were cuffed behind his back, but even so, he was trying to sit nonchalantly, cocky and self-assured, in the straight-backed wooden chair.

I said, "Special Agent Jim Hosty, with the FBI. I'm here to participate in the interview with the police. I want to advise you of some things. You have the right to remain silent. Anything you say may be used against you in court. You also have the right to have an attorney —"

I was interrupted by Oswald. His face had turned ugly, and his whole body jerked in my direction, as if touched by a hot wire. "Oh, so you're Hosty, the agent who's been harassing my wife!" he exploded.

Fritz and Bookhout exchanged puzzled looks. Oswald, clearly having lost his earlier complacency, ranted on. "My wife is a Russian citizen who is here in this country legally and is protected under diplomatic laws from harassment by you or any other FBI agent. The FBI is no better than the Gestapo of Nazi Germany. If you wanted to talk to me, you should have come directly to me, not my wife. You never responded to my request."

Fritz tried to regain control over the interrogation, to put Oswald at ease, which is very critical in the interrogation of any suspect. As any cop knows, you always want to keep a suspect talking. If a suspect gets riled he's likely to clam up on you. While Fritz was speaking to Oswald in the smoothest, most peaceful drawl he could manage, I paused to think for a moment.

I knew Oswald was spewing hot air regarding diplomatic law, but the other things he had said struck a chord. I had in fact on two occasions been to the house where his wife lived, once on November 1 and then again on November 5. The purpose of these visits was to make preliminary contact — introduce myself and establish the identity, address, and place of employment of the subject in the case, which was a counter-espionage concern. In these initial contacts with Marina Oswald, I was hoping to set up a time to conduct an in-depth interview with her. Both Oswalds — he being a former Marine who had defected to the Soviet Union and then returned the United States, she a Soviet citizen — made for a classic counter-espionage case. The question was: Could either of the Oswalds be Soviet intelligence agents? In November 1963, the Bureau had no direct information that the Oswalds were Russian agents, but this was the height of the cold war, and for national security purposes we had to be prudent.

What really struck me about Oswald's outburst in Captain Fritz's office, however, was the realization that it was Oswald who had left me an angry, unsigned note just ten days before. I had the note in my file drawer. It said, in effect: "If you want to talk to me, you should talk to me to my face. Stop harassing my wife, and stop trying to ask her about me. You have no right to harass her."

When I received this note from Nannie Lee Fenner, a former chief stenographer newly demoted to receptionist, I read it and, quite honestly, thought little about it. At the time I was juggling 35 to 40 cases, mostly on radical right-wing subversives, and had no way of knowing who might have written the note. I suspected it had come from a particular radical right-winger I had been investigating, simply because I had recently interviewed his wife.

At any rate, in law enforcement such notes are common. Occasionally I received abusive phone calls and notes from the targets of my investigations. All law enforcement officers do. It's what I called "getting guff." After reading the note, I had tossed it in my file drawer at the office and not given it another thought. That is, not until November 22 at approximately 3:18 P.M.

Oswald was squirming like a snared rat. He asked Fritz to remove the handcuffs. I quickly said that sounded like a reasonable request. Fritz compromised and told one of his detectives to cuff Oswald in the front rather than in the back.

Much more comfortable now, Oswald eased back into his chair and looked up at me. His intensity was starting to diminish. Oswald's outrage had unsettled everyone in the room, most of whom were already on edge. Now that Oswald was starting to settle down, Fritz, the two detectives, and Bookout were visibly relaxing. I was, too.

Then Oswald looked up at Fritz and said, seemingly sincerely, "Thank you, thank you." Turning to me, he somewhat sheepishly said, "I'm sorry for blowing up at you. And I'm sorry for writing that letter to you."

Bingo! That confirmed Oswald was the one who wrote the note.

Fritz took advantage of the moment to resume his questioning. Fritz came across as the quintessential southern good old boy. He had a soft-spoken approach, and his style proved extremely effective; in fact, Fritz had a much deserved reputation as a successful interrogator of homicide suspects, frequently getting both confessions and convictions. Rather short, Fritz loved the cowboy image that Dallas inspired, and always wore his white cowboy hat. All the detectives who worked under him in the homicide unit aped him by also wearing white cowboy hats. It was the only police unit that did, and you could therefore always spot a homicide detective from a mile away. Though Fritz had a soft approach with suspects, he also had unpredictable mood swings, which kept everyone who worked with him on his toes. In many ways, I thought of him as a smaller version of J. Edgar Hoover, a temperamental bulldog. As chief of homicide, Fritz had his own little empire, and no one dared cross him. Whereas Revill was part of the new breed of professional cop, Fritz was clearly a part of the old guard.

With his cowboy hat tilted back on his head, Fritz leaned back in his chair and asked, "Okay now, Lee, you work at the Texas School Book Depository, isn't that right?"

"Yeah, that's right," Oswald answered, very politely.

"When did you start working there?" Fritz asked.

"About October fifteenth."

"What did you do down there?"

"I was just a common laborer."

"Now, did you have access to all the floors in that building?"

"Of course."

"Tell me what was on each of those floors."

"The first and second floors have offices. The third and fourth are storage. So are the fifth and sixth."

"And you were working there today, is that right?"

"Yep."

"Were you there when the president's motorcade went by?"

"Yeah."

"Where were you when the president went by the book depository?"

"I was eating my lunch in the first-floor lunchroom."

"What time was that?"

"About noon."

"Were you ever on the second floor around the time the president was shot?"

"Well, yeah. I went up there to get a bottle of Coca-Cola from the machine for my lunch."

"But where were you when the president actually passed your building?"

"On the first floor in the lunchroom."

"And you left the book depository, isn't that right?"

"Yeah."

So far, things were going along pretty smoothly. Oswald was just one cool cucumber now.

Fritz continued. "When did you leave?"

"Shortly after I heard that the president was shot."

"Why did you leave?"

"Well, I figured with all the confusion there wouldn't be any more work to do that day."

"So what did you do?"

"I took the bus and went home, changed my clothes, and went to a movie."

"And you said earlier that you live at 1026 North Beckley?"

"Yeah."

"Did you rent that room under an alias?"

"Well, yeah. O. H. Lee."

"Were you carrying a pistol on you when you went to the movie?"

"Yeah."

"Why?"

"'Cause I felt like it."

"Because you felt like it?"

"Yeah, 'cause I felt like it." Oswald was almost snide.

"Now, when the police officers apprehended you, did you pull out this pistol?"

"Yeah. I admit I tried to fight the officers at first. I pulled out my gun, but an officer grabbed it and hit me above the eye. I guess I had it coming."

"Did you have a rifle at work?"

"No, I didn't," Oswald answered. "But the manager of the book depository, Mr. Truly, did."

"How do you know this?"

"'Cause he showed it to a bunch of us workers one day on the first floor."

"Do you own a rifle?"

"No, I don't."

"Did you ever?"

"No."

"Have you ever received any firearms training?"

"Well, yeah, in the Marines."

"What level of expertise did you achieve?"

"Marksman."

Fritz leaned in toward Oswald. "Lee, did you shoot the president?"

"No. I emphatically deny that." Oswald's jugular was popping out.

"What about that officer in Oak Cliff. Did you shoot him?"

"No. I deny that, too," Oswald said just as earnestly.

Fritz picked up a folded piece of paper from his desk. "We found this paper in your wallet. It talks about something called 'Fair Play for Cuba.' Now, what's this, Lee?"

Oswald nodded his head in my direction, and said, "Why don't you ask Agent Hosty?"

Fritz looked over at me, and I gestured to Fritz to continue. Fritz nodded and went on. "You said you have a wife who is a Russian?"

"That's right," Oswald said.

"So have you been to Russia?"

"Yes. My wife still has relatives over there, and she and I have many friends there."

"How long were you in Russia?"

"About three years."

"What did you do there?"

"Why don't you ask Hosty? He can probably tell you everything you want to know about me," Oswald said with a smart-aleck smile.

Fritz was starting to get a little frustrated, and again he turned and looked at me. I stopped taking notes and looked up at him. "Captain, I can explain all of this later. Why don't you just continue?"

Fritz shook his head and, clearly agitated, said, "Do you have any questions I should ask Lee, Mr. Hosty?"

I decided it was probably best to go ahead and ask some of my own questions. I thought for just a moment and decided to ask Oswald about the communiqué I had just received today relating that Oswald had been in contact with the Soviet Embassy in Mexico City. I started off with what I thought was a rather general and innocuous question. Out of deference to Fritz, I said, "Ask him if he has ever been in Mexico City."

Fritz turned toward Oswald and said, "Tell us about that, Lee."

Oswald hesitated for just a moment, then answered, "Sure. Sure, I've been to Mexico. When I was stationed in San Diego with the Marines, a couple of my buddies and I would occasionally drive down to Tijuana over a weekend."

"No, not Tijuana. Mexico City. Captain, ask have you ever been to Mexico City," I persisted.

Oswald was visibly upset. "What makes you think I've been to Mexico City? I've never been there. I deny that." He was shaking his head, and he was starting to sweat now. I knew I had touched a nerve.

The door next to me flung open, and another police detective poked his head in. "Captain Fritz, they're ready for the lineup now."

Fritz jumped up and said, "Okay, let's take a break and go do this lineup."

At that Oswald was escorted out of Fritz's office, and I was left wondering, why in the hell did they have to go and do that? Here we had Oswald on the ropes — he had lost his edge. That is typically a perfect opportunity to break a suspect's façade and get at the truth. We could have made some significant headway and obtained valuable information if we could have only pressed Oswald a little more.

It was clear to me that the Mexico City information was pivotal, and could be Oswald's Achilles' heel. If I just could have gone further with Oswald. Well, I figured, we'll pick up where we left off before the lineup. I left Fritz's office last, and looked at my watch: 4:05 P.M. I jotted down the time in my notes. While I had been furiously scribbling on what Oswald was reporting, I had noticed that I was the only one doing so. But then, that would be what I'd expect. Captain Fritz was an experienced homicide interrogator. The fact that he wasn't taking notes was standard operating procedure. Fritz was conducting his first run-through with Oswald, and the object was to keep a suspect talking. Note-taking by an interrogator can be inhibiting. I was enough in the background during the interrogation so that note-taking seemed appropriate to me.

I walked down the hallway a little more easily now, since the reporters had moved to where Oswald's lineup was taking place. I decided to watch. Pushing my way through the reporters and photographers, I gained a vantage point from which to watch the identifications at the lineup.

The police had brought in the eyewitnesses to the shooting of Officer Tippit in the Oak Cliff neighborhood. The witnesses were a waitress and a car salesman. I recognized the waitress, who worked in a restaurant where I often ate lunch.

I watched as both positively picked out Oswald as the person who had shot Tippit. I later learned these witnesses had watched in horror as Oswald shot Tippit four times: one bullet to the chest, then another, which struck a metal button on his shirt, driving it deep into Tippit's body and causing a larger than normal entry wound, then a bullet to the forehead, and finally, a fourth bullet to the temple of the officer, who was already lying on the ground, his gun still in his holster.

Oswald deserved the death penalty for the killing of Officer Tippit alone. With the positive identification by these eyewitnesses, and later with other eyewitnesses and the ballistics report matching the bullets in Tippit's body to Oswald's gun, we had Oswald cold for first-degree murder. We had the bastard. I felt a dark, brooding inner satisfaction knowing that Oswald was going to pay for his crime. No, for his crimes. I was already convinced that my initial surmise of barely two hours before — that the murders of Officer Tippit and President Kennedy were done by the same person or persons — was indeed correct. Little did I know that in the days and years to come, that all too simple conclusion would be doubted and dissected by hundreds if not thousands of investigators, many of whom came up with their own conclusions, all of which would seem to blur and cloud what seemed so clear to me that afternoon, the simple truth.

TIME: 4:25 P.M.

Harlan Brown, a senior agent in my squad, hurried up to me in the hallway. "Hosty! Come here. You are not to go back in on the interrogation of Oswald, and you are not to provide any information we have about Oswald to the police. Do you understand?"

I was dumbfounded, but I said yes, I understood. This was in direct contradiction to what Alan Belmont, Hoover's senior assistant, had ordered. But Brown was dead serious and was clutching my elbow tightly. It became clear to me that Belmont's order had been countermanded, and that probably meant that either the Old Man — Hoover — had taken over control of the investigation, or that the

White House had. I shuddered at the thought of Hoover personally supervising my work here in Dallas.

I decided nonetheless that I would remain at the police station. Just because I couldn't talk to the police didn't mean I couldn't learn things from them. I headed back to Fritz's office, where I knew the police were keeping Oswald's personal belongings. Nothing there, but in the second inner office, which belonged to Lieutenant Walter Potts, I spotted Oswald's things, which had been removed from his person and from his apartment at the Oak Cliff rooming house. Among the items on Potts's desk was Oswald's black address book. I pulled out my pad of blank police affidavit forms and started transcribing the entries in his book, thinking I might find some interesting leads or even some possible co-conspirators. A little way into my transcribing, I came across a line that made my heart crawl. There, scrawled in Oswald's handwriting, was the entry:

> Nov. 1 James P. Hasty, RI1–1211, MV8605,
> 1114 Commerce, Dallas

Jesus, I thought, what in the Sam Hill is my name doing in Oswald's address book? Then it hit me. As mentioned, I had met with Oswald's wife on November 1 and 5. During the first visit, I had given Marina's friend Ruth Paine my office telephone number and name. Oswald was so upset at me for making contact with his wife and asking questions about him that he had personally tromped down to the Dallas FBI field office to hand-deliver the angry note telling me to knock it off and stop harassing his wife.

It made sense that if Oswald would have taken those measures, he would also have made an effort to get my name, phone number, auto license plate number, and office address, which is what that entry reflected. He had misspelled my name, and he was off just one letter on my car tag, MU8605. But RI1–1211 was the phone number for the Dallas FBI office, and 1114 Commerce was the correct address. Oswald's date notation was clearly in reference to my first visit with Marina.

TIME: 5:30 P.M.

Having finished my transcribing, I replaced the last of the items belonging to Oswald on Potts's desk and walked back into the outer office.

In the hallway the press was still in a frenzy. Rubbing the back of my neck, I glanced over and looked through the glass wall to Fritz's office. I watched as a phone was placed in front of Oswald and watched as Oswald placed a call. I couldn't hear him, but I could see Oswald calmly speaking into the mouthpiece, occasionally pausing to listen. After a few minutes, he hung up and leaned back in his chair. I later learned that Oswald had called Ruth Paine, the kindly Quaker woman who was letting Marina and the Oswald children live with her in Irving, a Dallas suburb. Paine would later tell FBI agents that Oswald asked Paine to call John Abt, the chief counsel for the Communist party of America, to ask him to represent Oswald. Paine complied, but apparently Abt never returned her call.

Fritz's door opened and three Secret Service agents walked into the outer office. I recognized Forrest Sorrells, head of the Dallas Secret Service office, and Bill Patterson, another Dallas Secret Service agent. I didn't recognize the other agent, but assumed he was part of the president's permanent security detail. Sorrells, who was close to retirement, looked in shock. His hair was mussed, his shoulders drooping. Anguish was etched on his face: the president had been killed in his jurisdiction; he was a beaten man.

Sorrells asked to speak with Oswald. A police detective opened Fritz's office door, leaned in, and spoke to the captain. A moment later, Fritz walked Oswald into the outer office. Sorrells, standing in front of me, asked, "Who are you?" I was immediately struck by Sorrells's dazed and distant approach.

"Lee Oswald."

"Where do you live?"

"1026 North Beckley."

Sorrells asked Oswald a few other unnecessary questions, on matters that had already been established and known for hours. I noticed he was not taking any notes, not even bothering to conduct the interview with any sense of formality. Everyone stood during the five-minute interview, and when Sorrells finished, Fritz and Oswald went back into Fritz's office. Before Sorrells could leave, I walked up to him, tapped him on the shoulder, and gestured for him to come over to a corner of the room for a confidential conversation. I noticed Patterson trying discreetly to overhear our conversation.

"Mr. Sorrells, I can't tell you the full story, but have your headquarters call my headquarters. We have two items of secret information on some of Oswald's contacts that you should have."

Sorrells, not looking at me, or really at anything, mumbled, "Sure, I'll do that." Then he and the two other Secret Service agents left. I wondered what it must have felt like to be in Sorrells's shoes right then.

Still not wanting to leave, and still hoping to pick up some meaningful information, I resumed my vigil in Fritz's outer office while Oswald remained encloseted with Fritz and two police detectives one door away.

TIME: 7:10 P.M.

A couple of police detectives came in and talked with Fritz. Then the captain and the detectives escorted Oswald out and into the office next door. I followed. It was in this office that Justice of the Peace David L. Johnston arraigned Oswald for the first-degree murder of Officer Tippit. Oswald protested — with no legal basis — that he couldn't be arraigned for murder in the police station, that it could only occur in court. Still protesting, Oswald was led back through the gauntlet of reporters to Fritz's office.

Emmett Murphy, another FBI agent, came up to me and asked if I wanted to join him and a couple of detectives for a quick bite across the street. His invitation reminded me that I had never gotten to eat my lunch, and was actually hungry.

TIME: 7:45 P.M.

After a quick dinner, I drove back to the Bureau, figuring I could probably get more accomplished there than staring at Oswald through a glass wall. As I walked into the bullpen, which is what we agents called the squad room, a secretary told me I was wanted in Shanklin's office, pronto. When I arrived, I found Howe with him. They told me to shut the door.

"What the hell is this?" Shanklin asked, holding what appeared to be a letter.

I took it and immediately recognized the anonymous note I had received ten days before. The angry note asking me to leave the writer's wife alone and speak directly to him. The note I had just connected with Oswald less than four hours before. I shrugged. "It's no big deal," I said, "just your typical guff."

"What do you mean, 'typical guff'? This note was written by Oswald, the probable assassin of the president, and Oswald brought this note into *this* office just ten days ago! What the hell do you think Hoover's going to do if he finds out about this note!" Shanklin, more upset than I had ever seen him, was pacing to and fro behind his desk, puffing on a cigarette.

"What's the big deal? So what if Oswald wrote this note and left it for me? What does that have to do with anything?" I asked. He had not threatened the president.

"If people learn that Oswald gave you guff a week before the assassination, they'll say you should have known he'd kill the president," Shanklin insisted. "If Hoover finds out about this, he's going to lose it."

I looked over at Howe. His arms were folded across his chest, his expression grave. He obviously agreed that the note could spell big trouble for us with Hoover. I kept shaking my head, insisting that the note was no big deal. "If we simply explain everything: how we got the note, what it means, the background, et cetera, they'll understand there was no way in hell we could possibly have predicted or even guessed that Oswald was going to kill anyone, much less the president. I tell you, this little note is no big deal," I repeated.

Shanklin was rubbing his neck, still not convinced. Finally he said, "Okay, go do a memo right now explaining all the circumstances surrounding the note, and give it to me. I'll think about it."

I left his office and went to the first available steno I saw, Martha Connolly. I told her I had an urgent memo to dictate, so she interrupted what she was doing and took up her note pad. I dictated a memo explaining how Oswald had come into the Dallas FBI office on or about November 12 while I was out of the office.

Oswald had approached the receptionist, Nannie Lee Fenner, and asked to speak with me. She told him I was out and asked if he would like to leave a message. Oswald gave her an unsealed envelope, told her to give it to me, and left. Fenner reported that she had given the note to Kyle Clark, an assistant special agent in charge, who read it.

Clark handed it back to Fenner, told her it was no big deal, and said to give it to me. Fenner put the note in my in-box. When I came back to the office I read the note and saw that it was unsigned, which meant that it could have come from any one of the subjects whose cases I was working on at the time. I had spent not another minute thinking about it, until today.

Martha quickly finished typing the memo and gave it to me to proofread. I did, thanked Martha for her help, took the two-page memo back to Shanklin's office, and handed it to him. He thanked me and put the memo, together with the note from Oswald, in the "Do Not File" drawer in his desk.

In the Hoover FBI, every SAC had a "Do Not File" drawer. This was where he kept his personal notes on all his agents, so that when he did annual evaluations of each agent he had notes to work from. Personnel matters were treated confidentially, so everyone knew this was the SAC's most private drawer. The material kept in this drawer never entered the official record. Occasionally all the instructions and supporting paperwork for a particularly sensitive or controversial mission were kept in the drawer, and destroyed as soon as they were no longer needed. The absolute privacy of this drawer afforded Hoover "plausible deniability" — if an objectionable action or mission did reach the public eye, Hoover could claim to know nothing about it, since it had never officially occurred.

Shanklin maintained a file folder on each of us, so my file is where I assumed he placed my memo and the note. I left his office; across the squad room I spotted Howe.

"Ken, how did Shanklin find out about the Oswald note so fast?" I asked. Howe explained that after Oswald was arrested and his picture was shown on all the TV stations, Fenner recognized him as the guy who had brought the note in ten days ago. She reminded Clark about the note, but Clark couldn't recall it. Then Fenner told Howe and Shanklin.

In 1979 I learned from Clark that he had received a call the day of the assassination from Bill Sullivan, one of Hoover's other top assistants, who told him to make sure I did not see the communiqué from the D.C. field office about Oswald writing to the Soviet Embassy in Washington.

Clark then told Howe to keep the communiqué — which had just arrived the day of the assassination — and any others concerning Mexico City from me. Howe knew I had already seen the communiqué that afternoon, but he decided to remove it and other related memos from my file drawer so I couldn't see it again. Going through my file drawer, Howe came across the Oswald note and took it to Shanklin. Howe said Shanklin instantly became livid. How was this going to appear to the public, and especially to Hoover, he wanted to know.

I told Howe I still didn't think the note was that big a deal, and what we had to do was put it in context. Howe shrugged. I went back to my desk and began reviewing my Oswald file again.

TIME: 11:45 P.M.

"Okay, people, gather 'round. I want to discuss everything that's happened today," Shanklin said in a loud voice. We all stopped what we were doing. Almost all of the forty agents in the Dallas office gathered around Shanklin.

31

Shanklin spent about thirty minutes reviewing all the events of the day and the status of the Kennedy and Tippit cases. He explained that the police had discovered an apparent sniper's nest on the sixth floor of the Texas School Book Depository and how boxes had been arranged around one window looking down on Elm Street to shield the assassin from view.

The police had also found a high-powered Italian-made rifle with a telescopic sight on the sixth floor. The police had determined that all the employees were accounted for except Lee Oswald, who was seen on the sixth floor in the building shortly before the assassination. Immediately after the assassination he was seen on the second floor. Oswald had left the building, however, before it could be secured.

The police had recovered several prints from the rifle and the sniper's nest, which had been matched to Oswald.

The police had also interviewed a co-worker of Oswald's who had given him a ride to work that day. The co-worker reported that Oswald had been carrying a brown paper package, which Oswald said contained curtain rods. Police had found the paper packaging on the sixth floor, and the co-worker identified it as being consistent with what he saw. The paper was covered with Oswald's prints.

There was one eyewitness to the Kennedy shooting, a man standing directly across from the book depository, who saw a slender white male in his early thirties, between 5'8" and 5'10", wearing light-colored khaki clothes, shoot a rifle out of the sixth-floor window, the same window where the police had found the apparent sniper's nest. This physical description was immediately sent as an all-points-bulletin on all police radios.

The police had also gone out to Ruth Paine's home, where Oswald's wife and children were living. Marina Oswald said that Lee did own a rifle, but when she went to show where he kept it, it was gone. Oswald also maintained a rooming house apartment in the Oak Cliff neighborhood of Dallas, where Tippit had been killed.

Shanklin went on to say that the police had determined that at 1:15 P.M., Officer J. D. Tippit was shot five times by a white male matching Oswald's description at 10th and Patton in the Oak Cliff area.

Eyewitnesses had positively identified Oswald as Tippit's killer. Further, when Oswald was arrested at 1:45 P.M. at a movie theater, he pulled out a handgun, tried to shoot a police officer, and said, "It's all over now."

Police subdued him, then took him in for questioning. Oswald denied any role in shooting either Kennedy or Tippit. Police were conducting a ballistics study in the Tippit shooting, but the preliminary findings indicated that the gun that Oswald had on his person when he was arrested in the movie theater was the same gun used to shoot Tippit.

Shanklin said that, as he spoke, FBI agent Vince Drain had possession of the rifle recovered from the book depository and was en route to Washington with it, getting a ride on a two-seat Air Force jet fighter. This rifle was to undergo further forensic analysis at the FBI crime lab.

Shanklin said the county prosecutor had charged Oswald with the murder of Tippit, but as of now Oswald had not been charged with the killing of Kennedy. He said that we were to continue looking for any other possible suspects, though it was becoming clear that Oswald was the assassin. Police, with the help of the FBI, were trying to track down the ownership of the rifle.

Shanklin told us that FBI agents from all over the country were going to start pouring in tomorrow to assist in this investigation, and that tomorrow we were to all be here by 7:00 A.M. for our assignments. "That's all for now," he concluded. "I suggest you all go home and try to get some sleep."

As the agents all started to get up, I approached Bob Barrett and asked if I could catch a ride home with him. Barrett, a fellow University of Notre Dame grad, lived in the same Catholic parish as I did, St. Pius X on the northeast side of Dallas. He said sure, and we headed out the door.

As he was driving us home, Barrett said, "Did you hear Lieutenant Revill has written a memo to the chief of police saying that you and the FBI had Oswald under surveillance before the assassination?"

"What!"

"Revill says you told him all this today right after the assassination," Barrett said.

"That jackass has it all wrong."

"I know, but Chief Curry told the press that the FBI knew Oswald was in town, but didn't tell them, and you know what that means," Barrett continued.

I knew what it meant. It meant that it would be difficult to convince the media, the police, or the public that Revill's statement was a distortion of the truth. People would have already formed their own opinions. I also knew that Hoover was going to have something to say to me as well, and it was not going to be good. Either Revill had twisted my words in the police garage this afternoon or he had misunderstood me. Either way I would have a lot of explaining to do.

TIME: 2:00 A.M.

When I got home, the house was dark and quiet. Despite the day's traumatic events, all eight kids were asleep. As I crawled into bed Janet sat up. Relieved to see me, she said she hadn't been able to fall asleep and had been tossing and turning in bed for hours. She asked how things were going, and was genuinely more concerned about me than about all the momentous political upheaval of the day. I explained as much as I was allowed, then told her to get some rest. As I lay there in bed, I tried to will myself to sleep, knowing that tomorrow was probably going to be as trying and taxing as today had been. Maybe even more so.

3

Saturday, November 23, 1963

TIME: 5:30 A.M.

From an anguished, sporadic sleep, I woke up with a start. It was still dark outside. A dry Texas wind was howling at our bedroom window. Then it all came back to me: the president was dead.

I got up and quickly shaved and showered. I put on a fresh shirt and tie, and strapped on my .38 Detective Special snub-nosed revolver. When I went into the kitchen, Janet had put out cereal, orange juice, and coffee for the two of us. Eating quickly, I kissed her and told her I would call, but not to expect me home any time soon.

TIME: 6:30 A.M.

An hour later, I walked into the bullpen on the eleventh floor of the FBI offices and headed straight for my desk. I started reading the various memos that had been placed in my in-box during the night, and was still going through them when, shortly before seven, I was interrupted by Shanklin for the morning briefing and update. I took a seat on the corner of Bookout's desk. The agents had arrived in virtual silence, all of us in shocked mourning, whispering hesitantly about yesterday's event as we congregated. Our office had taken on the air of a funeral parlor.

"While you've been sleeping there have been some important

developments," Shanklin said. "Last night at about 1:30 A.M., the county prosecutor filed first-degree murder charges against Oswald for the killing of the president. Our agents in Chicago were able to trace the ownership of the rifle found on the sixth floor of the depository to Oswald. And one of our agents in New Orleans, DeBrueys, discovered that one of Oswald's aliases was A. J. Hidell. This alias was given to all FBI offices yesterday. Someone found out that rifles like the one found in the depository are advertised in certain magazines and can be mail ordered from Chicago. By using both Oswald's true name and his alias, the Chicago agents made a hit and traced the ownership to Oswald.

"This trace apparently tipped the balance for the prosecutor and they filed on Oswald after you all left last night," Shanklin added. He pointed out that as much as the FBI wanted to take over the investigation, the Dallas police had jurisdiction over all matters. But President Johnson and Bobby Kennedy had personally requested that the FBI conduct its own fact finding and report back to them.

Shanklin then proceeded to outline our assignments for the day. We began to disperse to our individual assignments, anxious for the distraction and purpose of our tasks. But Shanklin sharply raised his hand to keep us at bay. "Washington does not want any of you to ask questions about the Soviet aspect of this case. Washington does not want to upset the public."

"Washington" did not mean FBI headquarters; for Shanklin, "Washington" was shorthand for the White House, the State Department, and possibly the National Security Council.

As the meeting broke up, Bardwell Odum, a senior agent on the criminal squad, came over to me. He told me that at 2:00 this morning, Wally Heitman had gone to the Navy air base just outside of Dallas to meet Eldon Rudd, an assistant legal attaché at the U.S. Embassy in Mexico City. Rudd, who was actually an FBI agent, had flown in on a two-seat Navy jet fighter to personally deliver a surveillance photo and a phone intercept transcript. Heitman was chosen to receive this highly sensitive material because he and Rudd knew each other by sight. Heitman brought the material to the Dallas office and turned it over to Shanklin. I learned that Shanklin had never gone home last night, and that at about 4:00 A.M., a ten-page encoded teletype had been sent to headquarters.

Odum now had custody of the Rudd photo that was thought to be a shot of Oswald as he walked out of the Soviet Embassy in Mexico City. I took a look at it and knew immediately that it was not Oswald. Odum asked if I knew who the man was and if he had any association with Oswald. Not so far as I knew, I told him. Odum had orders to show

36

it to Oswald's wife, Marina. I took another look at the photo; I noticed something I felt I should point out to Odum.

"Bard," I said, "you can't show that photo to people outside the Bureau. Look, you can see the doorway to the Soviet Embassy. Here, take these scissors and crop out the doorway. That way no one will know where the photo was taken."

Odum quickly understood the implication of my remark: if the Soviets discovered that we had cameras outside their embassy, it would blow one of our vital surveillance methods. In this type of case, you go to great lengths to protect your sources and methods.

I took the police affidavit forms that had my notes from yesterday's Oswald interrogation, found the first available stenographer, and dictated a two-page report, what we called an FD-302. These reports were summaries of interrogations and interviews, and per Bureau procedure they had to be dictated within five days of the interrogation/interview. The steno then had five days to type up the report from her shorthand notes. The five-day requirements insured full and accurate reports. Any delay beyond that, and an agent or steno might inadvertently overlook or omit vital information.

TIME: 10:00 A.M.

During the morning briefing, Shanklin had given me the assignment of interviewing Ruth Paine at her home in Irving. After I finished dictating the Oswald report, I headed for Irving with Joe Abernathy, a senior agent on the criminal squad who was assigned to assist me. The Bureau always preferred to have two agents work together when interviewing. Thoroughness was the key, and the adage of two heads being better than one had generally proven to be true. It took us about 40 minutes to drive to Irving, and as we turned into Paine's street, we encountered dozens of reporters and photographers swarming the area in front of her house. As I walked up to the front door, an excited reporter ran up to me and asked if I was a law enforcement officer. I told him I was with the FBI.

"We hear Marina Oswald may be inside with Mrs. Paine, and I understand Marina speaks only Russian," the reporter said. "I speak fluent Russian, and I'll volunteer to act as your interpreter if you like."

"Thanks very much. If I need an interpreter, Mrs. Paine speaks Russian," I said, and left the crestfallen reporter, who had hoped to get a scoop on his colleagues, behind me in the driveway.

The Paines lived in a modest ranch house with two bedrooms, an attached garage, and a small, tidy lawn. Every house on the street looked alike, and it was clear the same developer had built them all, probably during the postwar building boom in the late 1940s. It was a middle-class neighborhood, a nice, quiet place to live and bring up kids. But today it was a madhouse.

When I knocked on the door, Ruth Paine answered. Abernathy and I identified ourselves and showed our credentials. Ruth was visibly relieved to see me. She said yes, of course, she knew who I was, since she remembered me from my two earlier visits this month. She ushered us into the house, shut the door, and told us to please sit down. Abernathy grabbed a straight-back chair and I grabbed a cushion seat nearest the sofa in the living room. Ruth introduced her husband, Michael, and then took a seat next to him on the sofa. Their kids, a five-year-old girl and a three-year-old boy, were playing with their toys on the living room floor.

Ruth, who was in her early thirties, was a tall, slender woman. On my two earlier visits, she had struck me as well-educated, soft-spoken, and compassionate. A Quaker, she taught Russian at St. Mark's School for Boys, a local Episcopal prep school. I could tell that the past 22 hours had taken a toll on her.

I quickly ascertained that Marina was not there; Lee's mother, Marguerite, had come by yesterday and spirited Marina away to a hotel room she had rented. Apparently Marguerite had decided to act as Marina's spokesperson and would later peddle both Marina's and her own stories to any members of the media willing to pay the price. *Life* magazine ended up footing their bill for choice accommodations at the Adolphus Hotel and providing them with ample spending money.

"Mrs. Paine, my partner and I would like to review with you how Marina and her children came to live with you. Then I would like to review Lee's activities in the days leading up to yesterday, as well as any other information about the Oswalds," I explained.

"Yes, of course. I want to cooperate as much as I can," she replied.

FBI procedure dictated that agents not use tape recorders in interviews, as it was thought that they would have inhibiting effects. So, with my note pad and pen ready, we began.

"Well, I guess I first became aware of Lee and Marina early this year through a local Russian immigrant group," Ruth told me. "But then in April, they decided to leave Dallas for New Orleans. Marina and I tried to maintain a correspondence after they had moved."

While Ruth was talking I couldn't help picking up the negative vibes from Michael Paine. I sensed he was uneasy and distrustful of me. He sat on the sofa, quietly taking in everything as a skeptical observer would. Like Ruth, he was tall and lanky and had an angular face. From my prior background check on him, I knew that he and Ruth were married but living separately. Obviously Michael was there to be at his wife's side during this turmoil. I later learned that Michael's father, George Lyman Paine, Jr., had telephoned him the night of the assassination. A long-distance operator, completely of her own volition, had illegally listened in on the conversation and later reported what she had heard to the FBI. George Paine was a well-known Trotskyite, and during his telephone call to his son, he said, "We all know who did this," and told his son to be careful. We at the FBI interpreted that comment to mean that George was speculating that the Soviet KGB had carried out the assassination, just as Stalin had the KGB assassinate his political rival Leon Trotsky. The FBI also knew that Michael Paine had little contact with his father; Michael's parents had divorced when he was four years old, and George Paine had essentially disappeared from Michael's life. This telephone warning may well have been the reason Michael was so leery of me now.

Ruth continued. "In late September, Lee was without a job in New Orleans. I am originally from Philadelphia and I knew of a job lead there, so I passed it on to Lee. Lee told Marina he was going out of town for a while. Marina was due to have her second child in a matter of weeks, so I drove to New Orleans and brought Marina and June back to Texas with me. Once I left New Orleans with Marina and June, Lee left town himself. I assumed he was going to Philadelphia, though he never told me for sure.

"Marina and June moved in to the second bedroom. After the baby was born, we put the crib in Marina's room as well. We got along well. Lee returned from his trip a few weeks later. He didn't say much, and I didn't ask, but I didn't notice anything unusual about him.

"Lee was still unemployed, and I got another job lead for him. One of my neighbors had a relative who worked at the Texas School Book Depository. The book depository had an opening for a laborer, so I told Lee about it. He applied and got the job. Then he moved into Dallas by himself. He rented a bedroom in a rooming house."

Ruth hesitated a little bit. "You know, Mr. Hosty, when you first visited on the first of November, you were asking us where Lee lived. We didn't know exactly, but we did have his phone number. Would that have helped you?"

"It would have been useful," I said. "I could have gotten his address from the phone company."

"Oh, I am so sorry. I should have realized that," she said with marked embarrassment.

"It's okay. Don't worry about it. Now just go ahead with what you were saying. Tell me what Lee did next."

"Well, for the most part, Lee stayed in Dallas during the week, and on the weekends he would get a ride out here to visit Marina and the girls. I never looked forward to his visits, because he could be really abrasive with Marina.

"Then you visited, Mr. Hosty. When Lee came that weekend and learned you had been here asking questions, he got very upset."

Ruth later learned from Marina that Lee gave her explicit instructions to get my name and car tag number if and when I returned. When I did so on November 5, Marina quietly sneaked out of the house while Ruth was talking to me and wrote down my license plate number.

"After your second visit, Mr. Hosty," Ruth said, "Lee came home again for the long Veterans' Day weekend. He went back to work in Dallas on Tuesday, and when I was cleaning the house I came across a handwritten letter from Lee to the Soviet Embassy. I thought this was an odd place for Lee to be writing a letter, so I read it, and then decided to keep it."

"Do you still have it?" I asked, trying not to sound too anxious.

"Sure, let me get it." The letter, on two sides of a piece of paper and written in Lee's hand, read as follows:

Dear Sirs:

This is to inform you of my interviews with comrade Kostine in the Embassy of the Soviet Union, Mexico City, Mexico.

I was unable to remain in Mexico City indefinitly because of my Mexican visa restrictions which was for 15 days only. I could not take a chance on applying for an extension unless I used my real name so I returned to the U.S. I and Marina Nichilayeva are now living in Dallas, Texas.

The FBI is not now interested in my activities in the progressive organization FPCC of which I was secretary in New Orleans, Louisiana since I no longer live in the state.

The FBI has visited us here in Texas on Nov. 1st. An agent of the FBI James P. Hasty warned me that if I attempted to engage in FPCC activities in Texas, the FBI will again take an "interest" in me. The agent also "suggested" that my wife could remain in the U.S. under FBI protection, that is, she could defect from the Soviet Union. Of course I and my wife strongly protested these tactics of the notorious FBI.

I had not planned to contact the Mexican City Embassy at all so of course they were unprepared and had I been able to reach Havana as planned the Soviet Embassy there would have had time to assist me. But of course the stupid Cuban consule was at fault here, I'm glad he has since been replaced by another.

This letter, I learned later, was an early draft of the letter Lee subsequently sent to the Soviet Embassy in Washington, the basis for the communiqué from the Washington field office that I read with Howe right after the assassination. I had now seen the name "Comrade Kostine" several times in relation to Lee's visit to Mexico City, and I wondered just who he was. All I knew was that he was the vice consul in the Embassy, a general administrative job. I wondered what in the hell Lee Oswald had been doing in Mexico City. My gut told me something smelled.

Ruth went on with her review of Lee's activities. "Lee always stayed in his apartment in Dallas during the week, and if he came to visit Marina, it was always on the weekend. Except last Thursday evening, the night before the assassination, when he came home to visit Marina."

Ruth's little boy wanted his mother to hold him, so she picked him up, put him on her lap, then said, "Lee was fairly quiet that evening, played with June a bit, and then went to bed at a decent hour. That evening, before I went to bed, I noticed the light in the garage was on. I knew Marina and I both had the habit of always turning the lights off whenever we left a room, so I guessed that Lee had been in the garage. The next morning Lee was gone before either Marina or I were awake. I believe he caught a ride to Dallas from my neighbor, who works with Lee.

"Later that afternoon, after the president had been shot and the police had arrested Lee, the police came by and asked if they could search my home for evidence. When they questioned Marina, I acted as the translator. When a police detective asked her if her husband owned a rifle, I expected her to answer no. So I was stunned when she said yes. Marina led the officers to the garage and pointed to a rolled-up blanket under the tool desk. When the officer checked the blanket, it was empty. Marina became very upset, and later that day confided to me that once she saw the rifle was gone she knew Lee had done it."

We had been talking for several hours, and Michael had gotten up to get the children some lunch. The interview was naturally coming to a close, so I told the Paines I appreciated their help and asked them if I could come back for follow-up interviews. They both said, "Fine."

Abernathy and I then left the Paine house and as we walked back to our car were mobbed by reporters eager to know if Marina was inside and what had been said. We waved them off, simply saying, "No comment. No comment."

TIME: 3:00 P.M.

As I entered the bullpen, all hell was breaking loose. Howe saw me and told me to go up immediately to the twelfth floor and see Shanklin in his office.

Shanklin, pacing back and forth behind his desk, was trying to light a cigarette when he saw me walk in. "Hosty! Headquarters is going nuts. They have a million questions for you, so sit down and listen.

"First, headquarters wants to know more about Oswald's allegations regarding you in a letter he wrote to the Russian Embassy about a week ago," Shanklin said, dragging long and hard on his cigarette. "Apparently, Oswald alleges that when you interviewed Marina, you were trying to persuade her to defect or something, and that Lee made a vigorous protest regarding your conduct. What do you have to say?"

"Well, first, I never asked Marina to defect. That's preposterous, since she's here legally for an indefinite period of time. Second, that vigorous protest must be that note I received from Lee ten days ago, if you can call that vigorous."

Shanklin nodded, apparently thinking what I said made sense. He then went down a list of the other questions headquarters had regarding my handling of the Oswald case. The majority of the questions dealt simply with routine matters, such as when was the case opened, by whom, why, and so on. Headquarters obviously wanted to know everything about the Oswalds, and so essentially they were picking my brain. Sitting there in Shanklin's office, I tried to remember everything I knew about them.

I remembered reading a front-page article in the Dallas newspapers in 1959 that a young former Marine, Lee Oswald, had defected to the Soviet Union. Upon reading this news, John Fain, one of our Fort

Worth agents, and the only agent working security cases there, opened a case on Lee in an effort to determine whether he posed any national security risks. Fain interviewed Lee's mother, Marguerite, and his brother Robert.

During that interview, Marguerite informed Fain that she did not believe her son Lee had defected, claiming it must have been an impostor posing as Lee who had defected. She seemed convinced that it was someone else using Lee's passport.

Fain checked this out and determined Marguerite's allegations were completely unfounded: it was in fact Lee who had defected to the Soviet Union.

In early June 1962, the Dallas newspapers ran another article indicating that Lee was returning to the States, and he was bringing back a Russian bride. Fain contacted Robert Oswald and asked him to let him know when Lee returned, since he would like to interview him.

On June 26, 1962, shortly after Lee had returned to the Fort Worth area, Fain and another agent, Tom Carter, were working in the Fort Worth office when Lee Oswald walked in and announced, "I heard you were looking for me."

Fain and Carter began the standard interview process. They wanted to know what Lee had done in the Soviet Union and what he planned to do in Texas. But before too long, Fain had lost control of the interview. Oswald was dictating terms and acting belligerently.

Oswald was reluctant to provide information, and when Fain persisted in asking why he went to the Soviet Union, Oswald snapped, "Because I wanted to." He also said he never denounced his U.S. citizenship, as the U.S. Embassy in Moscow had reported. For the most part, Oswald was vague about the details. The interview with Oswald had gone poorly, primarily because it wasn't conducted under the appropriate circumstances. It got so ugly, Carter told me after the assassination, that at one point after Oswald had baited Fain one too many times with his smart-ass remarks, Fain almost lost it; he was within a hair of clobbering Oswald.

Following this interview, Fain had called me at the Dallas office and asked me to run over to the Immigration and Naturalization Service (INS) office and review Marina Oswald's immigration file. I got a copy of her report, as well as a photo of her. I noted that Marina was college educated and a trained and licensed pharmacist. I also noted she was only twenty-two years old.

I had recently been to Washington for in-service training on security and counter-espionage cases, and during one of my classes I had learned of a new technique the Soviets were employing in the espionage wars. They were recruiting and training young, highly educated Soviets as intelligence agents in the United States. The Soviets used a variety of means to place their agents in the States. Sometimes they would blend into a wave of immigrants here; other times they would enter from a third country, using false names and documents. Once in the States, these people would lie low, sometimes for years, before being activated. In spy-talk, these agents were known as "sleepers." The Soviets were taking these measures in case the cold war escalated to the point where diplomatic communications were cut off. With dozens, if not hundreds, of agents in place throughout the United States, the Soviets would still have their eyes and ears here, and therefore be able to collect intelligence if diplomatic relations were ever severed.

Intelligence collection does not involve just getting "top secret" items. It includes a whole range of matters and techniques, including such mundane matters as reading newspapers and trade magazines for useful information. Soviet agents could also furnish "safe houses" for fellow agents, or act as mail drops and couriers, or service "dead drops" — a situation where one Soviet agent would place or "drop" intelligence matters at a place for a different Soviet agent to retrieve at a later time.

As I sat in my Dallas office in July 1962, the thought had struck me: Marina Oswald, as a Russian bride of a recently returned American defector, perfectly fit the criteria of a potential espionage agent: a well-educated young person who had left the Soviet Union under unusual circumstances.

After I gave Fain the information he wanted from the INS, I went to my supervisor in the Dallas office and asked if I could open a file on Marina Oswald. Howe said no. I persisted, reminding him that she fit the criteria for a sleeper. Finally he agreed, but said to open the file "pending inactive." That meant the file had a hold on it for six months, indicating no action could be taken. FBI procedure dictated that we should allow recent immigrants a six-month grace period to settle in before we began interviewing them.

As Fain in Fort Worth was nearer to the Oswalds, he was assigned the new file on Marina Oswald.

On August 16, 1962, roughly six weeks after the disastrous first interview with Lee, Fain decided it was time to try again. Along with agent Arnold Brown, Fain drove over to the Oswalds' home in Fort Worth. Timing their arrival for about 5:00 P.M., when they knew Lee would be walking home from work, they parked just down the street. Shortly after they arrived, Lee came strolling by. Fain asked Lee if they could talk with him again, to which Lee agreed. They decided to conduct the interview in Fain's Bureau car.

During this interview, Lee was radically different from the first time. He was polite and calmly answered the questions put to him. In short, Lee told Fain that when he was in the Soviet Union he had come to realize its flaws, which was why he had returned to the United States. Oswald said he no longer was an adherent to communism or the Soviet way, but instead simply wanted to work hard and take care of his wife and young daughter. In Fain's mind, Oswald seemed a reasonable young man. I think Fain heard only what he wanted to hear.

In September 1962, with his retirement just weeks away, Fain closed the case on Lee Oswald. Fain retired in October 1962, right in the middle of the Cuban Missile Crisis, and I inherited all his cases. Because of all the commotion and stress of the crisis, Fain and I never had an opportunity to sit down and discuss the transfer of his cases, one of which was the pending inactive case on Marina Oswald.

In late February 1963, after the six-month wait, I activated the Marina Oswald file and decided to locate her. I drove out to her last known address in Fort Worth, but learned from the landlady that the Oswalds had moved to Dallas, with no forwarding address. In mid-March I went to the INS office, because all aliens are supposed to update any change of address in January each year. Marina had done so; her new address was on Elsbeth Street, but when I drove out there, the Oswalds' landlady, Mrs. Tobias, told me she had kicked them out recently because of their constant fighting and yelling. She said they had moved nearby, but she wasn't sure where.

At the post office I learned the Oswalds were now living at 214 Neely Street. I drove out there and checked the mailbox: Oswald. That confirmed, I got back in my car and left. I had decided to give them a cooling-off period, once again per Bureau procedure, which dictated that all interviews should be conducted under tranquil circumstances. When it was known there were domestic disputes, an agent should know to back off for a while. We also never interviewed people at their place of employment, since we did not want to embarrass or antagonize anyone.

When I got back to my office I wrote up my report, for which I reviewed Lee's old file. It contained an intriguing memo: our New York office had discovered in one of its routine checks that Lee Oswald had recently taken out a subscription to the *Daily Worker,* the U.S. Communist party newspaper. The subscription started just after Fain had closed the file on Lee in September 1962.

I was also interested to see that the memo had been initialed by Fain in late October 1962 — after Fain had retired. I later discovered that when the memo came into the Dallas office, the relief supervisor mistakenly forwarded it to Fain rather than to me. Someone, for reasons unknown to me, forged Fain's initials on the memo, a false indicator that Fain had read the memo, and filed it away.

To me it was clear we needed to reopen the file on Lee Oswald. Lee had lied to Fain in the September 1962 interview when he told him he was disillusioned with communism, if subscribing to the *Daily Worker* was any indication.

I found Howe, showed him the *Daily Worker* memo, and told him that we really should reopen the case on Lee. Howe reluctantly agreed: I suspect Howe thought Oswald was a pest — Howe had been the supervisor of Oswald's case when Fain conducted his interviews — and preferred not having to deal with him.

About six weeks later, in May 1963, I decided that the Oswalds had had enough time to cool off. It wasn't as if the Oswalds were my only, or even my major, concern. I was heavily involved in investigating former U.S. Army general and leader of the Dallas-based Minutemen Edwin Walker for possibly inciting a riot at the University of Mississippi in Oxford during a tense confrontation over desegregation. I was under intense pressure from headquarters on the Walker case; they had made it my top priority.

When I returned to the house the Oswalds had been renting, I found they had moved out with no forwarding address. This time neither the INS nor the post office had a new address. All my other efforts to track them down proved fruitless. I wrote up a report on the Oswalds, noting that I was confident we would find them shortly.

About three weeks later, our New Orleans office sent me a memo informing me the Oswalds were now living there. An informant also advised the New York office that Lee Oswald was engaged in pro-Castro activities for the Fair Play for Cuba Committee, which had its headquarters in New York. I did not know it before the assassination, but the FBI knew that this group received most of its funding from the Cuban government. It seemed that Lee wanted to play an active role for this committee in New Orleans. The New Orleans FBI office was ordered to look into all this, and accordingly I transferred my files on Marina and Lee to the New Orleans office.

Milton Kaack was the FBI agent who took over my files on the Oswalds. A second agent, Warren DeBrueys, was also assigned to look into the Fair Play for Cuba Committee activities in New Orleans. DeBrueys later determined that Lee Oswald was the only member of the

New Orleans branch of this group; in other words, two FBI agents were assigned to monitor one person: Lee Oswald. It wasn't until after the assassination that I learned of reports showing that Oswald had made numerous contacts with the Soviet Embassy and other Communist organizations.

Sometime later in the summer and early fall of 1963, DeBrueys came up with what would turn out later to be valuable conclusions. DeBrueys not only figured out that Oswald was the only member of the Fair Play for Cuba Committee's branch in New Orleans, but concluded that Lee was using the alias A. J. Hidell and frequently signed Hidell's name to membership rosters and correspondence to double the size of his organization's apparent membership. DeBrueys's deduction of Lee's alias of A. J. Hidell made a trace of the rifle that killed the president possible.

On August 9, 1963, Lee was arrested in New Orleans when he got involved in a fistfight while passing out flyers for the Fair Play for Cuba Committee. The next day, in the city jail, Lee told a police lieutenant that he wanted to talk to an FBI agent. The lieutenant called the FBI and told them some guy in the city jail wanted to talk to them. Since it was a Saturday, one of the agents on call, Jack Quigley, was sent down to the jail. Quigley, a criminal agent, did not deal with counterintelligence or espionage cases. It is still unknown why Oswald wanted to talk to the FBI, but this type of request from men in city jails was not unusual. Frequently inmates would blab their crimes to cellmates, and sometimes these cellmates would provide key evidence to an FBI agent. Perhaps Oswald wanted to know what if anything the New Orleans FBI knew about him.

When Quigley sat down across from Lee, Oswald made a number of self-serving statements about his activities with the Fair Play for Cuba Committee, telling Quigley it was his patriotic duty as an American to distribute the flyers because Americans needed to back off Cuba. It soon became apparent to Quigley that Oswald was holding back: he refused to answer many of Quigley's questions about the pro-Castro committee, and was increasingly evasive about the identification found in his wallet for one A. J. Hidell. Because Quigley was unfamiliar with Oswald, the interview was completely unproductive. The following week, when he wrote up his report, he noticed that his office had an active file on Lee Oswald, so he routed his report to that file.

In October 1963, the New Orleans office sent me a communication reporting that the Oswalds had again disappeared. New Orleans had learned from a neighbor of the Oswalds that one afternoon in late September 1963, an American woman who spoke Russian drove up in a station wagon with Texas license tags and picked up Marina, her daughter, and their belongings. The next day, Lee left without paying his rent.

Later that month, shortly after I received the New Orleans memo, I returned to the INS office to check on another case. Jeff Woolsey, the chief clerk at the INS office, said, "Hey, Jim, what do you think of Lee Oswald being in Mexico City and making contact with the Russians a little while ago?"

"I didn't know that," I replied. "Can I see that communication?"

"I can't. Sorry, Jim," Woolsey said, somewhat embarrassed.

He couldn't show me the communication because of the third-agency rule. If agency A has information it chooses to share with agency B, agency B is not allowed to share that information with agency C. This is the rule because if agency A wanted C to have that information, it would have given it to C. The rule exists to assure security of classified and sensitive information. In this case, I represented agency C, Woolsey agency B. From the little Woolsey had let slip, I surmised that agency A was the CIA.

Back at the office, I sent an urgent overnight-air communication, what the FBI calls an Airtel, to FBI headquarters and the New Orleans office reporting what Woolsey told me. I asked the New Orleans office to respond. By return mail, I received information even more detailed than what Woolsey apparently had: FBI headquarters had been provided with information from the CIA, just as the INS, Navy, and State Department had. This information had logically been forwarded to our New Orleans office, which had the Oswald file.

When I received this information in late October from New Orleans, I saw the communication was dated October 18, 1963. The CIA report said that Lee Oswald had been in Mexico City and had made contact with V. V. Kostikov, a vice consul at the Soviet Embassy there. Per Bureau procedure, if Kostikov had been a KGB agent, or anything more, it was the duty of headquarters to note this for the agent in the field. They had not done this, so I figured Kostikov was just a simple administrative officer at the embassy. The communication was labeled "No Further Dissemination," which meant I was prohibited from discussing these matters with any other agency.

I guess my urgent interest got the New Orleans office moving. Overnight, they sent me the Oswalds' new address at Ruth Paine's home in Irving, Texas. New Orleans, however, maintained control over the Oswalds' files; they would not transfer them back to me until I had confirmed that the Oswalds were here in my territory.

On October 29, 1963, I drove to Ruth Paine's home at 2515

West 5th Street in Irving, Texas, and saw a station wagon with Texas tags in the driveway. I parked my car and strolled up to a neighbor's house. I asked the woman who answered the door if Ruth Paine lived next door. She said yes, and added that there was a Russian woman, who spoke no English and who had a little girl and a baby, living with her. The neighbor said that the woman who spoke no English apparently had no husband, as she didn't see one. I thanked her and left. I knew I had located Marina Oswald.

My objective was to conduct an in-depth interview of Marina to determine whether she posed any national security risk. But before I did I had to have a handle on matters. I decided I would first approach Ruth and Michael Paine to learn a little more about the Oswalds. Before any key interview, an agent needs to collect as much information as he can on the subject. Also, before I approached the Paines I needed to know a little about them. What if Ruth was a Communist? I wanted to know as much as I could about all parties concerned before I talked with them.

I ran credit bureau and background checks on Ruth and her husband, Michael Paine. Ruth taught Russian at a local prep school. Michael was an engineer at Bell Helicopter in Fort Worth and — reassuring to me — had a security clearance.

On Friday, November 1, 1963, I had a stack of cases based in Fort Worth that I had inherited from Fain. I made the 40-minute drive out to Fort Worth and worked my other cases first. Then, at about 3:00 P.M., I decided to pay a visit to Ruth Paine. Ruth lived right off the U.S. 183 expressway, the same expressway I would take back to the Dallas office, so it fit my plans logistically.

I parked my car on the street in front of the house. Ruth answered the door, and I introduced myself and showed her my credentials. She invited me to come inside.

We sat down in her living room and chatted casually for several minutes. I wanted to put her at ease: my objective today was simply to confirm that the Oswalds were living with her. She explained that Marina and her new baby and little girl were living with her and her own two children. Michael and Ruth Paine were separated, and so in effect were Marina and Lee. After some hesitation, she said that Lee was living in Dallas and working at one of the warehouses operated by the Texas School Book Depository. I was relieved to know Lee was simply a common laborer at some schoolbook warehouse. I didn't really care where his work was located, just the type of work. His job was not one that was a threat to national security.

Ruth said she didn't know exactly where Lee lived, but she

thought it was a small apartment in the Oak Cliff area of Dallas. She was letting Marina live with her while Lee tried to get settled down. I had a sense that Ruth truly felt for Marina, a young mother in a strange new land, and was simply trying to help her.

As we talked, a pretty young brunette with beautiful green eyes came out of one of the back bedrooms, stretching sleep off her bones. Ruth introduced me to Marina, speaking in Russian. Marina reacted instantly, her body language revealing her fear and anxiety. I was used to this reaction from immigrants from countries behind the Iron Curtain. Many of them immediately equated the FBI with the KGB or the MVD, which had a reputation for intimidating its own citizens. I did my best to put Marina at ease.

With Ruth translating, I explained that the FBI was not like the KGB or MVD, that the FBI was here to protect her, and that if she ever felt threatened by anyone, American or otherwise, she should let me know and I would try to protect her rights as a lawful alien. I assured Ruth and Marina that I was not there to harass them or Lee and that, per FBI procedure, I would never try to talk with Lee at his place of employment. This last was important to both women, because Lee had complained that the FBI had cost him jobs in the past. I told them I thought this very unlikely.

Marina, now sitting next to Ruth, seemed visibly to relax. The women told me that Lee was expected to visit this weekend, and they promised to find out exactly where he was living.

I looked at my watch, and saw I had been there just over a half-hour. I didn't have a second agent with me and I wasn't prepared to do my in-depth interview of Marina, so I asked Ruth to tell Marina that I would like to come back some time soon. Marina nodded and said that was fine. I wrote out my name and office phone number on a piece of paper, then headed out the door.

The first thing I did on Monday morning was to send an Airtel to the New Orleans office asking them to transfer the files on the Oswalds, as I had now reestablished my jurisdiction.

I didn't want to conduct an interview with Marina until I ascertained what New Orleans had done or not done. For all I knew, the Bureau might have conducted a series of in-depth interviews of both Oswalds. I decided I had to wait for New Orleans to send me all of its reports on the Oswald case. I didn't get the file, and the official transfer of the cases, until early on November 22, 1963. All New Orleans sent me was a New Orleans Police Department mug shot of Lee. No reports on any interviews or anything else.

• • • •

On Tuesday, November 5, 1963, I was out in Fort Worth working my other cases. I had a newly appointed agent, Gary Wilson, tagging along with me learning the ropes. I decided to run by Ruth's home and see if she had Lee's Oak Cliff address. I just wanted to get in and get out with this information, nothing else, while I was waiting for New Orleans to send me the files.

I pulled the car into the driveway this time, and Wilson and I went up to the house. Ruth chatted with us briefly at the front door. Ruth said she unfortunately didn't have the address for Lee, but she said Lee was a real character and that he had told her he was a Trotskyite. Ruth also said she felt that Marina would be moving out soon and in with Lee, probably in Dallas.

Wilson and I thanked her and left. We had been there less than five minutes, and we hadn't seen Marina until we were getting ready to leave. We left without saying a word to her. I didn't know then that while Wilson and I were talking with Ruth, Marina had slipped out of the house and jotted down my license plate number. I had earlier given Ruth my name and office phone number, and I later learned that she then gave these to Lee after my first visit on November 1, 1963, the information that later turned up in his little address book.

While I waited for New Orleans to send me the Oswald files, I was frozen. By FBI policy I was forbidden from interviewing Lee about his Mexico City trip prior to the assassination because we didn't want to compromise our sources and methods in Mexico City. If I had sat down with Lee and asked him about his visit to the Soviet and Cuban embassies in Mexico City, he would have learned more than I. Oswald would have realized that U.S. intelligence had monitoring systems in place in Mexico City. If Oswald had then forwarded this information on to the Soviets and Cubans, the CIA surveillance setup would have been blown. The CIA and FBI would have weighed what we knew about Oswald and would have decided it was better not to reveal our sources and methods than to interview Oswald. Even if I had interviewed Oswald, what would we have gained? He would have undoubtedly denied he was at the embassies. Oswald's track record as a witness for the FBI was poor. He was a liar and a belligerent. Actually, he really wasn't too different from all the FBI subjects. In any event, I continued working my other more pressing cases, in no way bothered by the fact that I couldn't yet act on the Oswald cases.

The day the president arrived in Dallas, I gave no thought to the connection between Lee Oswald and the fact that one of the Texas School Book Depository's two warehouses was on the parade route for the presidential party. At the time I had no information to indicate that Lee was violent or capable of killing anyone, much less the president. Lee had made no threats that I knew of. To me Lee and Marina were just routine espionage cases. All I was trying to find out was whether either one of them was a spy for the Soviets. Period.

Now here I was, sitting in Shanklin's office on Saturday, November 23, the day after Oswald had in all probability killed Kennedy, shaking my head. All around me, agents were shouting, phones were ringing off their hooks, the teletype machine was rattling feverishly, typewriters were banging and clattering. My head was throbbing, and despite everything I knew, one thought would not leave my mind: Could I have somehow prevented President Kennedy's assassination?

4

Sunday, November 24, 1963

TIME: 7:00 A.M.

As I was taking my coat off at my desk, I looked up and watched Shanklin come across the office, seemingly lost in some torturous thought. It looked as if he was wearing the same suit as yesterday; it was even more rumpled than usual. I couldn't believe it: the man had not been to bed since Friday. Just as I was sitting down, Shanklin called us all. He was holding a stack of papers, and his hand was visibly shaking.

He reviewed the latest news for all of us, though we pretty much knew it anyway. News travels swiftly among agents. Shanklin gave out the assignments for the day. When he came to me, he said, "Hosty, you're staying in the office today. God knows, headquarters will have more questions for you. I want you to handle walk-in and call-in reports."

I nodded, then leaned over to Barrett sitting next to me and whispered, "What a bunch of crap. Walk-ins and call-ins." That was an assignment for a junior agent. Or maybe even a clerk.

Shanklin raised his hand and said that the Dallas police had announced to the press, and to the world in general, that they were going to transfer Oswald from the police jail to the county jail and into the custody of the sheriff at 10:00 A.M. This meant transporting Oswald in vehicles while under heavy guard.

Shanklin went on to say that last night, at 2:30 A.M., Vernon

Glossup, one of our night clerks, had taken an anonymous phone call. Shanklin read Glossup's report: "I represent a committee that is neither right- or left-wing, and tonight, tomorrow morning, or tomorrow night, we are going to kill the man that killed the president. There will be no excitement and we will kill him. We wanted to be sure and tell the FBI, police department, and sheriff's office that we will be there and we will kill him." The caller, it seemed, was reading from a statement, and did so in a calm, mature voice. He hung up without identifying himself or his committee.

Shanklin said that when Glossup passed this information on to the night supervisor, Milton Newsom, he immediately reported it to the police, the sheriff's office, and FBI headquarters. The police and the sheriff's office reported to Newsom that they had received the same call. Shanklin said he then called Dallas Police Chief Jesse Curry and told him to move Oswald at once under cover of darkness. Some of Curry's assistants had reportedly recommended the same action. But Curry said that he was under pressure from the city manager and the press, and because he had promised the press that he would transport Oswald at 10:00 A.M., he told Shanklin he was keeping to schedule.

I knew what was going on behind the scenes. There was a power struggle between the city manager, Elgin Crull, and Curry, the newly appointed chief of police. A few months back, Crull had forced out the longtime chief, Carl Hansson, a man nationally recognized for his achievements. Crull and Hansson had had their philosophical differences, and Crull had come out on top.

Crull then moved Curry up to chief of police, but it was clear to Curry and everyone else that Crull was the boss. In late October 1963, United Nations ambassador Adlai Stevenson, who was also a liberal, visited Dallas, only to be roughed up by some right-wing radicals, one of whom hit him on the head with a placard. Following this, Crull hired the Sam Bloom public relations firm to advise the police department on how to handle the Kennedy visit. Many thought Kennedy's visit would be many times worse than Stevenson's.

After Kennedy was assassinated, the Sam Bloom agency, with Crull's backing, advised the police to be completely open to the press. The police were advised to show Oswald to the press as openly and as often as possible, which is why the Dallas Police Department had turned into a jungle of reporters and cameramen. I'm sure that even when advised about the threat to kill Oswald during the Sunday morning transport, Curry probably figured it was best to keep his promise to the press and transport Oswald on schedule.

During the morning briefing, Shanklin asked all of the agents present to be his witnesses; then he picked up the phone and dialed Curry's number. While we all listened, Shanklin said, "Chief, this is Gordon Shanklin again. Remember that phone call in which we were both warned that Oswald was to be killed during his transport this morning? . . . Well, you know it's my recommendation that you cancel those plans and try something else. . . . You're still going forward? . . . Well, I just wanted to warn you again." At that Shanklin hung up, turned to us, and angrily shook his head.

I heard the other agents muttering their astonishment at Curry's decision. I felt some pity for Curry, for I knew he was inextricably tied to Crull's directives. I was irritated at Crull's policies; a former newspaper man, he knew nothing about police procedure. To my mind, he was more concerned about the image of the police department than about what was prudent.

Before our meeting broke up, Shanklin ordered us, in no uncertain terms, to stay away from Oswald's transport. He didn't want any of us to get hurt, and he didn't want the FBI to take any flack if anything went wrong.

As the rest of the agents grabbed their coats and briefcases, I trudged over to the front counter to see if we had any walk-ins.

I took the first person who was sitting in the reception area and began taking notes of what he had to say. Most of the walk-ins and call-ins that day were people unsuccessfully trying to be helpful. For example, a man from Arizona called saying he had been watching news reports on television, and in one camera pan of the Texas School Book Depository he saw a chimney on the roof. He suggested that the FBI send a couple of men down the chimney, since an assassin might be hidden there. Another caller from somewhere in Texas said he thought he might have gone to school with Lee Oswald, but couldn't be sure. I took down the information and treated each item as a lead. In time, we would check each one out.

One walk-in proved interesting, however, and I spent about 45 minutes with her. Katyn Ford, a Russian-born refugee, and her American husband, Declan Ford, appeared in our reception area on the twelfth floor to offer some information about the Oswalds. I took them back to an interview room just off the main reception area. Katyn began by explaining that in Dallas there was a small Russian refugee community centered around a Russian Orthodox church. She told me that when they learned that Marina Oswald was in town, they had befriended her. Marina had grown up in Leningrad, and Katyn and many of the others in the community were also from Leningrad. Katyn told me she felt sorry for Marina because Lee was an abusive husband. Katyn explained that Lee annoyed all of the members of the Russian community in Dallas because he took a pro-Communist stand on practically everything, while the community was strongly anti-Communist. Generally, they had regarded Lee as an annoyance.

TIME: 11:21 A.M.

I had just finished the walk-in report from Katyn Ford and was going down the stairs to the eleventh floor, when I saw Ken Howe scrambling between the desks in the bullpen below. Howe's eyes were wild; he was grinding his teeth. He caught me on the last step. "Goddamn it, Jim, they've just killed Oswald!" Howe shouted. "And we told those police!"

I was stunned. My mouth opened, but no words emerged. Howe shoved me aside and charged up the stairs. My knees buckled and I collapsed on the stairs. My head was reeling and my lungs tightened. I couldn't believe it. The police had been warned and Oswald had been killed. Why in God's name had the police insisted on moving Oswald after they had been warned? Were the police involved in Oswald's death? I forced myself to say no, but I had a lingering doubt.

I must have remained there on the stairs for a few seconds. When I stood up, my leg muscles were slow and lethargic. Somehow I got to my desk and let my body slump into the chair. I picked up the phone and called Janet. The line was busy. I pulled a couple of papers together, put them in front of me on my desk, and stared at them. I didn't want to read them. I just wanted to be left alone so that my mind could adjust to this latest blast. I sat, then sat some more, feeling the world had gone mad. Remain calm, I told myself, you've got to remain calm.

TIME: 11:40 A.M.

My phone rang and I picked it up. It was the switchboard operator. "Jim, can you take a call from Captain Ganoway of the Dallas police?"

"Sure, I'll take it," I said. Pat Ganoway oversaw the police intelligence unit run by Revill.

The call was switched to me and I said, "Jim Hosty, what can I help you with, Captain?"

"Hosty, what do you guys have on a Jack Rubenstein, alias Jack Ruby? We've arrested him for shooting Oswald," Ganoway asked against a background of wild noise.

"Let me check. I'll get back to you, okay?"

"Sure. As soon as you can," Ganoway said, and hung up.

I jumped up and went over to our file cabinet and index system; it took only seconds to find Ruby's name. Our index system indicated that under the name Jack Ruby there were several insignificant references to organized crime matters. The most serious reference was that he was the subject of file number 137-681: Ruby was a potential FBI criminal informant.

I slammed the index drawer shut, searched for Ruby's file, grabbed it, and quickly read it. The file had only four pieces of paper in it. The first was a memo from Agent Charlie Flynn saying he was opening the file. The second was the "contact" page, which indicated Flynn had had several contacts with Ruby but no information had been developed. The third was a memo indicating the Ruby file was closed, because Flynn had been routinely transferred to another city. The final piece of paper was a misfiled item, dealing with an entirely different case!

Flynn had been a new young agent in our office, and part of any new agent's orientation to the Bureau was to develop informants. Bureau procedure dictated that all agents should have several informants. It is a fact of life that law enforcement is dependent on informants for a good part of its information. The FBI demanded that its agents aggressively seek out more and more potential informants. Since Ruby worked in a vice business, running a strip joint, he was considered close to the criminal elements. For a new agent in a strange new city, it's hard to find informants. That's why when I learned later that Flynn's use of Ruby as an informant had been more of a training exercise than the real thing, I understood that Flynn was just trying to keep Bureau higher-ups off his back and avoid disciplinary action rather than develop new information. Because Ruby never provided Flynn with any information, he was never regarded as anything more than a PCI, a Potential Criminal Informant.

With the file in hand, I went looking for Howe. I found him at his desk.

"Ken, Captain Ganoway just called and said they've arrested a guy named Jack Ruby for shooting Oswald," I explained. "Ganoway wants to know what we have on Ruby. Well, here it is: Ruby was one of our PCIs."

Howe snatched the file and quickly scanned it. After a moment, he ordered me not to call Ganoway back; he would take care of it.

I am sure Howe was concerned about two things. Because our informants are treated confidentially, it was exceedingly rare to reveal their identities. The moment you did you lost all credibility with all present and future informants. If we gave up Ruby, the next time we told an informant we would never reveal his or her identity, our credibility would be zero. Howe was also probably weighing the public relations aspect. How would this make the FBI look? Ruby was both an FBI PCI and Oswald's killer. The press would eat it up, distort it all to hell. I never did hear officially how headquarters decided to handle Ruby's PCI status. All I know is that no one was told about Ruby outside the Bureau and the Warren Commission, which did not publish anything about his PCI status; it did not become public until 1976, when it was released with and obscured by the flood of information in the Church Committee report.

Like many agents, I had joined the FBI as an idealistic young man. When it came to law enforcement, things were black and white to me. With time, my idealism waned, and I accepted the hard fact that law enforcement is basically gray. I also came to understand that one of our jobs was to protect the Bureau's image at all costs, even if it ran roughshod over individuals or principles. I kept getting up each morning because I knew that the vast majority of our work was just, and despite Hoover's quirks and weaknesses, I had to admit he ran a rather impressive machine.

TIME: 1:45 P.M.

I finally got through to Janet. My son Michael, who had just had his sixth birthday party Wednesday, answered the phone. After I explained to Michael that I would be home as soon as I could, Janet came on the line. She told me she had been watching television and had seen Jack Ruby shoot Oswald. Oswald, she went on, had died on the operating room table.

She also said that shortly after Oswald was shot, my parents called from Chicago. They were worried sick about me and wanted to know if they should cancel their trip to Dallas for Thanksgiving this week. Janet and I agreed they should still come; at least they could visit Janet and their grandchildren.

She told me to be careful, and I promised I would. I told her not to expect me until late again. After I hung up, I thought about my father and his father. My dad had been in the sugar business, but he had also been appointed police commissioner of River Forest, a small town just outside of Chicago. His father had immigrated to America from County Mayo, Ireland, and had become a police officer when he settled in Chicago. For 46 years, Luke Hosty had walked his beat on the streets of Chicago, keeping the hoodlums and no-goods in line. These past few days I had found myself thinking of my father and grandfather, wondering if they had ever been subjected to the level of stress I was now experiencing.

TIME: 6:00 P.M.

Since it was Sunday, Shanklin had let most of the clerks and stenos go home a little earlier. After they left, the agents working in the field were informed by radio or telephone to make sure they were back in the office by 8:00 P.M. for an all-agent meeting. I continued to work in the almost deserted office.

Howe told me Shanklin wanted to see me in his office. Throughout the day, Shanklin had been in constant telephone contact with his mentor, Johnnie Mohr, in Washington. Mohr, one of two deputy associate directors, was in charge of all non-investigative matters; in the pecking order, he was Hoover's number-four man. I had heard a story that years ago, when Shanklin was the SAC in another city, he had taken the fall on a matter for which Mohr was actually responsible, and as a result Mohr was greatly indebted to him. All the agents in Dallas knew that whenever Shanklin was in a tight spot or in need of advice, he turned to Mohr. Mohr understood Hoover's frequent tirades and was often called upon by different SACs to guide them through turbulent waters. As one SAC put it about Mohr, he may be an S.O.B. at times, but he's *our* S.O.B. Shanklin was a typical SAC in the Hoover FBI in that he wouldn't blow his nose until he first cleared it with someone. Shanklin almost always consulted Mohr for his clearances.

As I walked into Shanklin's office, Howe was right behind me. I stood in front of Shanklin's desk. Looking over my shoulder, I saw Howe standing in the doorway watching. I could tell by his expression that something was up. Shanklin cradled his cigarette in the ashtray and stood up behind his desk.

"Jim, now that Oswald is dead, there clearly isn't going to be a trial," he began, reaching down into his open "do not file" drawer. He pulled out the note that Oswald had delivered to this office ten days before the assassination, as well as the memo I had dictated on Friday explaining how I had come to receive the note. He thrust them at me, and said, "Here, take these. I don't want to ever see them again."

I took the memo and note from him and looked at him questioningly. Though I knew he was exhausted, he looked totally in control. Smoke from his cigarette billowed out of his nose. He was deadly serious, his eyes staring at me calmly.

I must have looked concerned or perplexed, which Shanklin instantly read.

"Look, I know this note proves nothing, but you know how people will second-guess us," he explained. I knew who those "people" were: Hoover and some of his lackeys. Monday morning quarterbacking was legendary in the FBI, with some of the higher-ups sure to run through a thousand "what-ifs."

Without really thinking any more about it, I began tearing up the note and memo right there in front of Shanklin and Howe.

"No! Not here! I told you, I don't want to see them again. Now get them out of here," Shanklin insisted.

I walked out of his office with the partially torn papers. Kyle Clark, the ASAC, was sitting at his desk in his office next to Shanklin's. When I walked by the open door to his office, I saw him look up quickly. As I walked on a few steps farther, Clark jumped up and went into Shanklin's office, shutting the door.

I was left alone with the job of destroying the papers. I walked past my desk, realizing I couldn't do it there. In fact, I thought, if I was going to do this, I needed to be alone.

I walked out to the stairwell and down half a flight of stairs to the landing where the men's bathroom was. I walked into the empty bathroom and went to the first toilet stall.

I didn't smoke, so I had no matches. I tore the papers into smaller pieces, and then threw the scraps of paper into the toilet. I pushed the flush handle and watched as the remnants of Oswald's note and my memo swirled around in the small whirlpool of water. Then they were gone. Forever.

Down the drain, I thought. Literally. I hoped the cliché didn't turn out to be prophetic.

I went back up the stairs, walked over to my desk, sat down, and tried to pull my thoughts together. There was no doubt that this note was ordered destroyed to keep Hoover from finding out about it. If Hoover had found out he would have blown up, and probably done something stupid. In my mind, I knew that Shanklin was operating under either the order or approval of someone back at headquarters. I figured it had to be Mohr. There was no way Shanklin would have ordered the destruction of the note unless he had first had some kind of go-ahead. He was just too damn cautious to give such an order without first running it by higher-ups.

In 1942, when I joined the Army as an eighteen-year-old, one of the first lessons I learned was that in battle a private had to blindly obey orders. He had to have full faith that the commander who gave the order knew what he was doing. The theory was that while it might appear to the GI in the trenches that the order was wrong or ill-conceived, he had to understand that he was only aware of his immediate surroundings, whereas the commander had a full view of the battlefield. When receiving an order, a private also didn't ask the colonel which general gave the order, or whether the colonel had given the order himself.

In many ways, the FBI was like the military, and I knew that the top brass back at headquarters had a full view of the battlefield. I also knew that Oswald had had some recent contacts with the Soviets, and therefore deduced that this whole sorry matter must have some serious international implications. I didn't know what was going on back in Washington, but Shanklin did. Something was afoot, and it smelled like cover-up.

At my desk, I said a prayer. I prayed that the people back in Washington knew what the hell they were doing.

TIME: 8:00 P.M.

All the agents had gathered for our meeting with Shanklin. Everyone was looking beleaguered, if not flat-out exhausted. We were a haggard bunch of men, but we were also a tight bunch of men, much like a fraternity. We stuck together and tried to look out for one another. Agents were also constantly sharing information, and everyone had a tidbit of unbelievable information they had come across the past few days.

One of our agents, Charlie Brown, said that when he heard over the radio that Oswald had been shot and was being transported to Parkland Hospital, he had turned his car around and dashed over there. When he arrived, emergency room personnel had wheeled Oswald into the operating room where the doctors were preparing to perform emergency surgery on the single gunshot wound to his chest. As Brown watched various doctors and nurses scrubbing up and gathering outside the operating room, he approached one of the younger doctors. He identified himself and told the doctor he needed to get in that room and stay next to Oswald in case he wanted to make a confession. No way, you can't go in there, the doctor replied. Brown persisted, telling the doctor that Oswald was charged with killing the president and that he had to stay near him in case he confessed. Finally the doctor agreed, but told Brown he would have to scrub up and put on a gown and mask.

Brown quickly scrubbed and dressed, then went into the operating room. Oswald was unconscious, and the doctors were working frantically to stop the bleeding. At 1:07 P.M., a doctor pronounced it was over. Oswald had died. The bullet had severed a major artery, and Oswald had bled to death. When he was shot, he had quickly gone into shock and lost consciousness. He never regained consciousness, and with his death, he was forever silenced.

Agent Bob Barrett also related his encounters with Oswald on Friday afternoon. When the report came over the radio that an "officer was down" in the Oak Cliff neighborhood, Barrett had sped to the scene. When he got there, the ambulance crew had already removed Tippit's body. Captain Westbrook and the Dallas police were in charge, but Barrett set about inspecting the crime scene. Near the puddle of blood where Tippit's body had lain, Westbrook had found a man's leather wallet. In it, he discovered identification for Lee Oswald, as well as other identification for Alek J. Hidell. Westbrook called Barrett over and showed him the wallet and identifications. Westbrook asked Barrett if the FBI knew anything about Oswald or Hidell. Barrett shook his head. Westbrook took the wallet into his custody so that it could be placed into police property later. Barrett told me that if I had been at the scene with Westbrook, I would have immediately known who Oswald was.

Although official police reports would later state that Oswald's wallet and identification were found on Oswald's person when he was arrested in the movie theater, Barrett insists that Westbrook found them near where Tippit was slain. I have to speculate that at the theater, Westbrook had handed the wallet to a lower-ranking officer, and in the confusion it was assumed the wallet had been retrieved from Oswald's person. The FBI decided to go with the official police version, even though Barrett's version was further proof that Oswald had in fact gunned Officer Tippit down. As Barrett said, the case against Oswald for killing Tippit was a "slam-dunk."

Also at the scene, Barrett inspected spent shell casings and listened to one of the numerous eyewitnesses to the shooting. Helen Markham, the waitress who saw Oswald shoot Tippit, was in near hysterics trying to relate the grisly scene to the police.

Another witness was a taxi driver, Willie Scoggins, who had been parked nearby eating his lunch when he saw the officer go down in the shooting. When the killer walked by Scoggins's taxi, the driver was hiding behind it, and could hear the killer muttering, "Poor dumb cop, poor dumb cop." Scoggins later positively identified Oswald at the lineup.

A carpet-layer who was eating his lunch nearby also saw Oswald shoot Tippit, and two ladies from the neighborhood heard the shots and saw Oswald standing over the dying officer when they came out to see what was happening. Five witnesses in all saw the shooting.

When a call came on the radio at the crime scene that a young, suspicious-acting man had ducked into a nearby movie without paying, Barrett and a bunch of police officers hightailed it to the theater. From what I learned later, the movie was stopped, the lights went up, and a shoe salesman who had seen Oswald duck in quickly pointed him out in the nearly empty theater. As Barrett looked on, the police officers moved in to arrest Oswald. Oswald yelled, "It's all over now," and pulled out his revolver. He pointed it at an officer and pulled the trigger. The officer instinctively reacted by thrusting the web of skin between his thumb and index finger between the revolver's hammer and bullet, thereby preventing the hammer from striking and firing the bullet. Oswald was wrestled under control, and in the melee was hit above his eye, causing a blackened swelling.

When the officers escorted Oswald out of the theater, a mob had already formed. Word had spread that a killer had been arrested, and many had already assumed it was the president's assassin. The police had to hold off the mob; the increasingly angry and ugly crowd was threatening to beat Oswald to death.

In addition to Barrett, agents Bardwell Odum and Jim Swinford were standing in the back of the theater at the time of the arrest. Odum told me that when Oswald was being escorted out of the theater, he shouted, "Police brutality! Police brutality!" — seemingly in an effort to get the mob on his side. Instead, Odum said, the mob was turning violent; one old lady even swatted her umbrella at Oswald.

Another story illustrating the total confusion and chaos that immediately followed the president's assassination was told by Doyle Williams, a senior criminal agent in our office. Williams was one of the other agents who, like me, had immediately responded to Parkland Hospital. While I was recalled to the office, Williams had been ordered by Bobby Kennedy and Hoover to find out what was happening in the emergency room.

When Williams got the report that the president had died, he grabbed a nurse and told her he was an FBI agent and that he needed a phone immediately. The nurse told Williams to follow her, and the two of them moved hastily down the emergency unit's hallway. The nurse came to a curtained-off corner and, pulling the curtain slightly aside, told Williams there was a phone in there. Williams stormed in, eager to place his call. The instant he walked inside the curtained area, a burly man cold-cocked him square in the nose. Williams slammed to the floor. When he looked up three dark-suited men were over him, glaring. They demanded to know who he was. He told them he was an FBI agent and showed them his credentials. After closely examining the credentials, one of the dark-suited men helped Williams up.

It turned out that President Johnson had been placed in the curtained area and the dark-suited men were all Secret Service agents. The Secret Service men were in a state of near hysteria. They had already lost one president today, and they would be damned if they would lose another. They weren't letting anyone but Secret Service agents anywhere close to Johnson. Apparently the Secret Service has a special ID system: each day a particular and distinct lapel pin is distributed for personnel to wear on their suit jackets; this allows agents to recognize one another immediately. Obviously, as an FBI agent Williams wasn't wearing one of these pins. When he came storming into the protective bubble of the new president, the Secret Service let him have it.

These past three days had been numbing for all of us. But I had an added burden. A giant vortex had angrily come to life and sucked me into it at 12:30 P.M., Friday, November 22. For all eternity, Lee Oswald and I would to a degree be linked. I knew that I would always be known as the FBI agent who had an active case on the man who would later kill the president. Now the bastard was dead before we could pump him for an answer to the question: Why?

Shanklin began the meeting tonight by telling us that Henry Wade, the Dallas district attorney who had filed murder charges on Ruby, had held a press conference announcing that his case on Oswald was now officially closed because Oswald was dead.

Shanklin continued by saying that President Johnson had ordered the FBI to take over the entire investigation from the Dallas police. This meant that the FBI would have to get from the police all the evidence in its custody. President Johnson wanted the FBI to conduct its investigation expeditiously and report back to him. The new president did not want any public hearings; he himself would report to the American public based on our findings.

That's interesting, I thought, no public hearings. Johnson obviously did not want the public to hear all the evidence. My feeling that there must be international implications got stronger.

Shanklin said that Division 6, the criminal division in the Bureau, would be in charge of the investigation. Division 6 was headed by Assistant Director Al Rosen, and he was sending to Dallas his top lieutenant,

Deputy Assistant Director Jim Malley. When Malley got here, he would be in charge in the Dallas office. Alan Belmont, a deputy associate director and Rosen's boss, would maintain overall control of the investigation.

Another interesting development, I thought. The cases I had on Lee and Marina Oswald had been counter-espionage or security cases, not criminal cases. Division 5 was the security division, which was headed by Assistant Director Bill Sullivan, a studious, academic type and a favorite of Hoover's. I wondered to myself, did this mean anything? I guess in a strict sense the assassination, when reduced to its basest level, was simply another violent homicide. Still, I knew that all of Hoover's top aides were constantly jockeying among themselves for power, and the pecking order was always in a state of flux.

I later learned, however, that when Belmont, who was in overall charge of both Divisions 5 and 6, would give his briefings to the supervisors of the two divisions, he would sometimes stop and have the supervisors from Division 6, the criminal division, step out of the room while he continued to brief the Division 5 supervisors. This angered the Division 6 supervisors: once again, it was the old need-to-know game. Obviously there were very sensitive security or espionage matters surrounding the assassination, and Belmont was being very cautious.

Shanklin said agents from all over the central states would begin pouring into our office tomorrow. In fact, many were en route right now. Because our ranks would be swelling to over a hundred men, the General Services Administration had granted an emergency approval for us to commandeer office space on the seventh floor of this building.

Shanklin said that we would be dividing up into two investigative squads tomorrow. One squad, known as the Oswald squad, would investigate the president's assassination, Tippit's killing, and Oswald's background. The other squad, the Ruby squad, would investigate Oswald's killing and Ruby's background. The Ruby squad would set up on the seventh floor, while the Oswald squad, which would be larger, would double up on desks in the bullpen on the eleventh floor. Office logistics should not be a problem, Shanklin explained, since all the agents would be spending most of their time in the field, not at desks.

With the out-of-town agents, Shanklin said, would come more clerks, stenos, typewriters, automobiles, teletype machines, and other office supplies. Agents, their clerks, and stenos had already literally packed their offices into their Bureau cars and started driving to Dallas. They were coming from all parts of Texas, Arkansas, Louisiana, Oklahoma, Kansas, and Colorado. All of them would be here for the duration of our investigation, and would be put up in nearby hotels.

Shanklin said he wanted everyone to go home and get some

sleep. He wanted us all there early tomorrow so that he could divide everyone into two squads and give out assignments.

TIME: 9:45 P.M.

The drive home seemed far longer than normal. I parked the car, climbed out, stiff and aching, and walked up to the house. Our home was a nice ranch house with off-pink brick and wood trim. We were on a short block of 12 homes, and in that block lived a total of 55 children. It was a vibrant and fun place to live. We had four bedrooms, a two-car garage, a den, and a backyard basketball hoop. It was my sanctuary.

Janet had been sitting in the den intently watching the news reports when I accidentally banged the door open. She jumped up and hurried to me. She told me to sit down, and we took seats on the sofa in the den. She looked into my eyes, saw their sorrow, and then her eyes started to water. For a few moments, neither of us said a word.

I was a fortunate man. I had been blessed with this woman as my wife, and today, as I have done each day since I first met her, I thanked God for bringing us together. I thought back to the first time I met her, at the front door of her parents' house. Janet was a junior at Rosary College, a Catholic school for women near Chicago, and I had been set up with her for a blind date for her junior prom. I had recently returned from the war and had just graduated from Notre Dame. When Janet opened the door that night, I thought, She's beautiful, how could she be unattached? I later learned that she had been a model and had been featured in a Coca-Cola advertisement as the all-American, athletic, girl-next-door type — drinking, of course, a nice cold bottle of Coca-Cola. On that first date we had what is called the "right chemistry." We talked for hours.

After Janet graduated from college with a degree in economics, we married. She said she wanted lots of children, and so far we had eight. Our oldest child, Jimmy, was almost twelve, and our youngest, Tommy, was just three months. Life had taken a magical turn when I married Janet. She had incredible strength and tenacity, and I was counting on those qualities now as I slumped in the sofa of our den.

She asked me if I was hungry, and I nodded. She got up and went in the kitchen to prepare something. My two oldest boys, Jimmy and Bobby, and the two oldest girls, Teri and Janet, were still awake, watching Walter Cronkite on television, saying something about something. I didn't care.

I closed my eyes, and smelled meat loaf in the kitchen. I let my mind and body go free, and drifted off to sleep.

5

When I walked into the bullpen, I was met by the sight and buzz of a hundred FBI agents. The reinforcements had arrived.

It was good, actually exciting, to see all these guys. I could see how quickly the out-of-town agents were starting to meld into our Dallas unit. They were highly trained professionals, and with the green light from the new president, anxious to hit the streets and get down to business. There was an aura of confidence in the room.

Someone pointed to the stairs, and the agents instinctively started to quiet and bring themselves to order. Shanklin was coming down the steps from the twelfth floor, followed by two other men. Shanklin called the room to order and introduced the men with him: Jim Malley, the deputy assistant director for Division 6, the criminal division, and Dick Rogge, Malley's aide from headquarters. I heard later that Malley's second aide, Fletcher Thompson, had also flown in, but he had immediately flown back to headquarters with a secret file. I speculated that it was the Mexico City phone intercept transcript that Heitman had retrieved from Rudd.

Malley, who was in his fifties, stood next to Shanklin. Malley had grown up in Kansas City, Kansas, a town of tough Irish and Eastern European immigrants who worked in the factories and mills six days a week and prayed in their respective churches on Sunday. Malley was a ruddy-faced Irishman with dark hair, and he looked like the kind of guy you would want by your side if you ever found yourself mixed up in a pub brawl. He looked all the agents over, as if he were sizing us up.

Shanklin stood in sharp contrast to Malley. Malley stood the way an admiral stands on the deck of a ship; Shanklin was like the ship's captain. The captain technically still runs the ship, but he takes his orders from the admiral. Shanklin began the meeting with a short reminder that matters were now fully in our hands, and that it was critical we do the best job possible.

Shanklin read names off some papers and divided us into the Oswald and Ruby squads. The majority of the agents were assigned to the Oswald squad. My name was conspicuously missing from this list. Then Shanklin read off the Ruby squad list, which included me. The agents on both squads were put into two-man teams, one man from Dallas or Fort Worth, and the second from out of town.

Why in the hell had I been placed on the Ruby squad? A number of agents had also noticed the oversight, and looked over at me sheepishly. Was I being treated like the proverbial "bastard at the family reunion"? I could imagine the thoughts running through the out-of-town agents' heads. Hosty: Isn't he the guy who was assigned to the Oswalds *before* the assassination? My face flushed and I started to perspire. Self-doubt began to gnaw at me again.

After Shanklin had finished dividing us up into the two squads, he gave out assignments to the individual teams. On the Oswald squad, Bob Barrett was put at the lead to investigate Tippit's killing, since he had been at the crime scene and the arrest of Oswald. Nat Pinkston, a senior criminal agent, was put in charge of the Dealey Plaza assassination site investigation. Shanklin was in overall control of all investigators.

On the Ruby squad, Manning Clements, the former ASAC from Alaska who was now stationed in Dallas, was put in overall control. I was given an assignment to interview an apartment neighbor of Ruby's. Whatever, I thought. When the meeting broke up I grabbed my partner and took off.

TIME: 9:00 A.M.

I rapped on the door at the apartment complex where Ruby had lived. A lady, Ruby's neighbor, answered. After my partner and I introduced ourselves, she invited us in. I looked around: it was a modest apartment, nothing extravagant. If this was how Ruby lived, then I guess Ruby didn't make a whole lot of money himself. I had heard that he owned a bar where girls stripped, a "classy" business. I took out my note pad and began to question the lady about everything she knew about Jack Ruby.

She told me that she dated a Dallas policeman, and through this relationship she knew that Ruby was close to the police department and the district attorney's office. She said everyone at both places knew Ruby well; he was a handshaking, gregarious guy. I thought to myself, Ruby is probably just a savvy businessman. He probably realized it's never a bad idea to be on good terms with the law, especially when you're in the vice business.

Other than this information, Ruby's neighbor didn't have much to offer. We thanked her for her assistance and left. My partner and I went back to my Bureau car to discuss our next step. As we were sitting there, Kyle Clark, the Dallas ASAC, called me over the radio: "7392, report back to the office. I'll explain when you arrive." My partner and I exchanged questioning looks. I put the car in gear and drove back to the office.

TIME: 11:00 A.M.

With my partner trailing, I entered Clark's office, which was just off the main reception area on the twelfth floor. Clark told me to sit down, then excused my partner. He shut the door behind him.

White-haired and dark-skinned, Clark favored his full-blooded Native American grandparent. A transplanted Wyoming man, Clark's western hat and wardrobe worked well in this Texas town. I liked and admired Clark; he was an enthusiastic and hard worker. Clark was a protégé of Bill Sullivan, the man in charge of the security and intelligence Division 5. With Sullivan frequently at odds with Johnnie Mohr, it was interesting to watch the dynamics between Clark and Shanklin, Mohr being Shanklin's mentor. Now that Sullivan was being iced out by Rosen and Division 6, the criminal division, I'm sure Sullivan was somewhat in the dark on how operations were specifically being handled. Clark became, in a sense, Sullivan's eyes and ears in Dallas, and had been keeping Sullivan abreast of matters.

"Jim, a little while ago I spoke to Bill Sullivan on the phone," Clark said. "He wanted to let you know that in his view you handled the Oswald cases appropriately. And I agree." The Oswald cases were counter-espionage or security cases, and if the chief of Division 5 was telling me I had handled things properly, I was greatly relieved.

"Sullivan and I think it's absurd for Shanklin to have assigned you to the Ruby squad," Clark continued. "We both want you immediately reassigned to the Oswald squad, as the lead investigator of Oswald's background." This was great news. Not only had Sullivan backed me up, he was entrusting me with a key post-assassination assignment. I was on the edge of my seat, nodding my head. "Now sit tight, and let me run this all by Shanklin and Malley," Clark said. I only hoped that they would now go along with Clark.

After a few minutes, Clark came back and told me that not only had Shanklin and Malley agreed to put me on the Oswald squad, but that I was in fact to be the lead investigator of Oswald's background. I took the Ruby squad roster and pointed out to Clark that Warren DeBrueys had investigated Oswald and the Fair Play for Cuba Committee in New Orleans, that it was his detective work that had made the rifle trace possible. Clark nodded and told me to take DeBrueys as my partner.

Before I went looking for DeBrueys, I decided to thank Malley. He was standing just outside Shanklin's office on the twelfth floor. I introduced myself and thanked him for my new assignment. He shook my hand, looked me over, rudely mumbled something, then turned his back and walked away. I got the strong impression that he had probably been the one to bury me in the Ruby squad.

I looked over and saw Rogge, Malley's aide, standing by a steno. I went over and introduced myself. Rogge was much more pleasant. After a few amenities, he said, with what seemed like carefully chosen words, "You had the Oswald case, but you didn't know he was dangerous."

My stomach knotted. Had Oswald in fact been a dangerous man, and I did not have this information? Presumably somebody did. Headquarters? The CIA? What exactly did our intelligence agencies know about Oswald? Was this one of those instances where the CIA and FBI did not share intelligence information?

I decided to go talk with Clark. I saw Howe was in Clark's office. I tapped on the open door and moseyed in.

"Kostikov was going to —" Clark was saying when I walked in, but when he saw me he stopped abruptly. Howe and Clark turned and looked at me. After a moment of awkward silence, Clark asked, "What do you want?"

"I wanted to talk to you. But it can wait."

"I'll come and get you later," Clark replied.

Kostikov again. Who was he, and what was going on? I was being kept from the full facts. The wagons were circling very rapidly: was I being left on the outside? There was undoubtedly some sensitive information involving Oswald's dealings with the Soviets and Cubans. It was that damn need-to-know rule.

TIME: 3:00 P.M.

It took a couple of hours for DeBrueys and me to hook up; when we did I told him that our first assignment was to retrieve all the assassination evidence from the Dallas police. We took my car and drove over to the police department. On our way, DeBrueys and I engaged in the typical introductory chitchat. We agreed it had been idiotic to place us both on the Ruby squad. Thankfully, we thought, we were both not only on the Oswald squad now but the lead investigators. DeBrueys turned out to be an amazing guy. Of Italian and French ancestry, he spoke fluent French, Spanish, and Portuguese, and was a dark-complected, tall, well-built man. I had heard that his security cases in New Orleans frequently involved working with the Cuban-American community. He had a reputation for being tough and not taking any guff. We hit it off well, which was good, because he and I would be partners in this investigation for quite a while.

After parking in the still bustling police garage, DeBrueys and I made it up to the third-floor detective bureau. We were told to go talk to the assistant chief of police to secure the release of the property. When we found him, he flatly refused to turn anything over to us. Instead, he said, we were welcome to look at the evidence in the station, but that was it. After several minutes more of trying to persuade the assistant chief to release the property, DeBrueys and I decided it was probably best to back off the release demand and go look over the evidence. Things were more testy between the FBI and the Dallas police than I had thought.

The night before, Hoover had publicly blasted the Dallas police for not heeding the death threats on Oswald that the police had received, as well as the warnings from the FBI. The media had a great time with these quotes, and the police were livid with Hoover. They were desperately trying to save face and naturally were trying to shift attention away from themselves. I thought it was poor judgment for Hoover to have made those comments. Talk about glass houses! For chrissake, I was now involved in some shady doings myself, having destroyed the Oswald note and my memo. It seemed as if everyone was scurrying to protect himself and shift the blame on to another.

I have to admit I was feeling some sympathy for the police. After Oswald was killed, the press heavily criticized the Dallas police for its lack of security. The newspapers and television laid it on thick, citing the police for incompetence and negligence. When I heard this, to a large extent it seemed like a lot of garbage. The press was equally to blame for Oswald's death. They had placed incredible pressure on the police to make Oswald available for all to see. In its frenzy, the press had swarmed all over the police building. The press had been extremely unreasonable these past few days. I know that their standard defense to these charges is that the public has right to see and hear from a suspect, but is it procedurally prudent to walk a suspect in front of the media and create a circuslike atmosphere? The police were unreasonable in transporting Oswald as they did after receiving the threat, but the press was just as unreasonable in demanding excessive access.

An officer showed DeBrueys and me to Lieutenant Potts's office, which was next to Captain Fritz's. Stacked in Potts's office was all the evidence. Two of our FBI agents, Ural Horton and Ron Brinkley, were already there reviewing it, and it looked as if they had been there for some time. When we told them we had been assigned to relieve them, Horton and Brinkley gave sighs of relief. They were criminal agents, with no expertise in counter-intelligence work, and were having a hell of a time making heads or tails of any of the evidence. They quickly grabbed their suit coats, bid us *adios* and good luck, and left.

DeBrueys and I surveyed the room. The evidence seemed to consist mostly of the personal papers of Lee and Marina Oswald. Nothing was organized; in fact, things were a mess. DeBrueys and I looked at each other, not knowing whether to laugh or cry. We decided it was best to divide the room in half and begin what was clearly going to be a tedious job.

Our objective today was simply to review everything, hoping we might discover some leads. President Johnson's directive to the FBI was to investigate Kennedy's death and determine who killed him and why. Oswald was clearly the prime suspect, but the emotions and drama of the past few days were over; now it was time to investigate matters objectively and make a fair determination of the facts. Nothing was to be assumed or taken for granted. If Oswald hadn't killed Kennedy and Tippit, we needed to know that. If others were involved, I felt damn sure we would get to the bottom of it.

After several hours, I came across Lee Oswald's "Historic Diary." I scanned a few pages. I couldn't decide if Oswald was trying to write his own *Mein Kampf* or if he just wanted to document his life's significance for posterity. I leaned back in my chair and began a thorough reading of his diary.

The first page had a heading, "Historic Diary, From Oct. 16, 1959 Arrival —." Under this Oswald describes his arrival in the Soviet Union from Helsinki, Finland. On his first day, he asks his Intourist guide, Rimma Sherikova, if he can apply for Russian citizenship. With his consistently poor grammar and spelling, Oswald writes, "She is flabbergassed, but aggrees to help."

In his next entry he informs Rimma he is a Communist, and it is clear she is stalling him on his citizenship request. In his October 18 entry, he indicates it is his twentieth birthday, and Rimma gives him a gift, a book, "'Ideot' by Dostoevski."

On his entry for October 21, Oswald indicates he has a meeting with a Soviet official about his citizenship request, but the official rejects the request and tells Oswald to go home. Oswald writes he has to leave the country at 8:00 P.M. that day and that he is shocked. He writes, "My fondes dreams are shattered because of a petty official." In this same entry, he writes, "7:00 P.M. I decide to end it. Soak rist in cold water to numb the pain. Than slash my left wrist. Than plaug wrist into bathtub of hot water. I think 'when Rimma comes at 8. to find me dead it wil be a great shock. somewhere, a violin plays, as I watch my life whirl away. I think to myself. 'how easy to die' and 'a sweet death, (to violins) about 8.00 Rimma finds my unconcious (bathtub water a rich red color) she screams (I remember that) and runs for help."

Oswald's entries continue, reporting that he is taken to the hospital, where his wrist is stitched up. He is initially placed on the floor for the mentally ill, but is soon transferred to a general floor.

Oswald records his eventual release from the hospital and a new round of meetings with Soviet officials, who tell him to sit tight while they consider his citizenship request. After several days, Oswald writes he is tired of waiting and decides he "must have some sort of a showdown!" In his October 31 entry, he describes a trip to the U.S. Embassy in Moscow, where he meets with American Consul Richard Snyder. Oswald throws down his passport and denounces his U.S. citizenship. He tells Snyder he intends to seek Soviet citizenship. Snyder tries to talk Oswald out of it, but Oswald persists. For the next few days, Oswald is visited by members of the American press, including *Time* magazine. In his November 15 entry, Oswald writes, "Again I feel slightly better because of the attention."

Oswald's diary displays another month of impatient waiting, until January 4, when the Soviet officials finally grant him a resident document, but not citizenship. Oswald writes, "Still I am happy. The official says they are sending me to the city of 'Minsk' I ask 'is that in Siberia?' He only laughs."

In his January 7, 1960, entry, Oswald says he leaves by train to Minsk and is given a good sum of rubles from the Soviet Red Cross to help him out. He writes letters to his mother and brother, telling them "I do not wish to every contact you again. I am beginning a new life and I don't want *any part* of the old."

On January 13, Oswald begins work in a Minsk radio factory as a "checker" metal worker, where he earns 700 rubles a month. With another 700 rubles a month from the Soviet Red Cross "to help," Oswald calculates that he now makes almost as much as the factory director. I raised my eyebrow at that. We at the FBI knew that the Soviet Red Cross was controlled by the KGB. Now why would the KGB be taking care of Oswald?

In his March 16 entry he writes that he received an apartment, "a small flat one-room kitchen-bath near the factory (8 min. walk) with splendid view from 2 balconies of the river, almost rent free (60 rub. a mon.) it is a Russians dream." Oswald was being treated royally in Minsk. Russians have a hell of a time getting *any* apartment, much less a nice one. Why the special treatment?

Oswald continued to write entries about his life in Minsk: his work, his dating, and surviving the winter. Then in a January 2, 1961, entry, he writes that he proposed to his girlfriend, Ella Germain, but that she refused to marry him. Oswald writes that he is "too stunned too think! . . . I am misarable."

Still reeling from Ella's rejection and starting to grow disenchanted with life in the Soviet Union, Oswald says that on February 1 he made his first request to the U.S. Embassy, saying "I would like to go back to U.S." On February 28, Oswald receives a letter from Snyder, telling Oswald he can come in anytime for an interview.

On March 17, Oswald attended a trade union dance and in the last hour is introduced to a girl "with a French hair-do and red-dress with white slipper." He writes: "I dance with her. than ask to show her home I do, along with 5 other admirares. Her name is Marina. We like each other right away she gives me her phone number and departs home. . . ."

In March, Oswald mentions his first date with Marina, and then, in an entry labeled "Apr: 1st–30," says they are "going steady and I decide I must have her, she puts me off so on April 15 I propose, she accepts." In an entry I assume is for April 30, after a seven-day delay with the marriage bureau, he and Marina wed in her aunt's home.

I scratched my head. Boy, was that quick! Meet a girl, a month later propose to her, and marry two weeks later! Interesting that *after* Oswald makes his request to return to the United States, out pops Marina, and presto they're married. In the next entry, for May 1961, Oswald hasn't told Marina of his desire to return to America, but still, this is a mighty curious set of circumstances. Just as our intelligence agencies can intercept a letter to the Soviet Embassy in Washington, the Soviets can also intercept letters to the U.S. Embassy in Moscow. I am sure Oswald's correspondence with the American Embassy in Moscow was intercepted by the KGB. Therefore, I am certain that the KGB was aware in February of Oswald's desire to return to America. Marina fit the criteria for being a Soviet sleeper agent, and she was now married to an American who had made known his desire to return to the U.S. Everything looked pretty damn suspicious regarding Marina's presence in Texas.

In a June 1961 entry, Oswald reveals to Marina his desire to return. She is slightly startled, but encourages Lee to do what he wishes. On July 8, Oswald visits the American Embassy in Moscow to request visas for him and his new bride. Snyder gives the Oswalds the necessary paperwork, but cautions them that although Oswald had never completed the paperwork to officially renounce his U.S. citizenship, it could take a while for the INS to decide if they want Oswald to return to the United States.

In an entry entitled "July 15 Aug 20" Oswald writes that many Soviets are trying to dissuade Marina from leaving, especially since she is now pregnant. Oswald next reports that in September, while awaiting word about whether they will get the passports, Marina leaves for four weeks to visit an aunt in the Urals.

In a November–December entry, Oswald says that Marina is beginning to waver about going to the United States, and he thinks this may be from the strain of waiting for his passport and her exit visa combined with being pregnant. On Christmas Day, Marina is granted a Soviet exit visa — which is virtually unheard of. The KGB-controlled visa office almost never granted exit visas to Soviet citizens, and never that fast. My suspicions about Marina were mounting by the minute.

On February 14, Marina gave birth to their daughter, June. Then, in a March 26 entry, Oswald writes that Marina is granted a U.S. visa, which is the last document they need to go to America. The last entry in Oswald's "Historic Diary" is for March 27, and here he receives a letter from his mother's employer saying she will support Marina if there is a need. It was my understanding that the INS did not want to grant Marina an immigration visa. But apparently the more politically conscious State Department intervened, theorizing that it would be good propaganda to let a defector return, so pressure was exercised on the INS to grant the visa.

•   •   •   •

I set the diary and my note pad down. I had written down some of the more important entries. I later learned that Oswald actually wrote this diary either right before he left the Soviet Union, on the way home, or when he returned to Fort Worth. Based upon a handwriting analysis, it was conclusively determined that Lee Oswald had in fact written the diary, but had done so in two days' time. The police had seized this diary among Oswald's personal papers at Ruth Paine's home.

Suddenly, DeBrueys exclaimed, "Thank God!" I walked over to his side of the desk and looked over his shoulder at the document he was reading. It was a letter that Lee Oswald had written to the national office for the Fair Play for Cuba Committee in New York City. In the letter, Oswald acknowledged that he was the only member of the New Orleans branch of this committee, and that he used A. J. Hidell as one of his aliases.

DeBrueys said that he had only deduced, not definitively concluded, that Oswald was the only member of the committee in New Orleans and used Hidell as an alias. This letter, in Oswald's own handwriting, completely validated DeBrueys's deductions. He was visibly relieved, because he knew that the rifle trace had largely depended on his deductions.

For the rest of the day, DeBrueys and I shuffled through the great mass of personal papers belonging to Lee and Marina Oswald. There were letters written by Lee not only to the Fair Play for Cuba Committee but also to the American Communist party and the American Socialist party. There were also personal letters from private citizens and countless pieces of paper that amounted to nothing. Obviously when the police had searched the Paines' home on Friday afternoon and seized these items, they decided to play it safe and take literally anything and everything connected with the Oswalds. In fact, some of the items seized clearly belonged to Michael and Ruth Paine and had no relevance at all to our investigation. It was slow and tedious, and both DeBrueys and I developed dull headaches.

Some of the more interesting evidence included the green and brown blanket from the floor of the Paines' garage (which had at one time contained Lee's rifle) and some photos of Lee standing near a house holding a rifle in one hand, some papers in his other, and a pistol holstered at his side.

At about 8:00 P.M., DeBrueys and I knocked off. I drove him to his hotel, and we agreed to return tomorrow to finish our reviewing. With any luck, we might even get to take the damn property out of the police station.

Tuesday, November 26, 1963

TIME: 8:30 A.M.

By the time DeBrueys and I arrived back at the police station to resume our work the next day, Henry Wade, the Dallas district attorney, had convinced the police that they should release all the evidence to the FBI. Because the transport of all the evidence was going to take a lot of work, Ken Howe came over to Lieutenant Potts's office to help us.

The police mandated several conditions for the release of all the evidence. They wanted two of their property men to accompany us to our FBI office to assure the chain of custody. They also wanted us to catalog and photograph everything, then provide them copies. That's mighty big of them, I thought, seeing they'd had the past four days to do that themselves.

With practically no help from the police, DeBrueys, Howe, and I boxed up everything and began lugging the boxes downstairs to the police garage and my car. About 90 minutes later, we packed the last box into the backseat. With the trunk and backseat crammed full of evidence, Howe and DeBrueys climbed into the front seat, and I climbed in behind the wheel. The two property officers got into their car, and with them following, I drove out of the garage.

I guess word traveled fast that the FBI was taking away the evidence from the assassination, because as my car reached the top of the garage exit ramp we were met by a dozen television cameramen and photographers. With bulbs flashing rapid-fire and television reporters solemnly announcing that the FBI was driving off with the evidence, I maneuvered our way out of there.

TIME: 11:00 A.M.

After unloading the evidence, we took the boxes up to the seventh floor, where we found a couple of long tables and set up shop. DeBrueys grabbed a Minox camera and propped it up on a kind of tripod so that it was about 12 inches above the table, its lens pointed straight down. While the two property officers looked on, I started feeding, one at a time, each of the items that had been seized. DeBrueys focused and snapped each item as they were fed through. When each item was photographed, we had to catalog and mark it. To say this process was time-consuming would be an understatement. It was particularly tiresome because of the sheer volume of personal papers belonging to Lee and Marina Oswald.

With short breaks for lunch and dinner, DeBrueys and I worked long into the night.

TIME: 12:45 A.M.

DeBrueys and I were just about finished when Vince Drain, one of our liaisons to the Dallas police, came into the room. The two police property officers stirred just a little in their chairs, cocking their heads to listen.

"Hey, the police still have some more evidence they forgot to give you," Drain said. "Captain Fritz has in his desk Oswald's wallet, one shell casing from the rifle on the sixth floor of the depository, and Oswald's notebook. Fritz said to run over to his office and he'll give this stuff to us. Hosty, Malley and Shanklin want you to go over there yourself and get it."

"Sure. I'll head over there right now," I said.

DeBrueys continued to work, feeding the items in one at a time, photographing them, cataloging them. I put on my suit jacket and left.

I had heard that Fritz was single and that he had an apartment just across the street from the police station. When I got down to the station about 1:00 A.M., Fritz was already there. He greeted me cordially, not the least upset that he had been roused from bed to hand over evidence. He walked me up to his office. It was quite a contrast to see his office and hallway at this hour: it was so empty and quiet compared to Friday afternoon's chaotic scene.

He unlocked his door, hit the light switch, and went over to his desk. He opened one of the drawers and pulled out the address book, wallet, and shell. I got out a piece of paper and wrote up a receipt of evidence:

> Received from Capt. Will Fritz at approximately 1:00 A.M. on 11/27/63:
>
> Billfold and 16 cards and pictures taken from Lee Harvey Oswald on 11/22/63.
>
> One notebook recovered from room of Lee Harvey Oswald at 1026 No. Beckley on 11/22/63 with names and addresses.
>
> One 6.5-mm rifle hull recovered at Texas School Book Depository, 411 Elm Street, Dallas, Texas, on 11/22/63.
>
> James P. Hosty, Jr., Special Agent, FBI

I signed the receipt and gave it to Fritz. Then I picked up the evidence and thanked the captain.

I quickly drove back to our office and rode the elevator back up to the twelfth floor. Before I took this evidence to DeBrueys, I wanted to show Malley and Shanklin the entry in Oswald's notebook where he had written my name. I still thought it incredible, myself. I walked into Shanklin's office, where I saw Malley sitting discussing something with Shanklin, who, true to form, was pacing behind his desk, smoking a cigarette.

"Excuse me, but I wanted to tell you I got the evidence from Captain Fritz," I said. I pulled out Oswald's notebook and pointed to the pertinent entry to Malley and Shanklin. "Here is the notebook I told you guys about earlier. Here's my name, office phone number and address, car tag number, and the date of my first contact with Marina."

Malley hesitated, peered up at me curiously, then nodded. He and Shanklin didn't utter a word, but exchanged what I thought were funny looks. I got an uncomfortable feeling that I should leave.

After this episode I was talking with a fellow agent, Emory Horton, who told me that he felt that Malley and Shanklin had sent me alone to Fritz's office to give me the opportunity to tear out the page in Oswald's address book that referred to me to keep the entry from reaching Hoover. I told Horton there was a perfectly innocent and logical explanation for that entry. He just nodded.

After leaving Shanklin's office with the evidence, I rode the elevator back to the seventh floor, and saw there were a number of agents working at their desks, undoubtedly reviewing their day's work. When I got back to where DeBrueys was, he had sealed up all the boxes. Some of the boxes had already been taken away, and DeBrueys said an Air Force jet was waiting at the nearby air base to whisk him off to Washington with the evidence. This was part of our prearranged plan. Once everything had been cataloged and photographed, DeBrueys was to transport it all to headquarters where the brass could review it and, if necessary, conduct lab tests. I was to remain in Dallas and continue working leads on Oswald.

"But, Warren, we have to photograph and catalog these three items I just got from Captain Fritz," I explained.

"No, there's no time. The jet has apparently been holding for me and I'm dead tired," DeBrueys said. "Here, just throw those things in this box and I'll take off. I'll catalog them in Washington."

"We can't do that, we have to do it here, the police want photos and catalogs of this stuff," I persisted.

"I am dead tired, and I'm leaving." DeBrueys was just as stubborn as I.

To hell with this. I was tired, too. Our nerves were starting to grate.

While DeBrueys resumed carrying boxes to the elevator, I hastily fed each item through the Minox camera's field of vision, snapped the pictures, and cataloged them myself. When I came to Oswald's notebook, the one with my name in it, I photographed only the exterior of the book, rather than each individual page. There was just no time. DeBrueys practically had one foot in the jet.

That done, I swept the last bits of evidence off the table, put them in the last box, and sealed it. DeBrueys snatched the box and told me he would see me in a couple of days. With a wave he was off.

TIME: 3:00 A.M.

Relieved to have that tedious ordeal over, all I wanted was to go home and sleep. But now a thought that had been festering in the back of my mind forced its way to the front. I was assigned to interview Marina Oswald in about six hours. I had better go talk this over with Shanklin.

I rode the elevator upstairs and walked over to Shanklin's office. He was alone, so I rapped on the open door and walked in.

"Is it okay if I go home and catch a little sleep before I interview Marina?" I asked, almost begging.

Shanklin, looking raw and frayed from the lack of sleep, abruptly exploded. "No, you have to do it now! The Secret Service is sending their Russian interpreter in, and when he arrives, which will be anytime now, the two of you are to go and interview Marina first thing. You're going to have to stay here and prepare for this interview, so don't you dare leave."

"For heaven's sake, I'm dead tired, can't this interview wait until later this morning? All I need is a couple of hours' sleep." I was desperate. "And why can't we use our own Russian interpreter? He's pretty good, I hear."

"No, goddamn it!" I thought Shanklin was going to have a coronary. "The Secret Service is providing the interpreter. It's already been decided, and that's the way its going to be. You will stay here, and you will get ready for the interview, because you're going to do it as soon as the Secret Service interpreter arrives."

Damn it! My ears were buzzing and my muscles were aching. I

needed to sleep. Damn stupid, I thought, being forced to interview one of the key witnesses in this condition.

I walked down the stairs to the bullpen. Looking around, I saw only one other agent still there. I cursed, because he was packing it in for the night. I slammed my body into the chair at my desk and pulled my files on Marina Oswald together.

6

Wednesday, November 27, 1963

TIME: 6:00 A.M.

I finished my paperwork preparation for the Marina Oswald interview, stuffed everything into a file folder, and went out to my car. I drove the short five blocks or so over to the Secret Service office at the U.S. Court-house.

It was still dark outside, and I again cursed Shanklin, and everything in general, for my present situation. I should have been home sleeping.

I had imagined the Secret Service office would be virtually empty, so I was surprised to see a number of agents still at their desks. I introduced myself at the front counter and asked to speak to Forrest Sorrells, the agent in charge. I was told where his office was and knocked on his door.

"Come in," a voice inside boomed. Sorrells introduced me to Tom Kelly, an inspector from Secret Service headquarters in Washington. Clearly all the federal agencies had their high-level officials down here overseeing every last detail.

Sorrells was known as a tough man to get along with, but he was cordial with me despite the early hour. I was immensely thankful for this — the last thing I needed was another irate supervisor.

I told Sorrells and Kelly that I was there to hook up with their

Russian interpreter, adding that I'd been up all night and hoped I wasn't too tired to do a proper job. Sorrells held up his hands as if he was trying to make me brake.

"Listen, Jim, our interpreter just flew in from California and he's been up all night, too," Sorrells said soothingly. "We aren't going to interview Marina until later in the day. Besides, the Immigration and Naturalization Service is sending down its number-one attorney, and they've insisted he talk with Marina before you do. Look, nothing is going to happen till this afternoon, why don't you go and get some sleep."

"Now that sounds like good advice," I said. "I'll come back at about noon and we'll get down to business then."

Sorrells and Kelly nodded reassuringly, and I left, my mind more on sleep than anything else.

I went back to my car and radioed in what Sorrells had just told me, reporting that I was going off duty for a few hours and was checking into the Baker Hotel near our office to catch a nap.

First, though, I had to eat and call Janet. I drove over to my regular lunch place, the Unique. At the counter I waved off the menu the waitress presented to me. I already knew what I wanted: two poached eggs, toast, and coffee. While she placed my order, I went back to the pay phone to call Janet. Even though it wasn't quite 7:00 A.M., I knew Janet would already be awake, tending to our three-month-old baby, Tommy. I apologized for not coming home last night, but Janet told me not to worry about it, she understood.

"How are you holding out?" she asked.

"Fine," I reassured her. "Tired but OK."

I told her about yesterday's collection of evidence, how painstakingly long it took, adding that I had orders to conduct an important interview today. I thanked her for insisting I take an extra white shirt and underwear in the event I didn't get home. I said I was grabbing some breakfast and was going to check into the Baker Hotel for a few hours of shut-eye.

"Take care of yourself," she said, adding, "Oh, by the way, I canceled Dick's therapy sessions for the rest of the week."

I cursed myself, for I realized I had our only car parked across the street from the office, and Janet had no way of taking Dick to therapy. Dick, who was three years old, had been born with cerebral palsy. He had been diagnosed with a fairly severe case, and already the little guy had endured six surgeries to correct birth defects. He was now going to physical therapy at a local rehab center four days a week, several hours each day. Normally everything worked out perfectly with the use of our single family car. I rode in the car pool with four other agents, and we rotated drivers each day. I drove the family car on Thursdays, the only day Dick didn't have therapy. All the other days, Janet had the car.

"Damn, I'm sorry," I said. "Somehow with all that's going on, I just didn't . . ."

"Don't worry," Janet said in her most soothing voice. "Actually, it's kind of nice. He got to stay home and watch cartoons on television, which he never does because he's always in therapy." She paused. "Do you think you'll be home tonight?"

"I think so. I'm pretty bushed. And I can't keep up this pace."

"Don't forget, your parents are coming by train today."

Of course they were! I'd completely forgotten. Which reminded me that my brother Ed, who was on leave from Fort Sill, Oklahoma, was also arriving tonight to spend Thanksgiving with us before heading off to Germany for eighteen months. I cursed again, and said I would do my damnedest to get home tonight. I only wish I knew when.

I walked back to the counter and found my breakfast and coffee waiting for me. I devoured it, put $1.50 on the counter, and hit the door. I was ready for some serious sleep.

TIME: 9:00 A.M.

I checked into the hotel at about 7:30 A.M., but I'd be damned if I could fall asleep. Daylight spilled into the room, even though I had drawn the heavy curtains as tightly as I could. There was also a constant hum out in the hallway, which was annoying the hell out of me. Nor did it help matters to hear the cleaning ladies cackling outside my door while they banged their cleaning carts around the halls.

I finally kicked off the sheets and bedspread and turned on the television. President Johnson was on all the channels addressing both houses of Congress. I stacked the pillows and lay back to listen. I found it harder and harder to concentrate on what he was saying, and before long his words were no more than incomprehensible blather. Thanks to President Johnson, I finally fell asleep.

The phone next to my bed blasted its bells. I sat up with a start and grabbed it. The clock said 10:15.

"Yeah," I answered, my voice slightly hoarse as I finally brought the phone to my mouth.

"Hosty, what in the hell do you think you are doing!" It was

Shanklin. "Get your ass out of there and back here! Why aren't you with the Secret Service interviewing Marina?"

Fully awake and irritated now, I explained as patiently as I could what Sorrells had said. Shanklin was still not satisfied. He wanted me back in the office that minute. I muttered I'd be there as soon as I could, and slammed down the phone.

I trudged into the bathroom, shaved, showered, and put on my clean underwear and shirt. Then I put on my same old tired suit. I combed my hair with my fingers, looked at myself in the mirror, and thought, Hosty, you look like shit. My eyes were red with strain and fatigue and my skin looked pretty awful.

I checked out, angry at myself for wasting twelve dollars for the room rent. I drove back to the office and reported to Shanklin. He was calm now, apparently satisfied just to have me in the office.

I went to my desk and decided I should dictate some reports to a steno. I noticed I hadn't dictated my interview yet with Ruth Paine, and this was day five. Better do it. I rattled off my FD-302 report, then examined again the draft letter Ruth had given me during our interview. This was the draft from which Oswald later typed his final letter to the Soviet Embassy in Washington about his Mexico City trip. In it Oswald referred to his meeting with "Comrade Kostine," and talked about the "notorious FBI" agent "Hasty" harassing his wife. I thought it a good idea to ask Shanklin if I should attach it to my report or make it a separate piece of evidence.

I walked into Shanklin's office and waved the letter in front of him. I asked what he thought would be the best way to handle this. He lunged to his feet. For a moment he looked as if he were going to jump over his desk and strangle me.

"I thought I told you to get rid of that damn Oswald note!" Shanklin yelled. "Get rid of it now. For God's sake, just do what I tell you, and get rid of it now!" I tried to tell him this wasn't the Oswald note, but he wouldn't listen to me.

The man appeared on the verge of a nervous breakdown. He had gone without sleep for God knows how many hours and had been working and worrying around the clock. The man knew a hell of a lot more than I did. I only wished I knew what that was. Were the international implications I had surmised actually true? Were the Soviets or Cubans — or both — involved in Kennedy's death? Had Oswald been recruited by the Soviets or Cubans to carry out this sniper attack on the man who had stared down the Soviets in the Missile Crisis of October 1962, and who had tried to overthrow Fidel Castro in the Bay of Pigs in 1961? What was going on back at headquarters? Why was Shanklin acting as if we were on the verge of a national collapse? There were no indications we were even close to going on a war footing. But I knew also that this kind of thing gets talked about and decided long before the public ever knows.

I backed out of Shanklin's office, leaving him to his demons, thankful I wasn't in his shoes. I had to admit he was carrying some awesome responsibilities right now; the strain had to be overwhelming.

Bardwell Odum, one of Shanklin's closest friends and one of the more senior agents in our office, approached me and asked what all the yelling in Shanklin's office was about. I decided to tell him.

"Shanklin is demanding that I destroy the draft letter I received from Ruth Paine," I said. "He's just damn irrational, and I'm starting to get worried that things are getting out of control around here."

Odum tilted his head back and let out a long, slow whistle. "Everyone seems to be assuming that there won't be any public hearings. If you ask me, I think Congress, among others, is pressuring Johnson for public hearings. My bet is Johnson has to give in.

"Let me tell you something else," Odum continued. "Saturday night, Shanklin sent me out to Ruth Paine's home after your interview with her. Shanklin essentially wanted to audit your investigation to date of the Oswalds. Once I got done talking with her, I knew you had done everything by the book. But when I was there she told me that she had given you Oswald's letter to the Soviets. She also told me that she had previously made a copy of this letter in her own handwriting. I got that copy — here, let me show you."

Odum retrieved Ruth's copy of Oswald's letter from his desk.

"When I reported back to Shanklin Saturday night and told him I had a copy of this letter, he hit the roof. He yelled at me — 'I thought I told Hosty to get rid of that letter!' I couldn't understand what he was talking about."

On that point, I just kept my mouth shut.

"Listen," I said. "I have an idea. Let's not destroy these letters like Shanklin said. Instead, let's dictate FD-302 reports and reference the letters in the reports. We can keep the letters in an evidence envelope here, just in case anyone needs them later."

Odum agreed, and we also decided not to mention any of this to Shanklin.

After Odum left, I felt a sharp pang of regret as I realized I should have treated the Oswald note addressed to me in the same fashion.

TIME: 12:30 P.M.

When I got back to Sorrells's office, the Russian interpreter was just waking up. He would be joining us shortly, I was told. At least one of us had gotten some sleep.

I was also told that the INS man had arrived: he was seated over in the corner, sipping coffee, keeping to himself. No one knew exactly what he was going to tell Marina. We all figured the INS was probably going to deport her. At least I hoped that was a possibility, because I could use that threat as leverage in getting at the truth.

I walked over to the table with the coffeepot and asked a nearby agent if I could help myself. "Sure," the man said, and I quickly poured myself a cup, which I downed like some forbidden elixir. To explain, drinking coffee in the FBI office by agents was absolutely prohibited by Hoover. I assume he thought it was unprofessional. I thought the rule was a bunch of bull. I drained the cup quickly and filled it up again. I needed all the help I could get to keep myself going.

TIME: 5:30 P.M.

Since DeBrueys was still in Washington, Shanklin had decided to send a partner over to help me, a senior criminal agent named Charlie Brown. By the time the Secret Service interpreter, Max Phillips, the INS man — a senior attorney — Brown, and I finally got together, it was late afternoon. Needless to say, I had cursed the powers-that-be more times than I could count for wasting all this time standing around rather than sleeping.

The interview with Marina was critical. We anticipated it would be the first of several, but it was vital to get off on the right foot with her. Not only would it set the tone for the rest, it could, if the agent was fortunate, provide the majority of the sought-after information.

Because the Secret Service had the Oswalds in their protective custody, they were calling the shots on the logistics for this interview. They told me they had secured Marina, her two daughters, and Marguerite and Robert Oswald at an undisclosed local motel. The Secret Service had been ordered by President Johnson to protect the Oswalds from possible vigilante attacks. A secondary objective, however, was to keep the Oswalds from the media. The reasoning behind keeping them from the media was two-fold: first, for the Oswalds' own protection, since the media frequently operated with a mob mentality; second, to keep the Oswalds from impeaching the integrity of the FBI's investigation by talking with the media. Time and again the press had provided the public with incomplete and inaccurate accounts of events. This was an extraordinary case, and it required extraordinary acts. We were trying to get a handle on the president's assassination, and the last thing we needed was an irresponsible or sensationalist press wrecking things.

Once we were all assembled, the Secret Service informed the INS attorney, Charlie Brown, and me where the Oswalds had been tucked away and told us how to get there. They instructed us not to "badge" our way on the tollway as we usually did. If the toll booth operators saw three carloads of FBI, Secret Service, and INS officials enter and then exit the tollway, the information could conceivably be leaked to the press, which could then focus its search for the Oswalds around our route.

Brown and I drove in my car. The INS attorney, whose name I never caught, drove by himself in a rental car. The Secret Service interpreter, Leon Gopadze, and his partner, Secret Service Agent Max Phillips, drove in their unmarked car. Phillips and Gopadze led us onto the Dallas–Fort Worth tollway and then took the Arlington exit. They pulled into a modest motel, the Inn of the Six Flags, which was immediately adjacent to the amusement park, Six Flags Over Texas. Driving around to the back wing, they found a spot and parked. Back here, our cars were out of sight from the road.

I climbed out of my car and looked around. The place was deserted, except for a few unmarked Secret Service cars. Across the way, I could see some of the rides at the amusement park, which was closed for the season. I figured the Secret Service made a pretty good choice, as this motel was virtually deserted at this time of year. They had probably commandeered the whole place. I wasn't sure, but I thought I could sense Secret Service agents staked around the perimeter of the motel's property, keeping watch.

When we had all assembled by our parked cars, Phillips and Gopadze led us to a first-floor room and knocked. Dusk was settling in, and the evening air was starting to chill my bones. A man in a dark suit opened the door, and when he saw Phillips, he let us enter. Phillips introduced Gopadze and the rest of us to this man. Then Phillips told Gopadze and the INS attorney that they could go ahead and have a private meeting with Marina Oswald first. Gopadze and the INS man were led to a back bedroom where they disappeared behind a closed door.

Standing next to Brown, I quickly scanned the motel accommodation, which I realized was a suite. Four men in suits were sitting at a little round table going through some mail. Much of this mail contained money, and they were counting and stacking this on the table. It turned out much of this mail was from Americans who had seen Ma-

rina on television, dazed and confused at the Dallas jail, holding her infant daughter. The letter writers were sympathetic to Marina, and the
money they sent eventually totaled over seventy thousand dollars. Reportedly, an FBI wiretap later picked up Marina laughingly telling one
of her friends that the Americans who had sent her all this money were
basically saps. The men counting the money were sitting in what was
the living room area of the suite; just off this area were three bedrooms. I figured Marina and her two daughters were living in one of
the bedrooms, while Robert and Marguerite had the other two. I knew
Robert had a wife and children, but I had heard he had sent them away
to his wife's parents.

Prior to driving out there, Gopadze and Phillips had informed
Brown and me that we would have ideal interview circumstances, since
Secret Service agents had taken Robert Oswald and the troublesome
Marguerite Oswald out shopping. Their removal was important for several reasons. First, in an investigation, you never want to interview one
witness in front of another, for this would have a tainting effect.
Second, we knew Marguerite Oswald was making a nuisance of herself
and potentially could have disrupted any interview with Marina. We
couldn't have any of that, because we desperately needed the wealth of
information locked away in Marina's head.

After just a few minutes the INS attorney and Gopadze came out
of the room. The INS attorney, acting jittery and nervous, headed
straight for the door and quickly left. Brown and I huddled with
Gopadze and asked him what that was all about. Shaking his head in
disgust, Gopadze told us that the INS man had just informed Marina
that the INS was most definitely not going to deport her, but that they
still wanted her to cooperate with the FBI. The INS attorney told Marina this even though she had committed fraud on her visa application
to the United States. It turned out that Marina lied on her visa application when she said she had never been a member of the Communist
party. She had in fact been in the Komsomol, or Communist Youth
Party, until the day she left for America. Less important, but still a technical violation, she had also failed to disclose the name she had gone
by before she married Lee: Marina Alexandrovna Medvedeva, her stepfather's name, which she had lived under until she was sixteen. Either
one of these fraudulent acts would have been grounds for deportation.

"Damn it, why did he go and do that!" I was furious. "Now we
have no leverage over her. She knows that she is not going to be deported and if she wants to she can lie as much as she wants."

With Lee Oswald the prime if not the only suspect, I had decided to stop pussyfooting. Prior to the assassination, I had taken great

pains to handle my case on the Oswalds with extreme care. Counter-espionage cases, or what we called security cases, were handled much like a chess match. An agent carefully considered his next move, always trying to anticipate every possible countermove by the opponent. On November 22, the chess board had been overturned. I felt we no longer had to act so delicately. That is why I cut to the chase in Captain Fritz's office and asked Lee Oswald about his contacts with the Soviets in Mexico City. Prior to the assassination, I would never have dreamed of asking Oswald about his Mexico City trip — Oswald would have learned more from my questions than I from his answers. Yes, the time to be careful and wary was past. It was time to turn the screws a little tighter. That was why the deportation issue was so important. I had been ready to play hardball. Now it felt as if that INS attorney had thrown me a sucker punch.

Brown and Gopadze were equally disgusted with the INS attorney, but before we could fester any longer, Marina entered the room. She had slipped out of the bedroom, gently closing the door. She came out alone, and I assumed she had just put her two daughters to sleep. Marina took a seat by herself on a sofa, and Gopadze and I pulled up two chairs in front of her. Brown sat to my left, while Phillips sat to Gopadze's left. This was my interview, and Gopadze was to act as the interpreter.

As I'd told Shanklin, I wanted our FBI Russian interpreter to assist me. Our man was a "white Russian" who had fled Russia with his parents and siblings when the Communists came to power. Gopadze was nervous about his role and told me he hoped his Russian would be good enough. He was born in Georgia, a province of the Soviet Union, and Georgian was his native language; Russian was a second language to him. As it turned out, Gopadze was a very modest man, and a very capable interpreter.

When I sat down on the sofa, Marina looked up and recognized me immediately. Her expression went cold and her spine went rigid. Setting my note pad on my lap, I asked, "Mr. Gopadze, why don't you introduce us all to Mrs. Oswald?"

Gopadze made the introductions in Russian, only to receive a curt response from Marina. "She said she already knows you because you have been out to her home before the assassination."

"That's correct," I said. Gopadze had a puzzled look on his face now.

I told Gopadze to advise Marina of her constitutional rights before we proceeded with the interview. "You have the right to . . ." he began before Marina interrupted him.

". . . to remain silent. Anything you say can be used against you in court. You have the right to an attorney, and if you cannot afford one, one will be provided," she spat out in Russian. Clearly Marina was not as naive as most people thought.

"Tell her I'd like to ask some questions about her husband," I said.

While Gopadze translated that, I reviewed my objectives for the interview. I wanted to pin down Lee Oswald's activities and movements in the days and weeks leading up to the assassination, information that might provide important clues about whether Lee was in fact the president's assassin, and if he had acted alone or as part of a larger conspiracy.

When Gopadze finished his translation, Marina threw a barb at him, replying, "I do not wish to be asked anything, as anything I had to say I already said before. I have no further information."

She was obviously referring to her interviews with the Dallas police.

"Tell her there are still many unanswered questions, and I would appreciate her answering them," I told Gopadze.

After he translated, she replied, "I am tired and I am worried about my child, who is slightly ill."

I looked over at Phillips and gave him a look that meant, "Is this true?" Phillips, his eyes on mine, gave me an ever so slight shake of his head, indicating Marina was bullshitting us.

Inwardly I cursed the damn INS attorney again. Thanks to him, we had no leverage on Marina, and she knew it. This was one tough broad. Wily and crafty. I hunkered down and told Gopadze to tell her that her cooperation was essential. I even gave her an option of having us come back tomorrow.

"No, I do not want to be interviewed," she insisted. Then she began to lose her cool, and bitterly spat out, "The government has all the information it needs from me. I am sick and tired of the FBI, and angry with them for causing my husband to lose one of his jobs in New Orleans after he was arrested."

"Do you intend to stay in the United States?" I asked.

With the assurance of someone who knows she has the upper hand, Marina shot back, "Yes, I intend to stay. I do not wish to uproot my children. I also want to stay close to where my husband is buried." She paused, and then challenged, "Are you suggesting that I can be deported?" She glared at me, waiting for my reply. She knew I was backed into a corner. I had no choice but to admit what she already knew.

"That is for the INS to decide," I conceded, hoping to cast a shadow of doubt over the INS attorney's assurances. Then I tried to bluff some leverage. "Mrs. Oswald, the U.S. government needs your help. Your cooperation with us could improve your situation with the INS."

She tossed her head back, tired of playing this game, and replied smugly, "Maybe I wouldn't mind leaving the United States after all."

Damn it! This woman had so much information locked away in her head and here she was teasing us, dangling the key in front of us. I tried to regain my composure, to prepare myself to take another tack.

"If you're going to stay in the United States, how are you going support yourself and the children?" I asked.

"I'll find some kind of work," she replied.

"If you cooperate with us, perhaps the government could be of some assistance to you," I said. When the stick fails, it's time to try some sugar. I had to leave that offer vague and open-ended, lest headquarters later veto it.

She didn't bite. Not even close. She was now visibly frustrated and repeated that she was tired of answering questions. Gopadze had been growing increasingly frustrated with Marina's obstinacy. Now he lost it. He started yelling at her in Russian. She yelled back with all the venom of a rattlesnake.

Seeing Gopadze and Marina locked in a war of Russian words, one of the Secret Service agents who had been at the table counting the money rose from his chair. "Here now, leave her alone. Can't you see she's tired of talking to you guys?" he barked.

My jaw dropped. Gopadze halted in his tracks, stunned that a fellow agent would interrupt us in this way. Gopadze and I looked at each other, shrugged, and tried to ignore him.

"Let's get to it," I said to Gopadze. "If we ask her some direct questions she may find herself answering them despite herself. Ask her if she and her husband ever had any conversations about President Kennedy."

"No," she said.

"Ask her if her husband in any way ever indicated that he intended to kill the president."

"No," she said.

"How about Texas Governor John Connally, who was also hit by a bullet? Did your husband have anything against him?"

She said, "I don't recall Lee ever saying anything against him. And I don't know if he had a grudge against Connally." Marina then interrupted Gopadze's Russian-to-English translation, and said indignantly, "I swear before God that my husband did not intend to kill President Kennedy."

"Do you believe in God?" I inquired.

"Yes, ever since my mother died," Marina replied.

"Who were some of the people your husband associated with?" I asked.

She told us that he was a loner, who kept largely to himself. "In Russia," she said, "he also kept to himself, preferring the company of his books on communism. For example, *Das Kapital* was one of his books. His constant reading of Communist literature got so bad, at one point I asked him, 'What are you trying to do, start another revolution?'"

Marina was now really opening up, perhaps having realized that talking to us was the only way to get rid of us. "Lee had an idea on everything," she said. "He was hotheaded, strong-willed, and stubborn. But he never really expressed his political views to me. He didn't feel women belonged in a political dialogue."

Noticing her willingness to talk now, I pressed into some more sensitive matters. I asked her if she had ever seen her husband with a gun. "No," she shot back, "I never have."

"What about hunting?" I asked. "Did he ever go hunting?"

She laughed. "There are no places to go hunting in Dallas or Fort Worth. Even if he had wanted to go hunting, he couldn't. He had neither a car nor driver's license."

She was irritated again. I hadn't been able to ask all the questions I wanted, but I decided I better start shutting down. I figured we could pick it up again tomorrow. I asked her if this was okay.

"There is no need for a second interview," she replied testily. "I have told you all I know and the government has all the facts. Besides, based on what I have been told, I am satisfied that my husband killed the president."

Interesting. Wanting to be fair, I told her that if there was anything that would exculpate her husband, the FBI wanted to know it. She said she couldn't think of anything, but if she did, she would tell us.

"The government knows more than I do," she retorted angrily.

At this point, the Secret Service agent who had interrupted us before got up again from his chair at the money table and again sternly warned us to back off Marina. "Quit badgering her," he said. Gopadze ignored him; I turned and scowled. What kind of people did the Secret Service hire? This buffoon had the audacity not only to interrupt our interview but to try to dictate our conduct.

Another Secret Service agent came in from outside the room and told us that Marguerite was due back from her shopping any second. I decided to wrap things up. I wanted to get out of there before Marguerite showed up. I had taken enough guff from Marina, and the last thing I wanted was to tangle with Marguerite Oswald, whose reputation preceded her.

I hastily got my things together and headed for the door. Brown stopped me. "Jim, hold on. I want to ask Marguerite a couple of quick questions on a lead I'm working on."

"Save it for another day, " I replied, turning back for the door.

"No, I want to ask my questions," he insisted.

While I argued with Brown, a short, stocky middle-aged woman with gray hair pulled back in a ponytail and wearing thick, black-rimmed, cat's-eye glasses walked in. She was followed by two Secret Service agents. The dragon queen had arrived.

Brown pulled out his note pad and quickly asked Marguerite his questions. "Mrs. Oswald, I received information from someone living in South Dakota who believed that he knew Lee when he lived there as a boy. Has your family ever lived in South Dakota?"

Marguerite sort of cackled. She said, "No, neither I nor Lee ever lived in South Dakota." Then she turned and addressed the man I had assumed was a Secret Service agent, the man who had kept interrupting our interview of Marina, telling us to back off. "Robert," she said, "did you ever know anyone who lived in South Dakota?" Robert shook his head no.

Oh, God! So that buffoon was Robert Oswald! Damn it, the Secret Service had said that they had removed him and Marguerite from the motel suite.

I grabbed Brown's coat sleeve and practically dragged him out of the suite, then followed Phillips and Gopadze back to the Secret Service office downtown. When we got to Sorrells's office, Gopadze beat me to the punch. He was fuming and demanded to know why his fellow agents had failed to get rid of Robert Oswald. Sorrells and Inspector Tom Kelly looked bewildered and said they didn't know anything about it. Now they, too, were angry and wanted to know how Robert had been allowed to be present during our interview.

A quick investigation showed that all of those men we had assumed were Secret Service agents — the ones sitting in the suite counting the money and ostensibly protecting the Oswalds — were actually *off-duty firemen from the Fort Worth area!* One of the local Secret Service agents, Mike Howard, had a brother on the fire department, and apparently through this connection a bunch of firemen had been hired, essentially as subcontractors to do the Secret Service's job. I also heard that when President Kennedy arrived in Fort Worth on November 21, 1963, the Secret Service had hired off-duty firemen to protect him while he slept. It seems the Secret Service agents who normally protected the president wanted to take the night off, and had gone out on the town. I was flabbergasted. Why did the Secret Service entrust off-duty firemen, and not other federal law enforcement agencies, with these highly sensitive duties? I understood that they needed nights off, and probably didn't have enough agents to protect the Oswald family, but why hire firemen with no law enforcement or firearms training? How could firemen react if someone had tried to attack the president in Fort Worth or the Oswalds at the Inn of the Six Flags? The only explanation I could think of was the Secret Service's jealous grip on its responsibilities and its arrogant lack of trust of any other federal agency.

Still fuming, Gopadze told Kelly and Sorrells that I had met with Marina on two occasions prior to the assassination. In disbelief, Kelly and Sorrells asked me if this was true. I said yes, of course it was true, and explained what I had done and why. They nodded and seemed to understand.

After Gopadze and I left Sorrells's office, Gopadze realized he would have to dictate a report of the Marina interview, but had taken no notes.

"Would you mind sharing your notes with me?" he asked.

"Be happy to," I said.

I sat down with one of the stenographers and dictated a report for Gopadze, knowing full well that when I dictated my FD-302, our two reports would be practically identical.

After I left the Secret Service office, I drove back to the FBI office. I was starting to have a letdown. I wondered how much longer it would be before I could sleep.

TIME: 9:00 P.M.

After I dictated my own report on the Marina interview, I was summoned to Shanklin's office. When I walked in, Shanklin was pacing behind his desk. Malley was sitting in a chair in front of the desk, thumbing through some files.

"What's up?" I asked.

"How did the initial interview with Marina go?" Shanklin asked in response.

"Rotten," I said. "Marina was adversarial. She refused to cooperate and didn't answer a lot of my questions. Fact is, she harbors hard

95

feelings toward me. So, much as I don't like to do it, I suggest you assign someone else to do the follow-up interviews. She's just too important a witness, and her feelings about me shouldn't get in the way of the information we need."

Shanklin didn't respond immediately, waiting for a sign from Malley. When he saw Malley nod approvingly, he piped, "Yeah. That's a good idea. I'll assign another agent first thing tomorrow morning."

"The Secret Service asked me if it was true I had been to Ruth Paine's and talked with Marina," I said. "I told them yes, I had."

"You said what?" Malley jerked in his seat and looked right at me for the first time. His fat face quivered in a display of surprise and anger.

"I told them I had been by twice, on November first and fifth," I said, not sure where I was treading now.

"Damn it, why'd you tell them that? You shouldn't have done that, Hosty!" There was no mistaking Malley's anger now.

"Wait a minute. How could I deny that? Ruth and Marina have both told the Secret Service and the police I had been out to the house on those dates," I reasoned.

Malley spun around in his seat with a huff and began to ignore me. Was this man an arrogant, hard-nosed S.O.B. or what? I had heard Malley was well respected by other agents, but I was certainly seeing his uglier side. Between Shanklin's tattered nerves and Malley's standoffish attitude, I had just about had my fill of supervisors. I got the hell out of their office and stormed back to my desk where I could stew in private.

As I sat at my desk, I tried to block out of my mind all the rage and frustration I was feeling. I was twisted, dazed, and confused. I felt I had done everything correctly, by the book, but more and more I felt myself under the hardest, most nit-picking scrutiny for every damn thing I had done that was even remotely connected with Lee Oswald. Somehow I was at the center of the storm, but I was being kept in the dark about some very significant matters. I had figured out that some very frightening facts were surfacing about the Soviets and the Cubans, but based on the need-to-know policy, no one wanted me to know what they were. Shit, if I didn't know *all* the facts, why was I having to go through the torture of being scrutinized and criticized for everything I did, or had done?

I looked at my watch, and saw it was nearly 10:00 P.M. I guessed my parents and my younger brother were probably at the house waiting on me by now. I was sure Janet had put all the kids to bed. My head was aching with pain and fatigue. I had to get some sleep, so I grabbed

my suit jacket and hit the door. I'd deal with Shanklin and Malley tomorrow.

Thursday, November 28, 1963

TIME: 4:30 P.M.

I wrapped up my dictation with one of our stenos, and apologized for
the tenth time for keeping her from her home and family on Thanksgiving Day. She just shrugged and told me not to worry about it, then
packed it up and left. I thought I should try to do the same, even
though I knew I couldn't afford to waste any precious minutes.

The steady rumors out of Washington were that President Johnson was going to retract his earlier comments about not having any
hearings and instead was setting up a fact-finding panel to review the
assassination. As this talk in Washington grew stronger with each passing day, the intensity level in the Dallas FBI office grew proportion-
ately. Each day the agents were pushing themselves harder and harder.
The nation's eyes were focused on Dallas, impatiently waiting for the
full facts.

I looked around the bullpen and noticed that most of the
agents from Dallas had stolen home for a quick bite of turkey. The out-
of-town agents, with nowhere to go, just kept plugging away. Well, I figured, a half-hour at home couldn't hurt, so I tidied up my desk quickly
and climbed the bullpen stairs to leave.

When I got home I realized I couldn't have timed my arrival any
better. Janet was literally placing the last few dishes of food on the table
as I walked in the door. My mother came over and hugged me, while
the kids clamored around my legs squealing, "Daddy's home! Daddy's
home!" For a moment I felt as if everything was all right. I was waking
up from a terrible nightmare: the president hadn't been killed. Lee Oswald was a mixed-up young punk, nothing more.

Then my father strode over to me, nodded gravely, and asked
how things were going, bringing me crashing back to reality. I didn't
want, nor did I have time, to discuss the case. "Things are going fine," I
said. He nodded, sensing I was keeping my feelings to myself. My
younger brother Ed was standing next to me, quiet out of deference to
our dad. We Hosty men tend to be the quiet sort. I guess we figured we
had to be stoic: chin up, no whining, keep pushing on. Emotions were
something we didn't know how to deal with, so we checked them away
as far as we could in the recesses of our psyches. I suppose if I had

broken down and started crying, my father and brother would not have been ashamed or embarrassed of me. They would have felt for me, but they also would have just stood there with their arms at their sides, incapable of doing much else. It was just the way we were.

I broke the awkward silence. "So, Ed, how's the Army? Tell me about your orders to ship out to Germany." Ed, in his early twenties, said he was looking forward to going overseas.

Janet, clearly anxious, discreetly edged into our conversation and asked how much time I had. I told her no more than thirty minutes. "In that case," she said, "we better sit down and eat."

I agreed, and started collecting the children.

Janet had moved our kitchen table into the den, and had placed the card table and chairs at one end to accommodate the overflow of people. After everyone was seated, I took my place at the head of the table and led us in grace. When I finished, Janet wanted to say an additional prayer.

She prayed for the Kennedy and Tippit families, and asked God to protect and help them. She prayed for all of the FBI agents who were working so hard. She thanked God for our wonderful family and asked for His blessing. "Amen," everyone murmured.

That moment, I came as close as I ever had in the past week to breaking down. Despite myself, my eyes watered and my throat tightened. I knew if I opened my mouth to try to speak, it would have been like opening a hole in the dike. So I began carving the turkey silently.

After I served dinner to the last of the children, I began to eat hurriedly. I looked at my watch and saw it was time to go. Apologizing to everyone, I dragged my coat on, straightened my tie, and trudged to my car to head back to the office.

I was tired as hell, but spending just thirty minutes with my family had given me new energy and courage. This was Thanksgiving after all, and for that gift I was truly thankful.

Friday, November 29, 1963

TIME: 3:30 P.M.

Earl Warren was called to the White House, and at the urging of President Johnson accepted the appointment to head the commission to investigate the assassination of President Kennedy.

TIME: 4:00 P.M.

President Johnson, in a press release, announced the establishment of a commission to be headed by Chief Justice Earl Warren to investigate the assassination of President Kennedy.

7

Wednesday, December 15, 1963

TIME: 10:00 A.M.

On December 6, 1963, as part of the FBI's internal investigation of the pre-assassination investigation of Oswald, Assistant Director and Chief Inspector James Gale had phoned in a set of questions to Shanklin and Malley regarding my handling of the Oswald cases prior to the assassination. Headquarters was obviously considering me for possible punishment, but this was a very unusual way to do things; in most cases, the inspector confronted the agent in person without going through anyone else. But I had dutifully written up my answers to Gale's questions and supplied them to Shanklin and Malley the same day, confident in my situation.

On December 8, Malley, Shanklin, and Howe had all met privately in Shanklin's office to review my answers. After more than an hour, Howe came storming out, his face red as a fire with anger. He marched straight up to me and thrust a stack of papers in my hands. "Here, Hosty. You may need these someday." Puzzled, I looked down at the papers and saw my answers to headquarters' list of questions.

Malley was still standing just inside Shanklin's office with Shanklin himself. Malley stared at me for a strange moment, then stepped forward to shut the door. I shrugged and went back to work. But not before I safely locked my answers away in my desk.

Malley and Shanklin mailed my typed-up answers to headquarters. One week later, Hoover sent me a letter of censure:

UNITED STATES DEPARTMENT OF JUSTICE
FEDERAL BUREAU OF INVESTIGATION
WASHINGTON, D.C.

December 13, 1963

PERSONAL

Mr. James P. Hosty, Jr.
Federal Bureau of Investigation
Dallas, Texas

Dear Mr. Hosty:

It has been determined that your recent handling of a security-type case was grossly inadequate. Specifically, there was an unwarranted delay on your part in reporting certain pertinent information and the investigation you conducted was most inadequate. Furthermore, the explanation which you furnished as to why you failed to conduct a certain interview was absolutely unacceptable and your judgment in connection with this aspect of the case was exceedingly poor. Moreover, in view of the information developed concerning the subject of this investigation, it should have been apparent to you that he required a status which would have insured further investigative attention.

In view of the slipshod manner in which you handled this investigation, you are being placed on probation. It will be incumbent upon you to handle your future duties at a higher level of competence so that further administrative action of this nature will not be necessary.

Very truly yours,

John Edgar Hoover
Director

Hoover composed all of his written communication with oblique, nonspecific references so that any non-Bureau person — or anyone not personally involved with the matter at hand — who happened to intercept the letter would have no clue to which case he referred. I knew he was referring to the Oswald case. What I couldn't figure out was what exactly he was complaining about in this letter of censure. What "certain interview" did I fail to conduct? And what was my "unwarranted delay" in reporting certain information? And what was that "pertinent information" supposed to have been? Finally, what other information was there that would have justified making the Oswald case a higher priority?

I decided to find Clark and ask him what he thought of Hoover's letter. He couldn't make head nor tails of it, either. It turned out that sixteen other agents, from Assistant Director Bill Sullivan on down, had also received letters of censure. Clark did tell me that he couldn't believe Hoover had acted this quickly, and for that matter this leniently. He advised me to ride out my 90-day probation, which meant I could continue working but should consider myself warned to correct any deficiencies in my work performance. Hoover would be stopped from punishing me again, and there were many worse things he could have done to me, justified or not. Hoover could be entirely irrational in his treatment of agents when the Bureau was publicly embarrassed.

The other reason I couldn't understand why Hoover was censuring me and placing me on probation was that the investigation had been going well. After DeBrueys returned from Washington, where he had turned over all the evidence we had collected, we continued our work. We had two primary tasks: first, conduct several additional interviews of Ruth and Michael Paine to learn more about Lee Oswald's activities up to the day of the assassination; and second, pull together the enormous amount of information all the field agents in Dallas had collected about the Oswalds' background. (Meanwhile, Bob Gemberling, a newly appointed supervisor, was in charge of pulling together all the information collected about the assassination and the Tippit killing.)

DeBrueys and I had to sort through hundreds of reports — thousands upon thousands of pages compiled by the different agents. We then had to write a synopsis for the collective whole of these reports. We were both proud to type our names on the cover sheet of the tremendously thick finished product.

Then Shanklin told me headquarters did not want my name on this report. Only DeBrueys would get credit. My name had brought public embarrassment to Hoover and the FBI because of the fact that the press had reported I had a case on Oswald prior to the assassination. DeBrueys objected on my behalf, but Shanklin cut him off. Headquarters had decided, and that was it.

After I had taken myself off the job of interviewing Marina Oswald, Shanklin and Malley chose Wally Heitman, a fellow security agent, to continue the task. Heitman's partner was Anatol Bogaslov, the FBI's top Russian translator. Bogaslov was born in Odessa, Russia, the son of a banker. His family barely escaped in 1922, when the city fell to the Communists. Once in the United States, his mother, father, and sister all worked as translators for the FBI; Bogaslov and his brother both became full-fledged agents.

During their first interview with Marina, Bogaslov had properly identified himself as an FBI agent, but she seemed to regard him as a fellow Russian immigrant, enlisted by the FBI to act as translator. She would tell Bogaslov things on the sly that she wouldn't tell Heitman, often directly contradicting what she had reported to Heitman. She would tell Bogaslov she didn't trust the FBI, and Bogaslov would just nod his head. Of course, right after he left her, Bogaslov would report to Heitman everything she had said.

Heitman and Bogaslov had at least seven or eight more interviews with Marina, none any more productive than mine. I was able to keep abreast of their lack of progress because Heitman and Bogaslov shared a desk with me, so I saw all of the paperwork and overheard all the briefings. Heitman and Bogaslov were nothing more than puppets. In the Bureau's own odd way of doing things, Bill Branigan, the section chief in charge of all Russian espionage cases, would telephone Heitman before each interview with a list of questions to ask Marina; afterward, Heitman would brief Branigan exhaustively. Then Branigan would dictate a completely new list of questions for Heitman to ask Marina. And so it went.

The most important thing to come out of all these interviews with Marina was not what she told the FBI, but what she didn't. Over a dozen times, in different ways, Heitman had asked Marina if she knew anything about her husband's September–October 1963 trip to Mexico City, where he had made contact with both the Soviet and Cuban embassies. Each time Marina denied knowing anything about the trip. We'd see what she would tell the Warren Commission, where she would have to testify under oath.

My dealings with Shanklin continued to slide into the bizarre. In early December, headquarters read my report on my November 23 interview with Ruth Paine. They noted my reference to Oswald's October hand-written draft letter to the Soviet Embassy in Washington. Headquarters, naturally, wanted Shanklin and the Dallas office to send them the letter. Shanklin scurried and got a copy of my FD-302 and read it. Then he went and got the letter from an evidence folder and read it. Next he called me into his office.

"Hosty, I see where I terribly misunderstood you about this letter you got from Ruth Paine," he told me. "You were right in not destroying it like I asked you."

I just nodded.

"But did you destroy, like I told you, that note Oswald left for you before the assassination?" he asked anxiously.

"Yes," I replied.

"Good," he said. "That will be all." Our meeting was over.

A few days later, I was summoned back to Shanklin's office. This time Malley was with him. They asked me to explain everything that happened in the interrogation of Lee Oswald in Captain Fritz's office. I began obediently, but when I got to the point when I began to ask Oswald questions about whether he had ever been to Mexico City, Shanklin literally screamed, "You asked him about that! Oh my God! I told you to go down to the interrogation and just observe, not ask questions!"

"No. You told me Belmont wanted me to go *take part* in the interrogation and give the police everything we had on Oswald."

"Goddamn it, I told you to *observe*. I never told you to give the police everything we had on Oswald!" Shanklin had totally lost his composure. "I'm ruined! Oh God, I'm ruined. I'll have to retire in disgrace!" He began sobbing uncontrollably.

I felt guilty watching him cry. Shanklin was a pitiful sight, and in this weak moment I tried to help him out. "Listen, I'll agree that you were right. I'll say that you told me just to go down there and observe, but that in the excitement of everything I forgot and asked Oswald about Mexico City." I said this reluctantly. I would regret it later.

Shortly after this meeting, Malley submitted a report to Belmont back at headquarters that I was unreliable, since I was always changing my version of events. The only example Malley was able to cite to prove this point was what I had volunteered to do for Shanklin. Malley reported that I first said I had orders to take part in the Oswald interrogation, as well as share with the police everything I knew about Oswald, and that I then changed my story when confronted with the truth and now said I had only been ordered to observe.

But Belmont didn't buy Malley's report. He told Hoover and

everyone else in the Bureau that he had in fact ordered me to take part in the Oswald interrogation and share with the police everything I had on Oswald. Shanklin never thanked me for volunteering to fall on the sword to save his ass, and Malley never apologized to me for distorting what he knew to be the truth.

In early December, Shanklin sent me over to the Secret Service's office to examine a potentially incriminating letter Oswald had written to his wife. Written in Russian, so Marina could read it, the letter was translated by the Secret Service's Leon Gopadze as follows:

1. This is the key to the mailbox which is located in the main post office in the city on Ervay Street. This is the same street where the drugstore, in which you always waited is located.
2. Send the information as to what has happened to me to the Embassy and include newspaper clippings (should there be anything about me in the newspapers). I believe that the Embassy will come quickly to your assistance on learning everything.
3. I paid the house rent on the 2d so don't worry about it.
4. Recently I also paid for water and gas.
5. The money from work will possibly be coming. The money will be sent to our post office box. Go to the bank and cash the check.
6. You can either throw out or give my clothing, etc., away. Do not keep these. However, I prefer that you hold on to my personal papers (military, civil, etc.).
7. Certain of my documents are in the small blue valise.
8. The address book can be found on my table in the study should you need same.
9. We have friends here. The Red Cross also will help you. [Red Cross in English.]
10. I left you as much money as I could, $60 on the second of the month. You and the baby [TRANSLATOR'S NOTE: baby's name illegible] can live for another 2 months using $10 per week.

11. If I am alive and taken prisoner, the city
    jail is located at the end of the bridge
    through which we always passed on going to
    the city (right in the beginning of the city
    after crossing the bridge).

While the Dallas police had been thorough in removing everything belonging to the Oswalds from Ruth Paine's house on November 22, they had missed two things in the kitchen. In early December, Ruth Paine discovered in her home a cookbook and a child care book of Marina's, both written in Russian. Ruth took them to the police, thinking they would give them back to Marina, who might need them. The police did not look at them, but instead gave them directly to the Secret Service, who still had Marina in protective custody.

These two books then made their way to Leon Gopadze, the only Secret Service agent who could read Russian. He decided to examine them before he gave them to Marina. While flipping through the pages, he came across a single, folded piece of paper, a handwritten letter in Russian. Though it wasn't addressed to Marina or signed by Lee, it was clear who the letter was for and who had written it.

After Gopadze had finished examining it, the Secret Service showed it to Marina to see what she had to say about it. "Oh, that letter," she reportedly said. "That was when he tried to shoot General Walker." She explained to the startled investigators that on the night of April 9, 1963, shortly after Lee Oswald had been laid off from his job, he had left her this letter. Then, with his rifle, the same one found on the sixth floor of the Texas School Book Depository, Oswald perched in the dark behind a tree across the street from Walker's Dallas home. Walker was home, visible through a glass window. From his sniper's position Oswald fired one shot. Just as he fired Walker bent down to pick up a piece of paper on the floor, and the bullet whizzed through the air where his head had been seconds before. Oswald stashed his rifle under some brush and ran from the scene. He caught a bus home and excitedly confessed everything to Marina. Marina told us that Oswald thought he had killed Walker. The next day he was shocked to read in the newspaper that he had missed. Marina said Oswald later returned to the scene to retrieve his rifle.

Marina said she had kept the letter in case she ever needed to blackmail her husband.

The police had had no clue on a suspect in the Walker case. During their investigation, the Dallas police knew I had been investigating Walker for inciting a riot in Oxford in protests over the desegregation of the University of Mississippi. The police asked me if I had any ideas on possible suspects. I had an informant who was a member of Walker's Minutemen who told me that the Minutemen were upset with Walker for going to Oxford in the first place. Through Walker's blunders there, he had caused himself and one of his aides to be arrested. When arrested, the aide had in his possession confidential documents revealing the strength of the Minutemen. My informant told me that because of all this, there was now talk among the Minutemen of replacing Walker as their leader. After I relayed all this information to the police, the police concentrated on Walker's own followers as suspects.

Following Marina's revelation, the FBI lab compared the bullet recovered from General Walker's wall to Oswald's rifle. Even though the bullet had been partly mutilated when it was removed from the wall, and even though rifles typically change ever so slightly over time, the lab was able to find five identifying matches between Oswald's rifle and the bullet. Because the FBI lab required seven matches before they could label it a conclusive match, it was only labeled "tentative." The Warren Commission had a second forensic lab, that of the New York State Police, check the bullet. While the FBI tended to be overly conservative in such matters, the New York State Police experts required only five matches for a positive and conclusive identification.

Finally, one of Oswald's acquaintances, George DeMorenschild, reported to us that a short time before the Walker shooting, he and Oswald had been discussing politics when Walker's name came up. DeMorenschild mentioned that Walker, who was fervently anti-Castro, was just another Hitler. He told Oswald that Walker was a menace to society and that maybe it wouldn't be such a bad idea if someone took a shot at him. DeMorenschild told us he had said this in the heat of passion — he hadn't been serious about that comment. But he might have inadvertently put the idea in Oswald's head.

The evidence was almost certainly enough to convict Oswald of taking a potshot at Walker. Oswald also would have had the motive, for Walker had called for the overthrow of Oswald's hero, Fidel Castro.

The most remarkable thing was Oswald's modus operandi. In shooting at Walker, Oswald had chosen a highly visible political target, had left money behind with Marina before his crime, had used the same high-powered rifle with scope, had shot from a sniper's position, had stashed the rifle near his sniper's nest, had fled on foot, then caught a public bus. And he had acted alone. This was, of course, startlingly similar to the behavior of Kennedy's presumed assassin.

8

Wednesday, March 25, 1964

TIME: 10:30 A.M.

A clerk dropped off my mail at my desk. Another letter from headquarters, a short one from Hoover telling me he was pleased to inform me that I was now off probation.

I tossed it in my file drawer

I was busy putting together some reports to comply with another request from the Warren Commission.

The FBI had been directed by President Johnson to continue its investigation but also to act as the primary investigative arm of the Warren Commission. By late December 1963, just before Christmas, the vast majority of the FBI's investigation was complete, so the out-of-town agents, stenos, and clerks were allowed to return home, leaving the Dallas agents to wrap everything up. The investigation had to be one of the most thorough and exhaustive in American history. We chased down every reasonable lead, and quite a few unreasonable leads for good measure.

The Warren Commission had begun its work even before the investigation was completed. After the first of the year, the Commission began calling key witnesses to Washington to testify. One of these witnesses was Marina Oswald.

When Marina was sworn in before the Commission, she had an attorney by her side. Marina had been elusive throughout Heitman and Bogaslov's interviews, but now that she was at risk of perjury, she came clean with the truth. While she had feigned ignorance to Heitman and Bogaslov about her husband's trip to Mexico City, she confirmed for the Commission that not only had he traveled to Mexico City in September 1963, but that he had met with officials in the Soviet and Cuban embassies there. When asked why she had lied earlier, she said she just wanted the FBI to look bad.

The Commission's chief of staff, J. Lee Rankin, was quoted in the press claiming there had been a major breakthrough in the case. The press went into a frenzy, demanding to know more. The pressure mounted to such a degree that Earl Warren was forced to comment personally; he told the press that in our lifetime the public would not know some of the things the Commission had learned about the assassination. His enigmatic and provocative statement satisfied no one and whetted the appetite of those who were convinced there had been a conspiracy, or at the very least a cover-up.

At this point, I still did not know what precisely had happened when Oswald was in Mexico City. Who exactly had Oswald met with? What had they discussed? How did the Soviet Embassy official Kostikov fit into all of this?

I learned that several Commission staffers wanted to get tough with Marina Oswald for being such an obstructionist, but Warren decided to take another approach. He asked the FBI to place a wiretap on Marina's telephone in Dallas and requested that visual surveillance be set up outside her home. I learned that the Commission suspected that Soviet KGB agents might try to contact Marina in Dallas, possibly with instructions on how to handle matters. The Commission hoped to catch Marina in a conversation with a Soviet agent. On February 29, 1964, in a letter signed by J. Lee Rankin, the Warren Commission requested a wiretap on Marina Oswald.

Alan Belmont, the number-three man in the Bureau, was livid when he received the Commission's request. Belmont felt that the Commission's suspicions were both outrageous and naive. Even assuming that Marina was a Soviet agent, the Soviets would not be stupid enough to make contact with the highly visible and carefully watched Marina Oswald. Why would the Soviets risk an international furor by contacting her?

Furthermore, if the public learned that the FBI had wiretapped her home, the public backlash would be swift and brutal. Marina, in the eyes of many Americans, was a poor grieving widow with young children.

But Hoover overruled Belmont's concerns. With the letter from

Rankin and the Warren Commission, Hoover insisted vocally that the FBI would be protected. If the wiretap backfired, Earl Warren, Chief Justice of the Supreme Court, would have hell to pay, not Hoover and the FBI.

Therefore, the first order of business was to secure the necessary warrant from the U.S. Attorney General's office. I found this interesting, since Bobby Kennedy was the attorney general. Once the warrant was secured, the Dallas FBI office was ordered to carry out the deed.

Every major field office was supposed to have a wire-man, someone who could place telephone and room wiretaps whenever necessary. Ours was Nat Pinkston, a good friend of mine. The redheaded, forty-something Pinkston had joined the Bureau during World War II and now primarily worked on interstate auto theft cases.

During the first week of March 1964, Pinkston was sent out to Marina's home to place the tap. Although he had received special wiretap training at the FBI Academy in Quantico, Virginia, he was nervous. He hadn't done many wiretaps and, further, hadn't done one for quite a while. Pinkston dressed in clothes to look like a utility worker and borrowed a utility service van.

A few hours after he left, Pinkston returned, successful. He had parked his van across the street from Marina's, and then, with his box of "utility tools," walked up to the house. Pinkston had already determined that Marina would not be home, so after walking around inspecting the house, he found an entry into a crawl space under it, out of sight of nosy neighbors. He wiggled his way into the crawl space and found just the spot to place the tap. Working quickly, he wiggled his way back out, got back in his van, and left.

He told me it went "as smooth as silk, no problem." He was clearly relieved to have the job over with. He told me he had initially been nervous that he would have to break into the house to place the tap. It was a stroke of good luck to discover the crawl space and avoid the break-in.

Now that the tap was in place, we had some agents set up a listening post nearby. For several weeks, agents monitored Marina's phone calls, recording each one. Because Marina still didn't speak English well, many of her conversations with her friends from the Russian community in Dallas were in Russian. The FBI had Anatol Bogaslov translate Marina's phone calls for the transcripts.

Ultimately, the wiretap was a bust. No Soviet agent ever tried to make contact with Marina. After a few weeks of monitoring Marina's phone conversations, the wiretap was discontinued.

Visual surveillance had also been set up, but it was deemed too risky and discontinued after a few days.

Still, the Warren Commission was asking itself the same question I was: Was Marina Oswald in fact a Soviet agent? Prior to the assassination I knew little about her. But over time I learned much. There was a real possibility that she was a "sleeper."

Marina was born on July 17, 1941, apparently illegitimately, to a young Russian woman, Klavdia Prusakova, in the village of Molotovsk, during the Germans' war on the Soviets. Molotovsk is in the Arctic Circle, not far from Archangel. Marina's mother moved into her parents' apartment, where Marina lived until she was six years old. Marina's grandmother was the primary caregiver, while Marina's grandfather worked as captain of a Soviet commercial ship.

During the war, Marina's mother met a young soldier named Alexander Medvedev, who was sent to the front shortly after he and Klavdia met. Before he was shipped out, Marina's mother and Alexander married. Marina was fourteen months old at the time, and was always told that this man was her natural father. After Alexander's return, Marina soon had a brother and a sister. During her early childhood, Marina was treated harshly by her stepfather, who favored his own children over Marina. She soon learned that Alexander was not her real father.

When Marina was eleven, the Medvedevs settled in Leningrad. At thirteen, she enrolled in pharmacy school. In the middle of this training, when she was fifteen, her mother died of cancer. Following her mother's death, life with her stepfather became worse, and she soon began to neglect her studies. At one point she was expelled, and it wasn't until she was almost eighteen, after having begged the school for a second chance, that she earned her pharmacy diploma.

A few months later, in August 1959, Marina was pressured by her stepfather to leave home. She packed a suitcase and took the train to Minsk to try to find a new home with her mother's brother Ilya and his wife. Ilya Prusakov reluctantly agreed to allow his niece to move into the spacious apartment he and his wife had never had to share, since they had no children of their own. Ilya, it turned out, was a high-ranking member of the Communist party and a lieutenant colonel in the Belorussian Republic's Ministry of Internal Affairs, the internal police security force also known as the MVD. The MVD worked hand in hand with the KGB and were frequently lumped together and known collectively as the Chekists, which is Russian slang for "secret police."

The lines between the two organizations were for the most part indistinct: personnel was frequently exchanged and, ultimately, both the KGB and the MVD were directed by the same group of people. Ilya Prusakov's apartment was in a complex set aside exclusively for high-ranking members of the KGB and MVD; thus Marina was now exposed almost exclusively to these people. The upper-class apartment complex was right across the street from the Surorov Military Academy, and one of the building's tenants was the head of the Belorussian Communist party.

While living with her uncle and aunt, Marina found a job as a pharmacist at a Minsk hospital. She also joined the Komsomol, or Communist Youth Party, from which future members of the Communist party were picked.

Marina, who was quite pretty, soon began attracting many suitors. Among them were several respectable young men, including two medical students and one young man from a prominent family. One Friday night, on March 17, 1961, Marina was asked by two young men to accompany them to a medical student's dance at the Palace of Culture, a huge building in the center of Minsk. With the orchestra playing, Marina danced with one of her suitors. Later, a medical student, accompanied by a dark-haired young man, approached Marina. The dark-haired fellow turned out to be Lee Oswald, who was living in Minsk and working at the local radio factory. He simply introduced himself by his Minsk nickname, Alik.

Marina danced with Lee several times. Marina was especially magnetic that night and had at least five other young men vying for her attention. After Lee and another young man escorted Marina home, he begged to know when he might see her again. She told him she might be at next week's dance.

Several weeks later, when Oswald was in the hospital to have his adenoids removed, Marina often came to visit him. She reportedly didn't regard him as a boyfriend, however. When he was discharged from the hospital, Oswald was invited by Marina to have dinner on April 11 with her aunt and uncle in their apartment. After dinner, MVD Lieutenant Colonel Ilya Prusakov quizzed Oswald. Following this examination, Ilya rose to leave for his work. He told Oswald to "take care of this girl, as she has plenty of breezes in her brain."

On April 18, barely a month after they met, Oswald asked Marina to marry him. Marina insisted he would have to talk with her uncle first. The next day, dressed in a suit, Oswald sat down with Ilya in Ilya's living room, while Marina and her aunt waited in the kitchen. Ilya asked Oswald several questions about his proposal, and finally gave the couple his blessing. The four of them toasted the occasion with cognac. On April 30, 1961, Lee and Marina were married in the Minsk marriage bureau office, followed by a reception at her Uncle Ilya's apartment.

Marina and Lee moved into Lee's spacious apartment, and with Lee's salary plus his Red Cross/KGB subsidy, were quite comfortable by Soviet standards. Soon after they married, Lee told Marina for the first time that he wanted to take her back to the United States with him. Marina agreed, but with some reluctance. While they waited months for the American government to approve the return of Lee with a Russian bride, Marina gave birth to their daughter, June, on February 14, 1962. The Soviets approved Marina's exit visa relatively quickly. It was the INS that dragged its heels. Lee was considered unworthy because of his public defection and his angry denunciation of his U.S. citizenship in 1959. It was only when the U.S. State Department intervened and said it would be better propaganda to allow Lee to return that Marina was granted her visa. Finally, in mid-March 1962, the Oswalds received her U.S. entrance visa and his passport. On June 15, 1962, Marina, Lee, and June arrived at the Fort Worth home of Marguerite Oswald. In short order, Lee would have his first encounter with the FBI when he was interviewed by John Fain in the Fort Worth FBI office.

I learned the vast majority of this information after the assassination. Beforehand, I simply knew that Lee had married a young Russian pharmacist. With hindsight, I felt even more strongly that Marina Oswald fit the FBI's criteria as a KGB-planted sleeper agent.

This criteria had been developed over time by the FBI's counter-espionage experts. In 1963, the cold war was deadly serious, and intelligence agencies on both sides were desperately trying to plant spies. Field agents, such as myself, were instructed to look for the following criteria in recent Soviet immigrants:

1. The immigrant is 20–30 years old.
2. The immigrant has no living relatives back in the Soviet Union.
3. While in the United States, the immigrant has no associations with Americans, except those that are unavoidable.
4. The immigrant's INS file reflects a sketchy portrait of the immigrant's previous life in the Soviet Union.
5. The immigrant strictly adheres to all laws, so as not to draw attention.

6. The immigrant's bank records indicate anonymous third-party cash deposits, which could indicate payments by the KGB.
7. The immigrant is not physically disabled in any fashion.
8. The immigrant is educated or highly trained in a technical field.

Marina fit these criteria. She was in her early twenties. She had no living relatives, other than a half-sister and half-brother. She really had no associations with Americans, except Ruth Paine, and that was out of housing necessity. Marina's INS file was sketchy and filled with lies. Specifically, she did not disclose the last name she lived under before moving in with her MVD uncle. She denied having been in the Communist Youth Party and conveniently failed to mention what her uncle did for a living. Marina kept a low profile and abided by U.S. laws. We did not know if she was getting a subsidy from the KGB through her bank. Marina was physically fit. Finally, Marina was trained and educated in a technical field, pharmacy.

Viewed from the other side of the Iron Curtain, Marina was a logical spy recruit. Here was a young, clever, educated woman with no family to speak of. She had never known her true father, her mother was dead, and her stepfather wanted nothing to do with her. I think it very possible that while Marina was living with her Uncle Ilya in the apartment complex housing only KGB and MVD officers that she could well have been recruited by the KGB.

When the Russians recently shared their files concerning their investigation of Oswald, it was determined that *all* of Lee Oswald's supposed friends in the Soviet Union were dutifully reporting everything they knew about Lee to the KGB. This included Oswald's "closest friend," Pavel Golovachev, who was the son of a Soviet Army general. If all of Oswald's "friends" were reporting to the KGB, then why not Marina as well? It would be naive to think otherwise. I am confident that Marina was, at the very least, communicating with the KGB about her activities with Oswald.

Then there is the intriguing series of events culminating in the marriage of Lee and Marina. In February 1961, Oswald wrote a letter to the U.S. Embassy in Moscow to make known his desire to return to America. It would be ludicrous to think that the KGB failed to intercept that letter. They had at least the same capabilities we did in 1963 when we intercepted Oswald's letters to the Soviet Embassy in Washington. If the KGB knew in February 1961 of Oswald's desire to return to America, is it just coincidence that one of Oswald's "friends" introduced him to the captivating Marina on March 17, 1961? While Marina surely could have married many men in Russia, including doctors and other distinguished young men, she chose to marry a high school dropout, a radio mechanic. He was not even a Russian. The clincher is that Marina's uncle, an MVD lieutenant colonel, consented to the marriage of his niece to the American in such short order.

Then another series of astounding events occurred. Marina supposedly learned that Lee desired to return to America shortly after their wedding. After a brief resistance, she agreed to go with him. Then, in amazingly short order, the Soviet immigration agency, known as OVIR, which was part of the MVD and known to be under the control of the KGB, approved Marina's exit visa. It was all too easy for Marina to leave the Soviet Union, especially as the niece of an MVD lieutenant colonel.

My suspicions about Marina were further solidified in 1976 by another piece of information published by the Senate Select Committee, commonly known as the Church Committee. This involved another young American who, like Lee Oswald, journeyed to the Soviet Union in search of a better life. James Mintkenbaugh lived in the Soviet Union in the late 1950s, but in 1959, disillusioned with communism's promise, decided he wanted to return to the United States. When Mintkenbaugh returned to Boston, he was routinely interviewed by FBI agents, just as Lee would be interviewed by John Fain upon his return. Whereas Lee was obstinate and elusive with Fain, Mintkenbaugh was forthcoming and honest with the Boston FBI. During his interview, Mintkenbaugh informed the agents that after he made known his desire to return to America, the KGB approached him to ask if he would marry a young Soviet woman and take her back with him to America. Taken aback by what he considered a ludicrous proposition, Mintkenbaugh refused and returned to America alone. (It would have been the responsibility of FBI headquarters to provide this sort of information to a field agent like myself.)

I acknowledge that there is a very real possibility that Marina was nothing more than an innocent immigrant with no connections to the KGB. Some people may regard my suspicions as paranoid or outrageous, but as an FBI agent I was trained to be suspicious. Counterespionage work was my trade. When Oswald killed President Kennedy, any chance of determining whether Marina was a Soviet agent was both pointless and moot. Typically, to catch a spy you have to catch him or her in the act. With Marina thrust into the public spotlight by her husband's crimes, there was no chance to catch her doing anything but living a normal, routine life. To put a KGB sleeper in the public spotlight is tantamount to cutting the umbilical cord back to the KGB.

I should also stress that there was absolutely no evidence that Marina Oswald was in any way involved in any of her husband's crimes. Regardless of whether Marina was a KGB agent or not, it is clear Oswald was acting independently of his wife. This said, one cannot help recalling that Oswald, after his abortive attempt to assassinate General Walker, confided his crime to Marina. Had she reported him to the authorities, he would doubtless have been behind bars when JFK came to Dallas.

9

Thursday, April 23, 1964

TIME: 10:30 P.M.

I don't usually get phone calls late at night, so when the phone rang I picked up the receiver and said hello in a less than cordial tone.

"Hugh Aynesworth with the *Dallas Morning News*," the caller identified himself. "Is this FBI Agent James Hosty?"

"Yes, it is. What do you want?"

"Well, we're running a story tomorrow and I wanted to see if you wanted to make a comment," Aynesworth said.

He explained his story. It would describe how I knew that Oswald was in Dallas prior to the assassination, that he was a Communist, and that he was capable of killing the president. Finally, Aynesworth said, I didn't share any of this information with the Dallas police. Aynesworth was basing this story on Lieutenant Jack Revill's memorandum of November 22, 1963. Revill had prepared this memo shortly after my conversation with him in the police garage immediately after the assassination. Detective Jackie Bryan was reportedly backing up Revill on this allegation against me. Aynesworth wanted my comment.

Strict Bureau policy absolutely prohibited agents like myself from talking with the media or making any public comments. I had no choice but to say, "No comment."

"Well, just wanted to give you an opportunity. Thanks." With that, Aynesworth abruptly hung up.

I wanted to wring Revill's neck. That story was all a fabrication. The Dallas police had continued to be assaulted in the media for their handling of both pre- and post-assassination matters and were desperately trying to shift the attention and blame to anyone but themselves. I was sure Hoover's public comments chastising the Dallas police for not heeding the phone call warning that Oswald was to be killed had a great influence on this latest wrinkle.

I had felt a growing hostility toward me from the Dallas police, but I had never taken it too seriously. Until now. It was apparent now that they were gunning for me.

I recalled a few words spoken to me back in December by a fellow FBI agent, Vince Drain: "Hosty, don't you know you're going to be the goat on all this?"

Friday, April 24, 1964

TIME: 2:30 A.M.

The phone next to our bed rang, startling me from my sleep. I grabbed the phone and hoarsely asked, "What do you want?"

"Hosty, this is Shanklin." Oh God, I thought to myself. "Listen, Aynesworth called me earlier to say they are running a story about you telling Revill you knew Oswald was capable of killing the president."

"I know, I know. Aynesworth called me, too," I said, sitting up in bed.

"Well, why in the hell didn't you call *me*?" Shanklin demanded. Before I could answer, he continued. "Listen, I'm down at the office now and I just had the night clerk run out and get an early edition of the *Morning News*. I want you to come down and help me prepare a teletype for headquarters."

"Now?" I asked, already knowing what the answer would be.

"Yes, *now*. I'll see you when you get here." With that Shanklin hung up.

Janet was awake and sitting up in bed now as well. I told her what Shanklin said. She sighed, wondering when it was all going to end. I figured I wouldn't be coming home until quitting time, so I shaved and dressed for the day.

Walking out to my car, I looked at all my neighbors' homes, wondering what they would be thinking later this morning as they sat in their kitchens, drinking their coffee in their robes, reading the

Morning News. I wished I could explain it all to them. I climbed into my car and quietly closed the car door. I didn't want to wake anyone up.

TIME: 3:15 A.M.

As soon as I walked into Shanklin's smoke-filled office, I saw the copy of the newspaper lying on his desk. I grabbed it. Staring back at me in bold, black print was the front-page headline: FBI KNEW OSWALD CAPABLE OF ACT, REPORTS INDICATE.

"Oh God," I groaned.

I quickly scanned the first few paragraphs while Shanklin sat quietly behind his desk puffing away. The story read, "A source close to the Warren Commission told the *Dallas News* Thursday that the Commission has testimony from Dallas police that an FBI agent told them moments after the arrest and identification of Lee Harvey Oswald on November 22, that 'we knew he was capable of assassinating the president, but we didn't dream he would do it. . . .' In a memorandum to supervisors on Nov. 22, Lt. Jack Revill, head of the Dallas police criminal intelligence squad, reported that FBI special agent James (Joe) Hosty had acknowledged awareness of Oswald in the basement of the City Hall at 2:05 P.M., Nov. 22. His remark was made as five officers brought Oswald in from Oak Cliff, Revill reported."

The article ended with some enlightening comments from the police: "Dallas police officers watched several known extremists prior to the Kennedy visit and even sent representatives as far as 75 miles to interview others thought to be planning demonstrations. Curry [the Dallas police chief] privately has told friends, 'If we had known that a defector or a Communist was anywhere in this town, let alone on the parade route, we would have been sitting on his lap, you can bet on that.' But he refused public comment."

The police were blatantly trying to wriggle out from under a rock. The implication was that if the FBI had just warned them about Oswald, they'd have sat on his lap just like they did with all the other Communists. I wanted to laugh. The police had a long list of well-known Communists in Dallas, and not one had a police officer sitting on his lap on November 22. In fact, Detective Sergeant H. M. Hart told me that the police neither picked up nor watched anyone the day of November 22. Clearly, someone from the police department had fed this story to Aynesworth.

I laid down the paper and took a seat in front of Shanklin. "This

119

article has got it all wrong. I don't understand how they can print crap like that," I protested.

"Well, this is what I want you to do. Prepare your version of what happened in the police garage that afternoon, and as soon as you get done, we're going to teletype it straight to headquarters. I've already called and told them all about the article and told them to expect a response from you in an hour or so."

I composed my version sitting in Shanklin's office. When I finished, Shanklin and I took it over to the teletype machine and sent it.

Later that day, Shanklin told me that in Washington that morning, Hoover had furiously demanded to know why I had been at the police station in the first place. Belmont stood up and told Hoover that he had personally ordered me to take part in the interrogation of Oswald and provide everything we had on Oswald to the police. Once Hoover knew this, he switched gears and said he would defend me.

Hoover came out blasting. He categorically denied the story's contentions. Revill himself partially retracted some of the article's allegations; he told the *Dallas Times Herald* that the comment that I never dreamed Oswald would kill the president was all someone else's fabrication. But Aynesworth and the *Morning News* had done the damage. It would prove to be irreversible regarding my relationships with the Dallas police and the Dallas media.

Two of my fellow agents, Bob Barrett and Ike Lee, later told me about their conversation with Revill after the story broke. Revill told Barrett and Lee that he had not wanted his November 22 memo to be released to the Warren Commission or the press, but police chief Jesse Curry threatened to charge Revill with filing a false police report if Revill wouldn't swear to the truth in his memo. The police then got a memo from Detective Jackie Bryan, who had been standing near Revill and me during this brief garage conversation. Contrary to Aynesworth's assertion, Bryan supported my version of the events. He reported that he did not hear me make any kind of comment suggesting I knew Oswald was capable of killing the president.

The first four paragraphs of Revill's five-paragraph memo were accurate. But the last paragraph, the incendiary paragraph, appears to have been added as an afterthought. The memo read:

November 22, 1963

Captain W.P. Gannaway
Special Service Bureau

Subject: Lee Harvey Oswald
605 Elsbeth Street

Sir:

On November 22, 1963, at approximately 2:50
P.M., the undersigned officer met Special Agent
James Hosty of the Federal Bureau of Investiga-
tion in the basement of the City Hall.

At that time Special Agent Hosty related to
this officer that the subject was a member of
the Communist Party, and that he was residing in
Dallas.

The Subject was arrested for the murder of
Officer J. D. Tippit and is a prime suspect in the
assassination of President Kennedy.

The information regarding the Subject's affiliation with the Communist Party is the first
information this officer has received from the
Federal Bureau of Investigation regarding same.

Agent Hosty further stated that the Federal
Bureau of Investigation was aware of the Subject
and that they had information that this Subject
was capable of committing the assassination of
President Kennedy.

Respectfully submitted,

Jack Revill, Lieutenant
Criminal Intelligence Section

Logically, that last paragraph should have been inserted into
the second paragraph where Revill is quoting me. The fifth paragraph's information is much more dramatic than everything else in the

memo, so why didn't Revill put it up higher? Could it be because he inserted it later?

I wasn't the only one to question the veracity of Revill's memo. The Warren Commission ordered the FBI's forensic document experts to analyze it to determine if the police had added the last paragraph after November 22. Unfortunately, the police had only supplied the Commission and the FBI forensic lab with a photocopy of the memo. Because they did not have the original memo on which to conduct a microscopic examination, the forensic lab could make no determinations.

On April 27, 1964, William A. Murphy, a retired FBI agent who had been the Dallas SAC, wrote Shanklin a letter. Murphy, just like the rest of the country, had read the press accounts quoting Revill's memo.

Murphy told Shanklin that on December 20, 1963, he had confronted Chief Curry about remarks he had made shortly after midnight the night of the assassination at a press conference. The chief had announced that the FBI knew Oswald was in town but had not warned the Dallas police. During the December 20 meeting, Murphy asked Curry what his basis was for that comment to the press. Later, in early January 1964, Curry asked Murphy to come to his office so that he could explain his November 23 comments. Curry pulled from his desk drawer the original copy of the Revill memo and handed it to Murphy.

Murphy took his time, and carefully read and reread the memo, which he described as "on Police Department memorandum stationery, from Lt. Revill to either Captain Gannaway or to Chief Curry." Murphy read Revill's comment that I had reported on November 22 that Oswald was a Communist and living in Dallas.

Most critically, Murphy insisted to Shanklin, "This entire memorandum consisted of approximately three to four brief paragraphs, and positively there was no information set forth in that memorandum indicating that Hosty had in any way represented that Oswald had any dangerous tendencies or that he was in any way considered capable of assassinating the president." Murphy was adamant on this point. He told Shanklin that if the memo had reported I knew Oswald was capable of killing the president, Shanklin could be assured that he would have immediately reported that to the FBI. Murphy also pointed out to Shanklin that Curry, during his press conference on November 23, made no mention about the FBI supposedly knowing that Oswald was capable of killing the president.

Murphy strongly resented that the Dallas police were trying to discredit me and the FBI. Murphy didn't say it, but he was directly implying that sometime after early January 1964, the police had added that explosive last paragraph to the Revill memo.

It was also interesting to see Revill note at the top of his memo Oswald's old address, 605 Elsbeth Street. Clearly, the police knew a few things about Oswald before the assassination themselves.

When Revill reported that I knew Oswald was capable of killing the president, either he grossly misunderstood me or had yielded to police pressure to make the FBI look bad. All I recalled telling Revill was that Lee Oswald, a Communist, had just been arrested and that I was fairly sure he was the guilty party. I said this based on information I knew at the time. I knew shots had come from the book depository where Oswald worked. I also knew Oswald was arrested for killing Tippit. I figured the two killings were related. I just wish Revill had hunted me down for a clarification rather than letting all this happen.

During their conversation with Revill, Barrett and Ike Lee asked him what he would have done if he had known what I knew about Oswald before the assassination. Revill admitted he couldn't think of anything.

To further illustrate the point that the Dallas police wouldn't have done anything themselves, it is interesting to review the case of Joe Molina. Molina was a bookkeeper in the Texas School Book Depository and had the unfortunate experience of being listed on the Dallas police subversive list. Although Molina was in fact an anti-Communist, he was a member of the Latin American Veterans Organization in Dallas, an organization that had been infiltrated by members of the U.S. Communist party. If the police thought Molina was a Communist subversive, and they knew he was working in the book depository, why didn't they pick him up or neutralize him when the president's motorcade passed by the depository? This despite Curry's idiotic statement in the *Dallas Morning News* about putting police officers in every known Communist's lap.

The *Morning News* article of April 24, 1964, infected my entire relationship with the Dallas police. Now it would be exceedingly difficult if not impossible for me to work with them. Those dark days in Dallas were bringing out the worst in people. A pity, because such times ought to have brought people closer together.

The emergence of Aynesworth's worst side, however, was hardly new. He already had some dubious achievements to his credit. One such: about a week after the assassination, Aynesworth, along with Bill Alexander, an assistant district attorney in Dallas, decided to find out if

Lee Oswald had been an informant of the Dallas FBI, and of mine in particular. To this end, they concocted a totally false story about how Lee Oswald was a regularly paid informant of the Dallas FBI. At the time, I had no idea what information the *Houston Post* was relying on; it wasn't until February 1976, in *Esquire* magazine, that Aynesworth finally admitted he and Alexander had lied and made up the entire story in an effort to draw the FBI out on this issue. They said Oswald was paid $200 a month and even made up an imaginary informant number for Oswald, S172 — which was not in any way how the FBI classified their informants. Aynesworth then fed this story to Lonnie Hudkins of the *Post,* who ran it on January 1, 1964. Hudkins cited confidential but reliable sources for his story's allegations. The FBI issued a flat denial of the *Post* story. I was once again prohibited by Bureau procedure from commenting. It was clear that they were pointing a finger at me, since I was known to be the agent in charge of the Oswald file.

The *Post* article identifying Oswald as an FBI informant helped fuel another fire with me trapped in its middle. In January 1964, Texas Attorney General Waggoner Carr stated before the Warren Commission that he had information that Lee Oswald was an FBI informant and that this was why neither the Dallas FBI nor I had told the Dallas police that Oswald was in town. It turned out that the manager of a hotel coffee shop had overheard a conversation between a few FBI agents and had reported this to the Dallas police, who then passed it on to Carr.

One day in early December 1963, Dallas FBI agent Will Griffin had been eating in the coffee shop at the Brown Hotel with a few of the out-of-town FBI agents. I guess those agents were asking Griffin whether it was true that Jack Ruby was an informant. Griffin, who was what I would call a party-guy — he was boisterous and loud, and thoroughly enjoyed having a good time in the off-hours — announced to these agents, "Yes, he was an informant, and his file was sent to Washington."

The manager of the coffee shop overheard only what Griffin had said, and because he knew Griffin was an FBI agent, he assumed Griffin was referring to Oswald. A few days later, the FBI got wind of the manager's report. We figured no one would take it seriously. But when Carr went before the Commission in January, it became clear the Commission was taking the coffee shop manager's report very seriously. Headquarters wanted any FBI agent with any connection to the Oswald case to sign affidavits swearing Oswald was not a Bureau informant. At the time headquarters' request arrived, I was in a surgery waiting room. My three-year-old disabled son, Dick, was in the middle of an eye operation. While we were sitting there sweating out the surgery, I was paged to the phone. It was Shanklin, and he was losing it.

"Hosty! Get your ass down here now. You have to sign an affidavit swearing Oswald wasn't your informant!"

"But my son is in surgery. Can this wait another hour or two?" I asked.

"You have to do it right now!"

Not believing I was actually doing it, I walked out of my little boy's life when he needed me most. I wouldn't be there when the anesthesia wore off. He would be crying the way he always did, softly. The bandages would be over his eyes, and he would be frightened. I wouldn't be there for him. I would be downtown, answering Shanklin's every irrational beck and call.

I swore out the affidavit, as well as a few choice words under my breath.

Fortunately, shortly after Carr brought this information to the Warren Commission's attention later in January, the FBI told the Commission about Ruby being a potential criminal informant for Flynn. The Commission carefully examined these allegations about Oswald being an informant for the FBI, but concluded it was not true.

I knew Aynesworth fancied himself an investigative reporter and desperately wanted to link Oswald to me in some sinister aspect. In the February 1976 *Esquire* article he admitted that in these efforts he had fraudulently obtained my home telephone records by posing as me. He admitted, however, that it was a total bust: in all of his dubious diggings, he never found any evidence linking Oswald to me.

After Jack Ruby had been arrested and charged with the first-degree murder of Lee Oswald, the clamor to restore Dallas's pride grew to a fever pitch. It was going to be satisfied only when Ruby was convicted and executed. The Dallas District Attorney Henry Wade, a good and generally reasonable man, assigned the controversial Bill Alexander to prosecute Ruby. Alexander was Wade's primary death penalty trial man, and he was coldly effective.

My fellow agent Vince Drain told me a story about how Alexander, in front of his son, shot the boy's dog dead to get a point across. Alexander was feared, not respected, by others. With his squinting, cold dark eyes, Alexander could have played the stereotypical villain from a Hollywood B-movie. All you'd have to do is place a black fedora on his head. Alexander had made the most fatal mistake any prosecutor can make — though he made no secret of his contempt for the FBI, he got too chummy with the local police. He was always out riding shotgun in the patrol cars and executing search warrants with them. In the off-hours, he was out boozing it up with the cops as well. For law enforcement to be effective, the prosecutor has to separate himself from the cops. Otherwise he loses his objectivity and slides into situations where he ends up pandering to the cops' whims and desires.

Within 20 minutes of Ruby's arrest, Alexander was down at the Dallas jail to take part in the interrogation of Ruby. Alexander, who was a friend of Ruby's and a frequent drinking customer at Ruby's strip joint, told Ruby he just wanted to ask some questions "off the record." Alexander then asked Ruby why he shot Oswald and how he got into the police garage. Ruby gave his famous response: he shot Oswald to save Jackie Kennedy from having to come back to Dallas for a trial. He said he also wanted to show the world that Jews had guts.

Ruby felt that he had done everyone a favor by killing Oswald, remarking that the police couldn't kill Oswald, so he did. I guess Ruby figured he would go down in history a hero, like the Army sergeant who gunned down John Wilkes Booth after he killed President Lincoln. Booth's killer was revered, receiving among his honors the post of sergeant at arms for the Kansas legislature.

Ruby explained how that morning, after he'd sent a telegram at the nearby Western Union office on Main Street, he walked toward the police station. He saw a crowd gathered around the entrance ramp to the police garage and decided to see what was going on. Ruby said that while the only police officer monitoring this entrance ramp was distracted, he just strolled down the ramp without anyone stopping him. When Oswald was being escorted out, Ruby was instantly infuriated by the "smirk" on Oswald's face. That was all it took for the notoriously quick-tempered Ruby to whip out his revolver and pump a bullet into Oswald's gut.

Ruby had been legally carrying a handgun, because under Texas law any businessman carrying his day's proceeds was entitled to carry a handgun until he could safely deposit his proceeds in the bank. Ruby was in fact carrying his nightclub's profits, and since it was a Sunday, he had to wait until Monday to deposit this money.

Alexander used all of Ruby's statements in the trial, even though he had elicited them by promising Ruby they would be "off the record." Ruby's flamboyant attorney, Melvin Belli, objected to their admission into evidence, but the trial judge, Joe Brown, allowed them. Judge Brown was a good old boy from Texas, and he not only allowed this clearly inadmissible evidence, but he denied a motion to change the trial's venue after Belli had argued strenuously that there was no way Ruby could get a fair trial in Dallas. Belli, who had been educated at the University of California at Berkeley and practiced law in San Francisco, was ridiculed by the Dallas press for his pompous manner and his fancy shoes, which were labeled "fruit boots." Ruby couldn't have hired a worse attorney to plead his case to a good old boy Texas judge.

On February 17, 1964, 900 potential jurors were impaneled. My wife, Janet, was one of those called to serve. When I told Shanklin, he lost his cool yet again and hysterically demanded I get her off the panel. He didn't want any agents or their spouses in the glare of the media's spotlight. Against her own wishes — Janet wanted to serve on the Ruby jury — she was forced by Shanklin to call the jury clerk and plead hardship. She was removed from the jury pool.

The trial lasted from March 4 to March 14. Needless to say, after Ruby was convicted and sentenced to the electric chair by the all-Dallas jury, two years later the Texas Court of Appeals reversed it all. A new trial was ordered, only this time the appeals court ordered the trial be conducted far away from Dallas. Further, the off-the-record statements made by Ruby to Alexander were ordered kept out of evidence.

But before he could be retried, Ruby died of cancer in prison. He died an unconvicted man.

Ultimately, Alexander had done Dallas a disservice in his handling of the Ruby case. A more careful and honest prosecution would have quickly and effectively closed the dark chapter involving Ruby, thereby allowing Dallas the opportunity to get on with its healing process.

A year or two after the Ruby reversal, Alexander was forced to leave the district attorney's office when he was reprimanded for some pubic comments he made about the Chief Justice of the Supreme Court. It was reported that while he was giving a speech before some group in Dallas, an audience member asked Alexander if he agreed with the growing Dallas sentiment that Chief Justice Earl Warren should be impeached. Alexander replied something to the effect that hell no, they ought to hang him.

However disgraceful the Ruby case may have been to Alexander, the Dallas FBI was guilty of complicity in what I considered a more disgraceful matter. Napoleon Daniels was a college-educated black man who had previously been a police officer in Dallas, a city that had tenaciously hung on to its Old South segregationist past. In 1953 when Janet and I moved to Dallas with our kids, there were separate bathrooms and water fountains for blacks. Department stores wouldn't let black women try on hats in the main section of the hat department. On the police force, all black officers were placed in black-only units and were allowed to work only in all-black neighborhoods. Further, no black officer held a rank above sergeant.

Daniels left the police force to go into the real estate business. After earning his real estate license, he went into business for himself. After the assassination, Daniels, like a lot of people, was curious about things. He wandered down to the police station on Sunday morning, November 24. He knew, like everyone else in the country, that Lee Oswald was due to be transported that morning and he wanted to have a look. Daniels found a spot on the sidewalk at the Main Street ramp to the police garage where he hoped to catch a glimpse of Oswald. He recognized Roy Vaughn, who, as the only police officer assigned to guard this entrance, was busy trying to keep out all the curious onlookers. Sometime between 11:16 and 11:21 A.M., someone tried to drive their car down the entrance ramp; Vaughn had to walk out in the street to divert the car. While Vaughn was distracted, Daniels watched a white man in a suit and hat casually walk down the ramp. Daniels thought the man looked as though he knew what he was doing and figured he must be a police detective, especially considering the noticeable bulge at his waist that could only be a holstered handgun. Thinking it was no big deal, Daniels didn't say anything to Vaughn.

Later, after Oswald had been shot, Daniels saw Ruby on television and immediately recognized him as the man he had seen walk down the ramp while Vaughn was distracted. Daniels went straight to the Dallas police to report what he saw. The Dallas police dismissed him without even listening to his report. He decided to tell the Dallas FBI.

Our agents concluded Daniels was telling the truth, for why would he lie about this seemingly innocent observation? So what if Daniels saw Ruby slip into the garage? It all made sense. But the Dallas police had a different agenda. They were getting torn up mercilessly by the press and the public for their breach of security. The police decided to do what a lot of agencies were doing at the time: they decided to cover up. After their own internal investigation, the police concluded that they had not been negligent; they concluded that because security had been airtight, there was no way Ruby could have gained entrance. Someone must have provided Ruby with extraordinary assistance. This was laughable, since half the reporters in the garage basement where Oswald was killed said that no officer had bothered to check their credentials when they entered it.

These conclusions were not only absurd but had been reached with great injustice. The police refused to accept Daniels's version of how easily Ruby had breached security and ignored Ruby's own state-ment corroborating Daniels's version. Instead, the police practically destroyed Daniels. During their investigation, the police strapped Daniels and Vaughn to a polygraph machine. The FBI's polygraph ex-pert, who was there observing, watched the police polygraph team threaten to cause Daniels trouble and take action to revoke his real es-tate license if he didn't tell them "the truth." Because polygraphs are designed to register a subject's heart rate, threats to one's livelihood can skew the results. It was no surprise to see that Daniels "failed" the polygraph. When it came time for Vaughn, he was simply asked whether it was true that Jack Ruby had sneaked past him into the po-lice garage. Of course Vaughn answered this was not true, because he didn't see it happen. His polygraph test naturally showed he was telling the truth. The police were then able to hold up the two test results tri-umphantly, one indicating that Daniels was lying, the other that Vaughn was telling the truth.

But what was just as shameful was the Dallas FBI's attitude and response. The out-of-town agents were clamoring for the Bureau to in-tervene in the Daniels affair and straighten it all out. They were dis-gusted with the Dallas police and DA's office. Many of the out-of-town agents had been assigned to the Ruby squad, and in their investiga-tions one witness after another told them that it was a well-known fact that Ruby was tight with these two departments. Many of these wit-nesses described how Ruby not only plied the police and members of the DA's office with free drinks at his strip-tease bar but pimped his hookers to them as well. Time and again, when these agents wrote up their reports, all negative references about the police or DA's office were deleted by the Dallas FBI supervisors. The FBI supervisors stressed that it was more important to maintain a good working rela-tionship with the police and DA's office than to humiliate them.

The Dallas FBI office refused to intervene in the Daniels matter and accepted the police conclusion with no objection. Whether Napoleon Daniels ever knew it, he was a martyr to the peace between law enforcement agencies. In the minds of many of the white officers, Daniels was a black man, and as such, had to be put back in his place. It made me sick that we had gone along with all this.

Meanwhile, Lieutenant Jack Revill was up to his old tricks. When a news photographer snapped a picture the instant before Ruby shot Oswald, he captured Ruby standing alongside Lieutenant William "Blackie" Har-rison of the Dallas Police Department. Harrison was a good guy, but this didn't stop Revill from accusing Harrison of conspiring with

Ruby. Revill suggested that Harrison had to be the one who helped sneak Ruby into the basement garage. I learned many in the police force turned against Revill, charging him with making a scurrilous and groundless allegation. To me this was just business as usual with Revill.

Many of the millions of Americans who watched Ruby shoot Oswald jumped to the conclusion that he had done it to silence Oswald. I suppose Ruby, with his fancy dark suit, fedora, and snub-nosed revolver, looked like a mobster. But an investigator is supposed to start from the beginning and work carefully and logically. You don't decide upon a guilty party first and then work backward to support your conclusion. Instead you follow the evidence until it leads you to a suspect and his motive. As much as I try to explain this to people, they still reply, "Well, it sure looked like a mob hit." They don't seem to care about the evidence.

When the FBI investigated the Ruby shooting, we began at the beginning. That he did it was documented on television and seen by millions. The questions were: 1) Had he planned this killing? 2) Was anyone else involved? The agents carefully sifted the evidence; it led to a logical and understandable conclusion.

One of the first things an investigator does is retrace the killer's steps. If Ruby had planned to kill Oswald, he would have been in the police garage at 10:00 A.M. sharp, because that was when Chief Curry had announced to the world that the transfer would take place. Instead, we know Ruby was home in bed at that hour: at 10:10 A.M. he received a person-to-person collect telephone call from one of his strippers, Little Lynn. The stripper was in Houston and needed a quick loan from her boss. We know Ruby got up, dressed, and went down to Western Union on Main Street, just a short walk from the police garage. At 11:16 A.M., Ruby wired $25 to Little Lynn in Houston. We recovered the time-and-date-stamped wire receipt from Western Union.

Ruby could not have known that Oswald's transfer would be delayed until 11:21 A.M., because neither the police nor anyone else knew it would be. While Curry was adamant that the transfer had to occur at 10:00 A.M. sharp as he had promised the press, Captain Fritz was just as adamant about proving who was really in charge. Shortly before the transfer was to occur, Secret Service Inspector Tom Kelly asked Fritz if he could ask Oswald some questions. Fritz obliged. Kelly wrapped up his questioning shortly before 11:00 A.M. Then Fritz granted Inspector Harry Holmes of the U.S. Postal Department an interview with Oswald. Holmes's request for an interview was completely unplanned. Holmes told us he had planned to go to church that Sunday morning as he always did, but at the last moment changed his mind: he had some questions for Oswald about his use of post office boxes with an alias. Holmes ended up keeping Oswald until just after 11:10 A.M.

When Fritz was ready, and not one second sooner, the transfer of Oswald began. By this remarkable set of coincidences, Ruby was able to get in a position to shoot Oswald.

It was an impulse killing, period. There could not have been any premeditation on Ruby's part. Therefore, Ruby was guilty only of second-degree murder. With some argument that like everyone else Ruby was distraught by the president's death and that he had lost his temper when he saw a smirk on Oswald's face, it is possible that the crime could have been labeled manslaughter.

No one else could have been involved. How could the Mafia or any other group have sent Ruby to kill Oswald? If Ruby had planned to kill Oswald for the Mafia or some other group, why didn't he do it on Friday night when he was at Oswald's press conference? If you're going to silence someone, you do it quickly, before the person has an opportunity to tell the police about any co-conspirators. By Sunday morning, Fritz and company had logged many hours interviewing Oswald. Furthermore, when the mob hits to silence a witness, they don't replace one guy in custody with another. If the mob had hired Oswald to kill the president, and then decided to bump off Oswald, they wouldn't have done it with the likes of Ruby; that would have been self-defeating, since now Ruby was in custody. You silence someone because you don't want that someone to lead the police back to you. With Ruby in custody, what's to stop him from leading the police back to the mob? It is completely illogical to believe that the mob, or anyone else for that matter, hired Ruby to silence Oswald.

A lot of people get caught up in irrelevant discussions about Ruby's connections to the Mafia. If the evidence shows that Ruby couldn't have planned his killing of Oswald, what difference does it make if he has any Mafia connections? Ruby was more like a character from *Guys and Dolls* — more a client and victim of the Mafia than a member of it. He was in the vice business, and he had no choice but to deal with the Mafia, whose "protection insurance" he needed.

There are some people who have tried to place Oswald and Ruby together in Ruby's bar. The FBI was interested in pursuing those leads. We also wondered initially if Ruby was in any way connected to the president's death. What we discovered was that there was a man who resembled Oswald, somewhat, who frequented Ruby's bar, The Vegas Club. No connection between Oswald and Ruby before the assassination has ever been documented. Ruby's shooting of Oswald was independent of Oswald's crimes. Anyone who thinks otherwise is just ignoring the evidence.

Pursuing every lead we had, I investigated another one of the many mysterious sightings of Oswald prior to the assassination. In late December 1963, I was assigned to follow up on an urgent lead. Someone had reported that there was a Cuban woman in nearby Irving, Texas, who had some good information about Oswald. Bob Gemberling, one of the FBI supervisors in charge of dispensing the leads, had Agent Bardwell Odum and me check it out.

The Cuban woman was named Sylvia Odio. Her co-workers had called in to report that one day at work, Odio had blurted out hysterically that she had seen Oswald before the assassination. Odio had been reluctant to have the FBI interview her, so we drove out to Irving to her place of employment. Odum and I sat down with her in a quiet, secluded spot. A strikingly beautiful woman who had fled Cuba when her father was imprisoned by Castro for disloyalty and her husband had joined Castro's ranks, Odio was from the pampered Cuban upper class. She spoke broken English, but Odum had some high school Spanish, so between the two of them we were able to get the information.

She told us that one evening in late September 1963, three men had come to visit her and her sister at her home. Two of the men were Latins, the third non-Latin. They claimed to be collecting donations for a moderate anti-Castro organization, Junta Revolucionaria Cubana (JURE). Odio was a member of JURE and was suspicious of them, so she turned them down. The next day, one of the Latins telephoned her, again asking for a donation. They struck up a conversation, and he identified the non-Latin as "Leon," an ex-Marine and *"loco."* He said Leon had wanted to shoot President Kennedy in retaliation for the Bay of Pigs fiasco.

Odio then told us that after the assassination, when she saw Oswald's face on television and in the newspapers, she recognized Leon as Oswald. She said she had been reluctant to come forward with this information because she did not want JURE to be blamed for Kennedy's death. It wasn't until she had a hysterical fit at work that she told anyone what she knew.

I later did a follow-up interview with Odio's psychiatrist, since Odio had told us she was under a doctor's care. Her psychiatrist told me that he had been treating her for what he called "grand hysteria," a condition he found to be prevalent among Latin American women from the upper class. The doctor did point out that Odio was generally truthful. Gemberling then farmed out a follow-up lead in Miami on the Odio information. Because I had a stack of other leads to pursue, I more or less forgot about Odio.

But then in late July 1964, the Warren Commission asked the FBI to re-interview Odio, this time with a Spanish translator to make sure Odum and I hadn't missed anything the first time around. She conveyed identical information.

By this time, however, a major flaw had become apparent in Odio's story. She said Oswald came to her home with the two Latins during a time period in which the CIA and Marina Oswald had both confirmed that Oswald was in Mexico City. After some digging, my fellow security agent Wally Heitman discovered the identity of one of the Latins. He turned out to be Loran Hall, a half-Indian who frequently passed as a Latin. Hall, Larry Howard, another non-Latin with dark enough skin to pass as Cuban, and William Seymour, a white man, were at Odio's home that night collecting money for their anti-Castro group, Alpha 66, which was more extreme than JURE. Hall described Seymour as an ex-Marine who had frequently "popped off" about Kennedy. Alpha 66 and JURE were actually rival groups that frequently spied on each other.

In law enforcement, there are two common problems with eye-witnesses such as Odio pointing out a suspect. First, members of one ethnic group tend to have a difficult time properly identifying suspects from another. Second, when an eyewitness has been bombarded with pictures of a suspect's face before a proper lineup can be done, they have trouble making a good ID. We concluded that Odio was mistaken. What was likely was that she mistakenly thought the non-Latin, Seymour, was named Leon, when it was actually Loran Hall who was being referred to. She had also mistaken Seymour for Oswald.

Heitman quickly put together his report, and it was sent to the Warren Commission just as they were closing shop in late August 1964. After the report came out, Seymour denied the story, at which point Hall withdrew his account.

Years later, in 1975, when assassination matters came to the surface again, so did Loran Hall's name. Hall refused to testify regarding what he had told the FBI back in 1964. He now refused to say that he had visited Odio's home. Looking at it from Hall's perspective, this was not a surprise. His organization, Alpha 66, had been held responsible for numerous terrorist acts including the bombings of airplanes. Back in 1964 he had broken a silence and identified for the FBI a fellow Alpha 66 member, a mortal sin in any terrorist organization. Also, because Hall also told the FBI that Seymour had "popped off" at

Kennedy, Alpha 66's donations had fallen off sharply. Any further co-operation with the law would assure Hall trouble, possibly even an early grave. After he surfaced briefly in 1975, Hall took to hiding in southern Kansas near the Oklahoma border.

Unfortunately, some people still hold on to Odio's story.

10

Tuesday, May 5, 1964

TIME: 9:00 A.M.

I had arrived in Washington the day before, and now I was climbing the stairs to the VFW building at 200 Maryland Avenue N.E. The U.S. Supreme Court's building was just across the street, and the U.S. Capitol was just a short walk away. I had fallen in step behind Alan Belmont, the man who had overall supervision of every FBI investigation. Belmont strode confidently and purposefully up the stairs, and I tried to keep up with his quick pace. Retired Fort Worth agent John Fain and New Orleans agent John Quigley were also following Belmont.

The four of us, all tall FBI men dressed in our finest suits with tightly starched white shirts and neutral ties, strode toward the office where Fain, Quigley, and I were to report for testimony. Belmont was leading us there. I couldn't help that I was starting to sweat.

Belmont pushed open the door to the office, then led us toward the back. We walked between the desks of secretaries working away, straight back to a small waiting area outside the door to the office's conference room. The Warren Commission had borrowed this room for the receipt of all witness testimony relating to its inquiry. The four of us took a seat just outside this conference room. We were early.

At 9:30 A.M., Samuel Stern, a Commission staffer, came out and told Belmont that the Commission was ready to take testimony from Fain. He and Belmont got up and followed Stern into the conference room. After the door shut, Quigley and I looked at each other.

Then, quite unexpectedly, a few minutes later, Belmont emerged from the conference room, his face flushed with anger. On his heels was Stern, who was apologizing profusely. "I'm sorry, I thought it would be okay for you to be present with the agents. I didn't know Justice Warren wouldn't allow you to be present."

Belmont gave Stern a few choice words — which I couldn't hear, but the tone was unmistakable — then turned and stormed out of the office. Stern went back into the conference room and shut the door again.

Quigley and I huddled and tried to piece things together. Apparently, Earl Warren had decided that FBI agents were not to have counsel when they testified. This, despite the fact that Warren had allowed police officers and Secret Service agents to have their own supervisors present as their counsel. The irony was that Warren was starting to establish himself on the Supreme Court as the eminent due process man. The right to choose your own counsel to assist you in adversarial hearings is fundamental to due process. Anyone doubting that I was placed into an adversarial situation with the Commission should read the Warren report. Warren had put Fain, Quigley, and me in a most unsettling situation.

On November 30, 1963, after taking heat for announcing that the FBI would conduct an investigation into the assassination of Kennedy and the killing of Oswald and report the facts, President Johnson, acting on the advice of a wide spectrum of political advisors, appointed a "blue ribbon" panel to conduct the investigation. Politics undoubtedly played a role in his decision: after President Garfield was assassinated, the assassin was tied to a faction of the Republican party identified with Garfield's vice president, Chester Arthur. With Garfield's assassination, Arthur became president. When Arthur ran for reelection, he couldn't even gain his party's nomination. I am sure President Johnson's advisors feared any perceptions of misconduct in the inquiry into Kennedy's death, since Kennedy had been killed in Johnson's home state of Texas and the 1964 election was already imminent.

To placate Congress and also head off any rival congressional probes into Kennedy's death, Johnson allowed each political party to pick one senator and one representative for the panel. The Republicans chose Senator John Sherman Cooper and Representative Gerald Ford; the Democrats chose Senator Richard Russell and Representative Hale Boggs. At the suggestion of Attorney General Bobby Kennedy, Johnson also appointed Allen Dulles, the former CIA chief, and John J. McCloy, one of the founders of the CIA; both were now in the private sector. All the congressional members appointed to this Commission were from the CIA watchdog committees in their respective houses. With the participation of Dulles and McCloy, it is safe to conclude that the Commission knew exactly what the CIA had been up to prior to the assassination and what the CIA had uncovered and covered up afterward. To head the Commission, Johnson made the logical choice: he appointed U.S. Supreme Court Chief Justice Earl Warren. Logic aside, this appointment was a disaster of the first magnitude for J. Edgar Hoover, since Warren and Hoover were mortal enemies.

When Dwight Eisenhower became president in 1952, he instituted a program (still in force today) that mandated FBI background checks on all federal appointees. So when Eisenhower appointed Warren as Chief Justice of the Supreme Court, the FBI was ordered to make his background check. Warren had been nominated as a reward from Eisenhower. In the 1952 presidential election, Eisenhower had emerged as the leader for the Republican nomination, but was critically short on the number of delegates to put him over the top at the Republican convention. Warren, then governor of California, had also run for the Republican nomination and had accumulated his own group of delegates. At the convention, Eisenhower asked Warren to pledge his delegates to him, which would put Eisenhower over the top. Warren asked for a favor in return; he wanted Eisenhower to appoint him to the next vacancy on the U.S. Supreme Court. Eisenhower agreed, received Warren's delegates, and went on to win the nomination and the presidential election.

When Chief Justice Frederick Vinson stepped down, Eisenhower kept to his word and appointed Warren the new Chief Justice. The appointment was made when the Senate was in recess, and Warren was allowed to assume his position on the Supreme Court, contingent on the Senate's later approval. With Warren on the bench, the FBI began its background check.

The FBI's investigation unearthed some rather serious personal indiscretions on the part of Warren — most notably an affair with someone on his staff. The report of this investigation was supplied to the Senate Judiciary Committee, which had initial jurisdiction to review Warren's appointment. The chairman of this committee, Senator William Langer, held up Warren's appointment for months, creating an embarrassing situation for Warren, already sitting on the bench. The press got hold of the investigation's findings and hinted — in the 1950s the press didn't report the sordid details of public officials' private lives the way they do today — that Warren's appointment was being held up by some dark, mysterious secret. Finally, President Eisenhower exerted pressure on Senator Langer to report Warren's appointment to the full Senate, where it sailed through. Eisenhower would later call the Warren appointment the biggest mistake he ever made as president.

Now safely confirmed, Warren sought out Hoover at a Washington cocktail party and publicly chastised him for the background check that had apparently held up his appointment. With all the indignation he could muster, Warren called Hoover a "Boy Scout."

When President Johnson first asked Warren to head the Commission investigating the assassination, Warren refused. But after Johnson called Warren to a private meeting in the Oval Office, Warren emerged with tears in his eyes. Johnson had told Warren that if certain items of information regarding the Soviets and Cubans were not dealt with responsibly, millions of lives could be lost in an atomic war.

Now that Warren was at the helm of a commission with direct oversight of the FBI's handling of the assassination investigation, I figured Hoover had to be shaking in his boots. It was payback time.

After the Commission was assembled, Warren wasted no time choosing the staff members. These staffers would play a critical role in amassing, evaluating, sorting, and reviewing the voluminous amounts of evidence. Warren chose J. Lee Rankin, a former U.S. solicitor general, to act as his chief of staff. Rankin in turn played a large role in choosing the remaining staff members, clerks, stenographers, and other personnel. Once Warren and Rankin had assembled their thirty-two–member staff, they announced their appointments to the public. *Then* they asked the FBI to conduct the staff background checks.

The background checks unearthed the fact that two Warren Commission staff members belonged to an organization on the U.S. attorney general's list of subversive organizations. The organization was a civil rights group, which by itself was perfectly legitimate, but this particular civil rights group advocated support for Soviet causes, which earned it a spot on the attorney general's subversive list. However loyal and patriotic these two staff members may have been, they ordinarily would have been summarily dismissed or denied employment. No federal appointee with that type of background would stand a chance of being approved. But Warren intervened, saying that if these two were denied their appointments after they had been publicly announced, they would be hurt and humiliated. Warren persuaded the other Commission members to support him on the point, and the two staff members remained. Agents in the FBI and CIA were appalled, and a rift of distrust slowly began to develop. In the eyes of many Commission staffers, this made the FBI the enemy. Warren and Rankin should have submitted the names of the chosen staff members to the FBI for background checks before making any public announcements, so that anyone with a problem, such as the two staff members in question, could have been dismissed discreetly.

However, when the Warren Commission received highly classified information from the CIA or FBI, they made sure they were the only ones who saw it. The staffers were denied access to the most sensitive information.

Once the Commission was fully in place in January 1964, it took over the direction of the FBI's investigation. All of the original out-of-town agents had returned to their homes right before Christmas 1963. Now that the Commission had a whole new set of investigative requests, more out-of-town agents were brought into Dallas in early January to help handle the deluge.

By early May 1964, the Commission was ready to hear from the FBI. The Commission took testimony from Hoover, Belmont, and several other high-ranking FBI officials. But of all the field agents involved with the case, the Commission only wanted to hear from three: Fain, Quigley, and me.

As soon as I received my orders to appear before the Warren Commission, I began to prepare my testimony. I retrieved the Oswald file and began a tedious but thorough review of everything in it. To my consternation, two key items were missing. Someone had removed the two secret communications from FBI headquarters. One was the October 18, 1963, communiqué that indicated that the CIA, during routine surveillance, had observed Oswald making contact with vice consul V. V. Kostikov at the Soviet Embassy in Mexico City. The second item removed was the November 19, 1963, communiqué (received on November 22, 1963) that indicated that Oswald had written to the Soviet Embassy in Washington, reporting that he had been to Mexico City and made contact with Kostikov.

Fain, who was in retirement in Houston, was allowed to come up to the Dallas FBI office to prepare to testify, but was only allowed to review the file up to October 1962, when he retired and closed the case.

The day before our testimony, Fain, Quigley, and I — in the company of Belmont, our chosen counsel — had to brief the Commission staff on exactly what we intended to testify. The staff member in charge of our testimony, Samuel Stern, was one of Warren's law clerks at the Supreme Court and had been hand-picked by Warren to join the Commission staff. Stern and his staff partner, Howard Willens — both of whom were recent law school graduates — seemed to be the staff members in charge of handling intelligence agents and related matters. Though both young attorneys were bright and qualified, they had little experience dealing with the intelligence bureaucracy.

To ensure that my testimony went as smoothly as possible, Stern ran me through a pre-testimony series of questions. As I had anticipated, Stern particularly wanted to review Secret Service Agent William Patterson's report on a conversation he had overheard between Forrest Sorrells, the Dallas chief of the Secret Service, and me in Captain Fritz's office the evening after the assassination. Patterson contended that I had told Sorrells I knew of two contacts Lee Oswald had with secret agents prior to the assassination, and that Sorrells should check into this. I knew that I had told Sorrells that he should have his headquarters contact my headquarters because there were two items of secret information that the Secret Service should have, referring of course to the two communiqués from FBI headquarters. Clearly Patterson, like Revill, had misunderstood me during the chaos and tension following the assassination. I now explained all of this to Stern, who seemed to understand.

Belmont, however, looked startled when I was explaining to Stern that I had read these two communiqués. He leaned over and muttered in my ear, "Damn it, I thought I told them not to let you see that one from the Washington field office." I was stunned. Here was the head of all FBI investigations admitting that the FBI was deliberately trying to conceal matters from me. I understood the need-to-know policy, but what was going on? Who *was* this Kostikov, this character from the Soviet Embassy who seemed to touch a raw nerve with the higher-ups? Kostikov must be more than a simple administrative assistant.

Quigley and I sat outside that hearing room for about two hours while Fain testified alone. Fain appeared unfazed by the hearings. For all practical purposes, as a retiree he was untouchable now. I figured the only heat Fain might feel would be if the Commission grilled him on his decision to close the file on Lee Oswald. Unbelievably, the Commission did not ask Fain anything about why he had done this, and therefore was not subjected to any criticism for it. Fain left immediately after he finished. He was already on his way to the airport when Quigley was called in to testify.

TIME: 2:45 P.M.

Quigley walked out of the hearing room, and I jumped to my feet.

"How did it go?" I asked, desperate for any kind of reassurance.

Looking greatly relieved, Quigley said, "For me, okay. But I just heard the staffers say to each other 'Hosty's next.' It seems like you're the star attraction today."

Great. That was not what I wanted to hear.

Stern, standing at the open door to the hearing room, beckoned me in.

I walked in and looked around. It looked like a typical conference room, one you would find in any prestigious law firm, nicely furnished, and against two walls were stacks of what looked like law books. Another wall was almost entirely windowed. I didn't notice the view. In the middle of the room was a long conference table. At the far end was a large executive-type desk, and sitting on it was the windshield from President Kennedy's limousine. The day before, Stern had shown this windshield to Belmont, Fain, Quigley, and me. We could see pockmarks on the inside of the windshield. Stern explained that forensic experts had determined that the pockmarks were consistent with high-speed bullet fragments hitting it. On the floorboard just beneath these pockmarks, bullet fragments had been recovered. These fragments were determined to be consistent with the headshot Kennedy had suffered. I shivered when I looked at the windshield.

I turned my attention to the men sitting at the conference table. They were all staring at me expectantly. I was shown my chair at the head of the table. Stern took the seat just to my left, and next to Stern on that side of the table was Earl Warren. The Chief Justice looked at me for a moment, then started scratching his pen on some papers in front of him. Next to Warren was an empty chair, and next to this chair sat Stern's partner, Willens. Just to my right was Congressman Ford. When he saw me he gave me a benign, discreet nod of his head. Next to Ford was McCloy and next to him, Senator Cooper. The Commission's chief of staff, Rankin, sat next to Cooper, and Commission staff members occupied the remaining six or so chairs around the conference table. Directly opposite me, next to the wall, sat two men I did not recognize. I learned later that the Commission had allowed the Texas attorney general to designate two observers to the hearings as a courtesy to the state of Texas: the two observers were the Southern Methodist University law dean Robert Storey and Houston attorney Leon Jaworski, who would turn up in the spotlight during the Watergate controversy in 1973.

Seated to my immediate left, away from the conference table, was a court reporter. Once he readied himself, he nodded to Warren to proceed. Warren told me to raise my right hand to be sworn in. He then turned the questioning over to Stern.

Stern cleared his throat, double-checked some notes, and then ran me through some typical preliminary questions: name, job description, and so on. He asked a series of questions to explain how I came to inherit the pending inactive case on Marina Oswald from Fain, and how I had asked that the file on Lee be reopened after Fain had chosen to close it. I told how I tried to locate the Oswalds, but seemed always to be just a few days behind their constantly changing addresses. Then Stern asked Warren to admit into evidence my report, prepared in the middle of September 1963. In this report I requested that the New Orleans office try to verify whether the Oswalds were living there. Once it was established that the Oswalds were in New Orleans, I transferred jurisdiction of the files to that office.

Stern asked me about October 1963. I explained how I had received a communication from the New Orleans office indicating that Marina Oswald, who was eight months pregnant with her second child, had been picked up by a Russian-speaking woman who drove a station wagon with Texas tags. Lee had reportedly stayed behind till the next day, then disappeared.

"What happened next in your effort to locate Lee Oswald?"

"I received a communication on the twenty-fifth of October from the New Orleans office advising me that another agency had determined that Lee Oswald was in contact with the Soviet Embassy in Mexico City in the early part of October 1963."

"Did they tell you anything else?" Stern asked curiously.

Not catching the significance of his question, I answered, "No. Just very briefly that there had been contact."

I then explained how I got the lead on Ruth Paine's home address — the Oswalds' mail was being forwarded there from New Orleans — where Marina Oswald was reportedly living. I drove out to Ruth's home, and in early November I met twice with Ruth and Marina in an effort to verify that Marina and Lee were back in Dallas. I went into detail explaining my November 1 and 5 visits with the two women.

When Stern reached the part where Ruth Paine told me, during the November 1 meeting, that Lee Oswald worked at the Texas School Book Depository at 411 Elm Street, he asked if this had meant anything to me, whether I remembered the building.

"No, sir. I knew of the building in the outskirts of the downtown area. That's about all. I looked up the address, and I recognized the address, but it meant nothing to me," I replied.

I explained that after I left Ruth Paine's home on November 1, 1963, I returned to work on my other cases. Congressman Ford asked me to clarify this.

"I run anywhere from twenty-five to forty cases any one time," I explained. "I have to work them all, fit them in as I go."

"These other checks did not involve this case?" Ford asked, referring to the Oswald case.

"No, other cases I was working on," I explained. Ford nodded, indicating he understood.

McCloy interjected, a little viciously, "May I ask at this point, did Ruth indicate whether there were any belongings of Lee Oswald in the house?"

"She did not, but of course she did tell me his wife and children were there, and I assumed that their personal effects would be there. We didn't go into that."

"You made no search of the house," McCloy shot back.

"No, sir. That would have been illegal. I couldn't have done it without his consent. There was no attempt to do that."

After another series of questions by Stern on my second meeting, November 5, with Ruth Paine, Allen Dulles, who had just arrived back from lunch, chimed in. "I wonder if I could just interrupt. This is on the record. I am not quite clear, maybe because I came in late. Are you from the Dallas or New Orleans office?"

"I am from the Dallas division," I replied.

"From the Dallas division?" he asked again, clearly confused. He couldn't be confusing me with Quigley; Quigley had a head full of white hair and was tall and lanky. I had dark hair and was stockily built.

"Yes, sir," I said patiently. "The man right before me was from the New Orleans division. I am from the Dallas division."

"You are from the Dallas division?" Dulles persisted, still not tracking.

"Yes, sir," I said again.

Ford took back control of the questioning from Dulles, but after a bit Dulles interjected again, still confused. Probably because he was very late in getting back from lunch, Dulles asked me a question that had already been answered about whether the Lee Oswald file was closed or open when I inherited it from Fain.

Stern tried to come to Dulles's rescue, and asked, "I wonder if I might summarize this?"

Dulles replied, "It is not clear to me." Just the year before, this clueless, senile old man had been the director of the CIA. So much for our vaunted Warren Commission, I thought.

While Stern patiently recounted the relevant facts for Dulles, I couldn't avoid wondering how seriously the Commission was taking its business. Not only was Dulles late and confused, but two Commission members, Senator Russell and Representative Boggs, had not even bothered to show up. And this was supposed to be a blue ribbon panel, charged with the sacred mission of getting to the bottom of one of the greatest crimes of the century?

Stern resumed questioning and began to grill me on my handling of the Oswald cases. He asked me what had I planned to do with the Lee Oswald case after my November 5 meeting with Ruth Paine.

"Well, as I had previously stated, I have between twenty-five and forty cases assigned to me at any one time. I had other matters to take care of. I had now established that Lee Oswald was not employed in a sensitive industry. I could afford to wait until New Orleans forwarded the necessary papers to me to show me I now had all the information. It was then my plan to interview Marina Oswald in detail concerning both herself and her husband's background."

"Had you planned any steps beyond that point?" Stern asked, apparently suggesting he would have expected me to do more.

"No. I would have to wait until I had talked to Marina to see what I could determine, and from there I could make my plans."

Acting as if he were giving me my last chance to justify my pre-assassination handling of the case, Stern asked, "Did you take any action on this case between November fifth and November twenty-second"

Firmly, I replied, "No, sir."

Stern cleared his throat, shuffled some files, and then moved the line of questioning to the day of the assassination. He asked me to review the meeting Shanklin had with all the local FBI agents the morning of the assassination.

"Mr. Shanklin advised us, among other things, that in view of the president's visit to Dallas, that if anyone had *any* indication of *any* possibility of *any* acts of violence or *any* demonstrations against the president, or vice president, to immediately notify the Secret Service and confirm it in writing."

"Did you know that there was going to be a motorcade on November twenty-second?"

I could see where this questioning was heading. I answered, "I found out about nine P.M. the night before that there was to be a motorcade in downtown Dallas. I read it in the newspaper. That was the first I knew of it."

"Did you know that the motorcade would pass the School Book Depository building?" Stern asked. This was the question Stern had been waiting to ask. Not very subtly, he was trying to determine if I could have been in a position to prevent the assassination.

"No, sir," I told him.

"Did you know the route of the motorcade?" Stern persisted.
"No, sir."

Dulles piped up, "Had there been any contact between you or the Dallas office with the Secret Service on this point?"

Hmm. Dulles was tracking now. Again, I answered, "No."

I explained that I had seen a map of the motorcade route in the newspaper, but that I didn't study it in any detail. I saw it would pass down Main Street, near the FBI offices, and that was all I was interested in, since I had hoped to catch a glimpse of President Kennedy.

Stern continued. "So the fact that Lee Harvey Oswald was working in the Texas School Book Depository meant nothing . . ."

Before he could finish, I answered, "No."

". . . in connection with the motorcade route?" Stern finished his question.

"No."

"Did you think of him at all in connection with the president's trip?" Stern continued.

"No, sir."

Ford interrupted. "Did you have any other cases assigned to you that came to your attention in reference to the president's visit?" It was clear that the Commission had been trying to ascertain whether or not I had been negligent in my handling of the Oswald case. Now able to demonstrate that I was not asleep at the wheel, I pointed out to the Commission that I had turned over to the Secret Service some information touching upon the president's security. As this line of questioning concluded, I felt confident that my responses adequately handled matters, so I pushed those concerns out of my head.

Stern next steered the questioning to my incident with Lieutenant Revill in the police garage on November 22. I explained everything as clearly as I could, and specifically denied the allegations printed in the *Dallas Morning News* on April 24, 1964. "Prior to the assassination of the president of the United States, I had no information indicating violence on the part of Lee Harvey Oswald. I wish the record to so read." I was starting to get my Irish up at the thought of Revill and the *Morning News* article.

Then Warren asked to go off the record. While I sat there, the Commission members and the staff had a discussion about Revill, the Dallas police, and the *Morning News* article. Apparently the Commission had examined the original copy of Revill's memorandum (the basis for the *Morning News* article), and they could see that someone had added that incendiary last paragraph to the memo at a later time. The Commission talked about all of this in front of me; by their discussion, it was clear that they concluded that the Dallas police had tried to dupe the Commission into believing Revill's memo. The Commission, much to my relief, took my side and dismissed Revill's memo. The Commission was especially incensed that the police waited six months before coming forward with this memo, and when they finally did, that they brought it out through the press first, rather than through the Commission. The Commission was openly disgusted with the police and the *Morning News* for their outrageous and irresponsible behavior.

Stern then led the questioning to my participation in the interrogation of Lee Oswald at the Dallas police station. When he admitted my report from the Oswald interrogation into evidence, he asked if I had retained my handwritten notes. My usual practice was to destroy handwritten notes once the report of any interview was finalized. So, in response to Stern's question, I answered that I had indeed destroyed the notes. At that time I truly believed that I had destroyed them, and therefore I testified truthfully, but several months after the Warren Report was released, I discovered the notes among my papers in my desk. Realizing their significance, I chose to hang on to them, and I now keep them safely stored away.

I explained my taking part in the interrogation of Lee Oswald in Captain Fritz's office at 3:15 P.M. on November 22, 1963. I explained how Oswald reacted violently to meeting me. I went into the details of what Oswald had said, focusing on Oswald's emphatic denial of killing Kennedy and Tippit.

When I finished this narrative, McCloy leaned forward and peered at me. "I didn't hear you repeating your testimony that he denied ever having been in Mexico."

"Oh, yes," I said, embarrassed at my oversight. "He was being questioned about his activities outside of the United States, where he had been outside of the United States. He told Captain Fritz that he had only been to Mexico to visit at Tijuana on the border, and then he did admit having been in Russia."

"He only admitted to having been at Tijuana in Mexico?" McCloy's eyes were still locked on mine.

"Right," I said.

"Not to Mexico City?"

"Not to Mexico City, that is right," I said.

Ford leaned forward and spoke up. "There was no recording made of this interrogation?"

"No, sir, it was notes I took," I replied.

At that point Warren interjected himself again, and I noted the rest of the Commission reacted deferentially. "Mr. Hosty, I think the answer to this question is implicit in your testimony, but I would just like to ask it directly. Did you or anyone in the FBI to your knowledge, for compensation or any manner whatsoever, use Oswald as an informant in any way, shape, or form?"

I was thankful for the opportunity to put my answer to this question on the record. "I have previously furnished a sworn affidavit to this Commission to the effect that I had never seen or talked to Lee Harvey Oswald prior to the twenty-second of November 1963. I had never made payments of any kind to him, and, in addition, I had never made any attempt to develop him as an informant or source of information. I have made a sworn affidavit to that effect."

"Your answer to my question then is no," Warren asked.

"Correct."

After Stern admitted my affidavit on this point into the record, Warren asked if that was all, acting as if it was a wrap. Stern responded there were a few other points to cover with me. "Let's hurry them along," Warren replied with some agitation. I looked at my watch. It was 4:30 P.M. I wondered what the big hurry was, since the Commission ordinarily took testimony until close to 6:00 P.M.

Stern then led me through my conversation with Forrest Sorrells, the Dallas chief of the Secret Service, a conversation reportedly overheard by fellow Secret Service agent William Patterson. I explained how I told Sorrells to have his headquarters contact my headquarters because there were two items of secret information that the Secret Service should get about Oswald's activities. Patterson had written a memo saying I claimed Oswald had met two "secret agents" in Mexico City. I explained that Patterson was mistaken.

Ford then started asking me questions about my dealings with Lieutenant Jack Revill, which, from my point of view, was obviously a vital subject. Immediately after I answered one of Ford's questions, Warren cut Ford off: "Have you any further questions, Congressman Ford?" Warren seemed desperate to wrap things up. Ford ignored Warren and continued his line of questioning.

Then, much to Warren's consternation, McCloy began asking questions about my interview with the supervisor at the book depository, Mr. Truely. I explained that I interviewed him in January or February 1964, and he explained that when the *Dallas Times Herald*, which hit the stands before noon, printed the planned motorcade route for the president, all the employees got excited because the president would pass right in front of the book depository. Truely said all of the employees learned this around noon on Thursday, November 21.

147

Senator Cooper then took over with a new line of questioning. "On November 5, did Mrs. Ruth Paine tell you that she thought Lee Oswald was an illogical person?"

"Yes, sir," I responded.

"And that he admitted to her being a Trotskyite Communist?" Cooper continued.

"Yes, sir."

"Did you know that he had engaged in this Fair Play for Cuba demonstration in New Orleans and had been arrested?"

"Yes, sir."

"You were told on November first that he was employed at the Texas School Book Depository?"

"Yes, sir."

"Considering that he was a defector — you knew he was a defector?"

"Yes, sir."

Then Cooper lowered the boom — something I could see coming a mile away. "And considering that he had been engaged in this demonstration in New Orleans, and the statement that Mrs. Paine made to you, did it occur to you at all that he was a potentially dangerous person?"

"No, sir," I answered firmly.

"Why?" Cooper asked. He seemed to be trying to understand.

"There is no indication from something of that type that he would commit a violent act. This is not the form that a person of that type would necessarily take. This would not in any way indicate to me that he was capable of violence."

Cooper seemed to be tracking with me, and asked, "I believe you testified that you didn't know the route of the . . ."

"That is correct, sir," I said.

". . . of the procession which passed the Texas School Book Depository?"

"That is correct, sir."

"Did it occur to you to communicate this information to the Secret Service or the Dallas police about Oswald?" Cooper asked.

"No, sir. There would be no reason for me to give it to them," I replied.

McCloy jumped in. "You did know he was lying, though, didn't you?"

"Yes, sir."

"Don't you think the combination of the fact that you knew that he was lying and that he was a defector and that he had this record with the Fair Play for Cuba, that he might be involved in some intrigue that would be, if not necessarily violent, he was a dangerous security risk?" he pressed.

"He was a security risk of a sort, but not the type of person who would engage in violence. That would be the indication."

Ford then interrupted, "What are the criteria for a man being a potentially violent man? Is this a subjective test?"

"You mean to the point where we would report him to the Secret Service?" I asked.

"Yes."

"It is instructions we had as of the twenty-second of November. We had to have some indication that the person planned to take some action against the safety of the president of the United States or the vice president," I responded.

"How do you evaluate that? Do you have any criteria?" Ford asked.

"No, at that time there had to be some actual indication of a plan or a plot."

"There had to be conspiracy of some sort?" he asked.

"Well, or a single person doing something if anyone was going to take any action against the safety of the president or vice president."

Ford then slightly redirected his line of questioning: "I think you testified earlier that at the time of the motorcade you were at your lunch hour."

"Right," I confirmed.

"And were you actually eating lunch? When a president visits a community, is the FBI or its people assigned to any responsibilities as far as the security of the president is concerned?"

"Prior to November twenty-second, I know of no incidents where the FBI was called in to help the Secret Service, to my knowledge," I answered.

"And particularly on this day none of the —" Ford began.

"Definitely not," I replied, a bit eager.

"— of the people in the FBI of the Dallas area were given any assignments —"

"That is correct," I answered again.

"For the security of the president?" he asked, finally finishing his question.

"That is correct," I repeated.

Once again, McCloy took over the questioning. "Mr. Hosty, let me ask you this: Suppose you had known that the motorcade was going to go past the School Book Depository, do you think your action would have been any different?"

"No, sir, it wouldn't have been any different."

"Even though you knew that he was located there?"

"Right."

"And that he was a defector?"

"Right," I answered.

After a few more questions, Warren gave a signal to wrap it up. I overheard Warren tell Ford that he had a dinner engagement to get to, so my testimony was ended at 5:10 P.M. The court reporter starting packing away his equipment, and as other people started gathering up their papers and pushing back their chairs, I wondered why they hadn't asked me several key questions about what I might have been able to shed some light on. Why hadn't they asked me about the note from Oswald that I had destroyed on Shanklin's order? I know they knew about it. Marina Oswald and Ruth Paine had both reported that Lee Oswald had delivered some kind of abrasive note to me at the office before the assassination.

"Excuse me, Mr. Warren, but will you be needing me in the morning?" I asked.

"No, that's quite all right, you're excused," he quickly responded. Then he headed out the door.

I headed back to FBI headquarters at 9th and Pennsylvania, a good walk across the Mall. As I walked, I started feeling better. I was relieved to have finished the testimony, and I felt I had done fairly well. I was confident I had provided reasonable responses. Feeling better, and glad this was over, my step became a little lighter and I enjoyed the lush green grass and beautiful blooming trees on the Mall.

11

Wednesday, May 6, 1964

TIME: 2:00 P.M.

"It will just be a moment."

"Thank you," I replied to J. Edgar Hoover's aide, Sam Noisette. I was sitting in a chair in the reception room of Hoover's office. Noisette was a black FBI agent, a rarity in 1963. For all practical purposes, Hoover had made Noisette an agent to do nothing more than act as his personal assistant and chauffeur.

I had requested a private meeting with Hoover. While it is every agent's prerogative to make these requests, Hoover didn't always oblige. The day before I testified for the Warren Commission, I had asked Belmont for a meeting with Hoover. Belmont said that he would wait and see how I testified before he put in my request. This morning, after I briefed Belmont on my Warren Commission testimony — although I could tell he knew just about everything I'd said — I asked again if I could meet with Hoover. Apparently satisfied with my performance, Belmont agreed to put in my request. Later that morning, his secretary informed me I would be able to meet with Hoover after lunch, at 2:00 P.M. This was another encouraging sign: one of the most significant prerequisites for meeting with Hoover was to have earned his favorable regard. The meeting itself indicated that my handling of the Oswald case had met with Hoover's approval.

A few minutes after two o'clock, Noisette ushered me into

Hoover's office. As I walked in — the first time I had ever been there — my eyes immediately rested on a massive executive desk, elaborately ornamented and highly polished, resting on an elevated platform in the center of the room. Then I saw the Old Man himself. At a smaller desk, off to one side, against one of the walls, Hoover had his head buried in foot-high stacks of paperwork. Next to this desk was a single chair, which he waved for me to take when he looked up and saw me. I sunk into the low chair, descending significantly lower than Hoover. I am sure this was the desired effect.

I didn't need this trick to be made aware that I was sitting in front of a legendary man, the man who had built the FBI from scratch and still controlled it from the bottom up. In 1917, after graduating from law school, Hoover went to work as a departmental attorney in the U.S. Justice Department. In 1921 he was appointed assistant director of the FBI, an obscure federal agency with little jurisdiction. When the Teapot Dome scandal broke, the FBI director and U.S. attorney general at the time were both implicated and forced from office. Harlan Fisk Stone was appointed the new attorney general, and he in turn appointed Hoover as the director of the FBI in 1924 — incidentally the year I was born. Hoover took this corrupt agency and turned it around, totally rebuilding and professionalizing it.

It had been the middle of the Prohibition and gangster era. Gangsters bribed and corrupted all the law enforcement agencies with relevant jurisdiction. Because the FBI had little role in fighting lawbreakers during Prohibition, when it ended the FBI stood alone as one of the only agencies not corrupted by gangsters. Hoover took this window of opportunity and began his crusade to rid America of gangsters, bank robbers, and kidnappers. Hoover brought down John Dillinger and "Pretty Boy" Floyd, making himself the "fair-haired boy" in President Franklin D. Roosevelt's eyes. Roosevelt's attorney general, Homer Cummings, realizing that the press had glamorized the gangsters, figured it was time to turn the tables. Cummings influenced several national newspaper columnists, including Walter Winchell, to puff up Hoover's public image. The Hoover superman myth had begun.

During World War II, while the Soviets were allied with America and much of America held the Soviets in trust and high regard, Hoover pushed his recently granted jurisdiction, counter-intelligence. Even when many mainstream Americans were cozying up to "Uncle Joe" Stalin during World War II, Hoover relentlessly pursued Communists. When World War II ended and the cold war began, he gained accolades for his pursuit. At this point, Hoover seemed to begin to believe his own propaganda, to believe that he was, indeed, Superman,

Valerie Vladimirovich Kostikov, ostensibly the Soviet vice consul in Mexico City, worked for the KGB's Department 13, which dealt in international terrorism, sabotage, and assassinations. Kostikov met with Oswald in the Soviet Embassy in Mexico City on September 28, 1963, shortly after Oswald had told Cuban Embassy officials he intended to kill President Kennedy. *PBS Frontline*

The CIA maintained visual and audio surveillance of the Soviet Embassy in Mexico City and was able to confirm Oswald's meetings with the Soviets from September 27 through October 1, 1963. *James Werth, FBI Special Agent*

(*Above*) The CIA, under orders from President Kennedy, enlisted Rolando Cubela (center), code name AMLASH, in their efforts to overthrow Fidel Castro. Cubela was one of Cuba's highest-ranking officials. On September 7, 1963, the CIA met with Cubela in Brazil to discuss a possible coup against Castro. By this time, Castro had discovered Cubela's intentions and had him arrested for treason once he returned to Cuba. On September 9, 1963, Castro was quoted in the *New Orleans Times-Picayune* as saying that if the United States persisted in its plans to assassinate Cuban leaders, Kennedy's life was in danger. Oswald, an avid newspaper reader, was living in New Orleans at this time; less than three weeks later, Oswald went to the Cuban Embassy in Mexico City and told officials he intended to kill President Kennedy.
National Archives and Records Administration, Washington, D.C.

(*Facing page*) Around noon on October 1, 1963, the CIA intercepted Oswald's phone call from the Cuban Embassy in Mexico City to the Soviet Embassy. A KGB officer invited Oswald to come by, and Oswald did. The CIA attempted to photograph him as he entered and exited the Soviet Embassy, but was only able to take this picture of an unidentifiable man. At Hosty's suggestion, before they showed this photograph to anyone, intelligence agents carefully cropped out the background, which would have shown the embassy and revealed the ongoing surveillance.
National Archives

Ruth Paine's home in Irving, Texas, where Marina
Oswald and her two children lived during October and
November 1963. Hosty visited Ruth and Marina here on
November 1 and 5. On November 21, Lee Oswald, who
was living alone in Dallas, came here to retrieve the rifle
he then used to kill President Kennedy.
National Archives

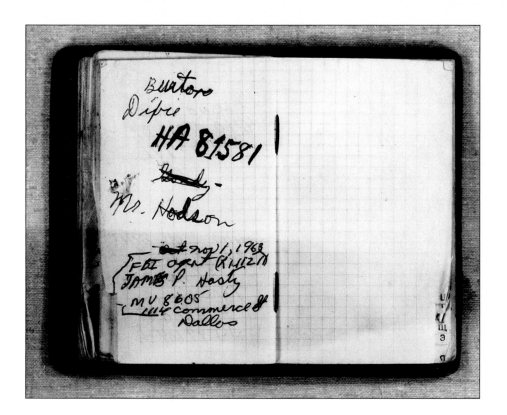

While Hosty was talking with Ruth Paine at her front door on November 5, Marina Oswald snuck out the back door of the house and wrote down Hosty's license plate number. She gave this number to Lee, who then copied it into his notebook, along with Hosty's name, office address and phone number, and the first date that Hosty had visited Marina, November 1.

James P. Hosty, Jr.
License plate photograph courtesy
of Vleisides Photo Studio

Hosty suspected that Marina Oswald, seen here standing on the balcony of the Oswalds' apartment in Minsk, was a KGB plant in the United States because she fit the FBI's criteria for KGB deep-cover agents. *National Archives*

CERTIFICATE OF SERVICE
ARMED FORCES OF THE UNITED STATES

THIS IS TO CERTIFY THAT
ALEK JAMES HIDELL
HONORABLY SERVED ON ACTIVE DUTY IN THE

United States Marine Corps

DD FORM 217 MC   1 JAN 51

Oswald used the alias Alek Hidell to order the rifle he used to kill President Kennedy. The Hidell identification card was found in Oswald's wallet when he was arrested following the shooting of Dallas police officer J. D. Tippit. *National Archives*

WANTED

Exhibit - 4

FOR

TREASON

THIS MAN is wanted for treasonous activities against the United States:

1. Betraying the Constitution (which he swore to uphold):
   He is turning the sovereignty of the U. S. over to the communist controlled United Nations.
   He is betraying our friends (Cuba, Katanga, Portugal) and befriending our enemies (Russia, Yugoslavia, Poland).
2. He has been WRONG on innumerable issues affecting the security of the U.S. (United Nations- Berlin wall - Missle removal - Cuba- Wheat deals - Test Ban Treaty, etc.)

3. He has been lax in enforcing Communist Registration laws.
4. He has given support and encouragement to the Communist inspired racial riots.
5. He has illegally invaded a sovereign State with federal troops.
6. He has consistantly appointed Anti-Christians to Federal office: Upholds the Supreme Court in its Anti-Christian rulings.
   Aliens and known Communists abound in Federal offices.
7. He has been caught in fantastic LIES to the American people (including personal ones like his previous marraige and divorce).

This flyer, which was widely circulated in Dallas just prior to the president's visit, and which Hosty gave to the Secret Service on the morning of November 22, reflected the popular sentiments in Dallas toward President Kennedy.
National Archives

PHOTOGRAPHS OF LEE HARVEY OSWALD
AFTER HIS ARREST
(COMMISSION EXHIBIT 2964)

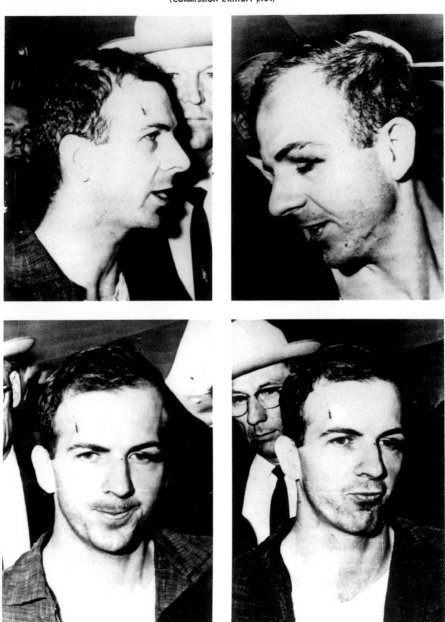

Photographs of Oswald taken shortly after his arrest on November 22.
National Archives

BASEMENT

DALLAS POLICE DEPARTMENT, DALLAS, TEXAS

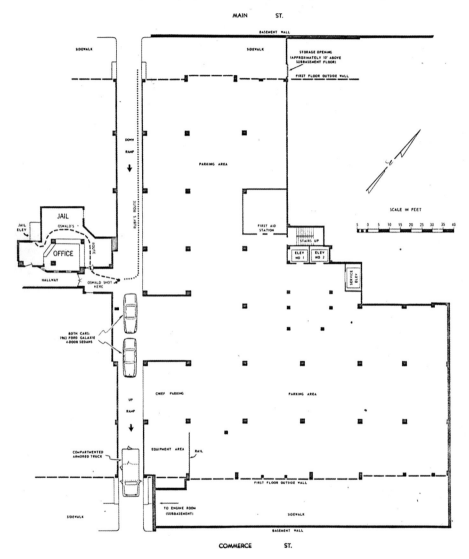

A diagram of the basement of the Dallas police station where Hosty and police lieutenant Jack Revill discussed Oswald and his arrest before the police interrogation of Oswald. It was here that Jack Ruby shot Oswald on November 24.
National Archives

At 3:15 P.M. on November 22, Hosty went to Captain Will Fritz's office to take part in the first interrogation of Oswald. Oswald lost his temper when he was introduced to Hosty, claiming that Hosty had been harassing his wife.
The Sixth Floor Museum Archives, Dallas

Hosty was the only person to take notes during the police interrogation of Oswald, since no one anticipated the assassin's imminent death. These pages, which Hosty intended to discard after typing up his final report, fortuitously survived. *James P. Hosty, Jr.*

The FBI assignment cards that made the counter-espionage cases on Lee and Marina Oswald part of Hosty's caseload one month before the assassination of President Kennedy. *James P. Hosty, Jr.*

Edwin Walker, a retired Army general who led the Minutemen, Dallas's most prominent radical right-wing militia group, was one of Hosty's cases at the time of the assassination. On April 9, 1963, Oswald tried to assassinate Walker with the same rifle he later used to kill President Kennedy. Oswald had not even been a suspect in this case until after Kennedy's assassination, when Marina told the Secret Service that her husband had done it. *UPI/Bettmann*

Oswald's single rifle shot at Walker missed because the bullet was deflected by a window frame. Hosty, who had an informant in the Walker group, remembers being told that Walker thought his life was saved because he bent down just as the shot was fired. Had Oswald lived, he might also have been charged with attempted murder in the Walker case. *National Archives*

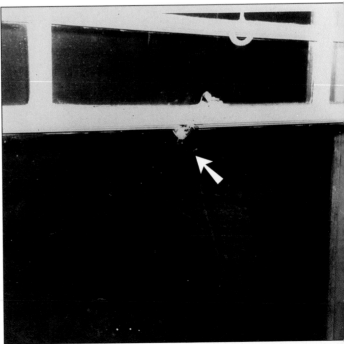

J. Edgar Hoover built the FBI from the ground up, and managed to take personally all criticism of the FBI's pre-assassination handling of the Oswald case. He ultimately meted out the harshest discipline he could against Hosty, even breaking federal regulations by punishing him twice for the same offense. Later FBI directors exonerated Hosty from any responsibility for President Kennedy's assassination. *AP/Wide World Photos*

Gordon Shanklin, Hosty's FBI supervisor in Dallas, made one of the most controversial decisions in the FBI's investigation of Oswald when he ordered Hosty to destroy the note Hosty had received from Oswald ten days before Kennedy's shooting. When he appeared before the House Judiciary Subcommittee, Shanklin said he did not recall such a note. *Farris L. Rookstool, III Collection*

At the time of the assassination, Hosty was 39 years old and an eleven-year veteran of the FBI.
James P. Hosty, Jr.

Jack Revill was in charge of the Dallas police intelligence unit, which handled mainly organized crime and racial matters. Revill alleged that Hosty told him at 3:00 P.M. on November 22 that the FBI had had Oswald under surveillance and knew he was capable of killing Kennedy. He has stuck to his story despite the testimony and evidence against it that led the Warren Commission to disregard it.
AP/Wide World Photos

Dallas District Attorney Henry Wade outlining the evidence against Oswald for the news media at the Dallas police station the evening of the assassination. Security was extremely lax because Dallas's city manager Elgin Crull had ordered Jesse Curry, the police chief, to accede to all media demands for access to information. *National Archives*

Oswald at the press conference in the assembly room of the Dallas police department on the night of November 22, 1963. *National Archives*

The members of the Warren Commission seated around the conference table where they received testimony, including Hosty's. From left: Representative Gerald Ford, Representative Hale Boggs, Senator Richard Russell, Chief Justice Earl Warren, Senator John Sherman Cooper, John J. McCloy, former CIA director Allen Dulles, and Chief Counsel J. Lee Rankin. *National Archives*

In September 1975, the news media learned that Hosty had destroyed a note he had received from Oswald two weeks before the assassination. In December 1975, Hosty was asked to testify about the matter before a subcommittee of the House Judiciary Committee. Seated next to Hosty is his attorney, Jack Bray. *AP/Wide World Photos*

or as longtime House speaker Sam Rayburn put it, "Hoover is a myth in his own time."

This megalomania began to creep into Hoover's persona, and by 1964 truth and myth had completely blurred. But at almost seventy, it was getting increasingly harder for Hoover to live up to his own legend. He had become a crusty old man, given to unpredictable mood swings and irrational outbursts. Agents quaked in his wake, not out of respect but out of fear, for if an agent fell out of favor with Hoover, he would have hell to pay. It didn't matter if the agent had done nothing wrong, or if the judgment of wrongdoing was premised on faulty logic. All that mattered was that Hoover had deemed the agent in the wrong. Whenever agents in the field did a remarkable job, the press release announcing these achievements would always begin, "J. Edgar Hoover announces that he has . . ." and then explain the deed, but with no mention of the agent individually; when something bad happened, the press release would state that FBI agent so-and-so had screwed up, with no mention of Hoover's name. He was quick to take all the glory for himself, and even quicker to push the blame on the individual agents. There are countless examples of what we came to call Hooverisms, but agents, including myself, endured these irrational acts because we loved our jobs. We prided ourselves on what we considered good and noble work.

I give Hoover all the credit for building the FBI into the vast, efficient, hardworking, crime-fighting machine that it was. But I also have to acknowledge that Hoover was a real S.O.B. Because of this, many of the field agents not only feared but loathed him.

Belmont had warned me to take a notebook and pen in with me — in case Hoover dictated any orders or tasks for me. He also advised that if I had anything I wanted to say to Hoover, say it first thing. Otherwise, forget it.

So when Hoover put down his pen, swiveled in his chair to face me, and leaned back, I burst out with the only thing I really wanted to say. "Mr. Hoover, I just wanted to thank you in person for really standing by and publicly defending me on the Revill memo a couple of weeks ago."

Hoover just smiled, and, futilely struggling to act modest, said, "Oh, that was nothing."

Then Hoover took over the conversation, and for the duration I could not really speak, except for the obligatory nods, of courses, and yes, sirs.

Hoover told me that he had just come from lunch with President Johnson. It was easy to see that he was bursting with good news.

Hoover said that he really liked Johnson and was glad he was president. He said it was really tragic about Kennedy's assassination, and a great loss for the nation. Hoover said he had really liked President Kennedy, and mentioned his acquaintance with his father, Joseph Kennedy. Almost without a pause, he added that he did not feel the same way about President Kennedy's brother, Bobby — who was his boss. As I recall, he said Bobby Kennedy "disgusted him." He gave me the impression he thought Bobby was a young whippersnapper who shot from the hip too often.

For most of his career as the director of the FBI, Hoover had always had direct access to the presidents, even though the FBI fell under the umbrella of the Justice Department, which was led by the U.S. attorney general. Hoover operated the FBI much like the U.S. Marines are operated in relation to the Navy: the Marines are a fighting force under the umbrella of the Navy, but often operate as though they are a separate and distinct fourth branch of the military, equivalent to the Army, Air Force, and Navy.

When Bobby Kennedy became attorney general, he informed Hoover that he would not be allowed access to the Oval Office; instead, Hoover was to report directly to Bobby, who would then report anything Hoover had to say to the president. This drove Hoover crazy.

Further, Bobby placed a "hot-line" phone on Hoover's desk, which gave him direct access to Hoover whenever he wanted it. Hoover initially scoffed at this, and placed the hot-line on his secretary's desk. But Bobby Kennedy won this turf battle, and the hot-line was put back on Hoover's desk. Hoover had never been treated this way before, and as I listened to him talk about Bobby Kennedy, it was easy to hear how much he loathed him.

Then, like a child who had just discovered one more nickel in his pocket to spend at the carnival, Hoover gleefully told me his good news. At lunch, President Johnson had informed Hoover that he was going to waive the mandatory retirement requirement for Hoover. At age seventy, just around the corner for Hoover, all federal agency directors had to retire. This was mandated by federal law. Only the president could waive it, and now as I sat with Hoover I realized that I was probably one of the first people to learn of Johnson's extraordinary decision.

"The president told me that the country just couldn't get along without me," Hoover said.

I wanted to roll my eyes, but I restrained myself.

Early in his administration, President Kennedy had decided to force Hoover to retire at seventy. Kennedy had carefully set the stage by not granting retirement exceptions to the directors of the Secret Service, the Bureau of Prisons, the Immigration and Naturalization Service, and the Narcotics Bureau. Hoover was next. Now that Johnson had made his decision, I wondered what Bobby Kennedy was thinking.

Bobby Kennedy had placed Courtney Evans — a confidant of his — in the upper ranks of the FBI as the assistant director of the newly created Organized Crime Division. As attorney general, Bobby Kennedy had made curbing organized crime his number-one priority. Bobby Kennedy and Evans worked hand in hand in their relentless hounding of the Mafia and other organized crime, and before the assassination it was widely discussed in the Bureau that once Hoover was forced to retire, Evans would be nominated to replace him.

Hoover changed the subject to the Warren Commission and their proceedings. He told me that the FBI had a source on the Commission (I later found out it was Congressman Ford, among others), and that Hoover's information, which he considered reliable, was that the Commission would clear the FBI of any mishandling of the Oswald case by a 5-to-2 margin. Only Warren and McCloy would vote against the FBI. Hoover told me how Warren detested him, and recounted the story of the cocktail party, telling me himself, with some enjoyment, how Warren had spit out that Hoover was a "Boy Scout."

Hoover proceeded to McCloy, who "was nothing more than a broken down Philadelphia lawyer with holes in his shoes before he married that Zinsser girl." That Zinsser girl was from a wealthy German-American family and, according to Hoover, after the marriage McCloy's career took off like a rocket. McCloy now had access to the most elite social circles, and this had carried him all the way to his present position. I later wondered if Hoover had unearthed something relating to McCloy, much like he had with Warren, which would explain why he could be counted on to vote against the FBI.

Then, I guess because Hoover knew I was presently stationed in Texas, he began rambling about all his good friends in the Texas oil business, whom he had recently visited in California. I endured this inane monologue, realizing Hoover did not know I did not consider myself a Texan (I was born and reared in Chicago, and considered myself a Chicagoan and midwesterner). Hoover, at least, was trying to relate to me. He tried for another good half-hour.

He only returned to anything relevant as we stood as he showed me to the door. In his best esprit de corps manner, Hoover said that I was to go back to Dallas and keep my mouth shut. I wasn't to talk to the press or the Dallas police. He wanted me to lie low while we waited for the Warren Commission's report, which President Johnson was pushing for a late summer release. "Remember what Calvin Coolidge used to say to the press, 'No comment, but don't quote me on that.'" Hoover laughed heartily at his joke. I responded with an obligatory chuckle.

The director had spent an hour chatting, confiding, and joking with me — the surest indicator for any agent that the Boss was standing behind him. Most important, Hoover had not even discussed my handling of the Oswald case, and he had absolutely no criticism for me. Everything had been upbeat. Grinning at this thought, I walked down to Belmont's office to let him know I was heading back to Dallas. I told him how well my meeting with Hoover had gone. He confirmed my optimism: "Well, it looks like you're all set."

And with that I was off.

Monday, May 11, 1964

TIME: 10:30 A.M.

I decided to get out the Oswald file to double-check a few things I had testified to before the Commission. The file had now grown to several volumes. I pulled out volume I, which contained my original file on Oswald. When I opened it I was shocked to see the two communiqués about Oswald's meetings with the Soviet and Cuban officials at their respective embassies in Mexico City, resting right on top. They had been replaced in the file during one of the days I was in Washington for the Warren Commission.

"What in the hell?" I asked out loud.

I noticed Ken Howe's initials on the bottom of the communiqués, indicating that he had removed these from the file on November 22, 1963. This was the same time that Howe had discovered and removed the Oswald note from my desk.

Howe had told me he had removed the communiqués temporarily, since FBI headquarters did not want me to see these. But why were these back in the file now? I suspected that someone had not wanted me to see these until *after* I testified before the Warren Commission. Apparently the FBI was trying to orchestrate my testimony in some fashion.

What exactly happened down there in Mexico City? Why in the hell was I being kept in the dark about these obviously weighty matters?

12

TIME: 7:00 P.M.

The television networks were all breaking simultaneous special reports to announce the first revelations of the Warren Commission's final report on President Kennedy's assassination. The networks had received some precious advance copies, so I spent my evening glued to the television, waiting to hear what Walter Cronkite had to say.

In his most solemn voice, Cronkite announced that after ten months the Commission had come to the same conclusion the Dallas police had in less than twelve hours, namely that Lee Oswald was the president's assassin. More important, the Commission had concluded that he had acted alone as a "lone assassin."

During his summation of "this most distinguished report," Cronkite evenhandedly announced that the Commission had concluded that the FBI had been unduly restrictive with its information on Oswald and should have provided it to the Secret Service prior to President Kennedy's visit to Dallas. The clear implication was that if the Secret Service had been provided with all the information we had on Oswald, they would have used it to good effect.

My parents were in town visiting, and even though they, Janet, and several of our older children were sitting with me in the family den watching Cronkite, I couldn't restrain myself. "Ah, hell!" I was steaming, and when Janet tried to say something to me, I waved her off, telling her, "Forget it, just forget it!" Janet had a pained expression on her face.

How could the Warren Commission conclude that Oswald fit the criteria that would have qualified him for the Secret Service's list of potential assassins? And for that matter, how could the Commission imply that the Secret Service would have done anything anyway?

The Secret Service had provided the FBI with very restrictive criteria by which to identify potential assassins: the suspect had to present a direct threat against the president or vice president before the Secret Service wanted to be bothered with further details. Though I don't necessarily blame the Secret Service, it was running a bluff, hoping no one noticed the gaping hole in its security bubble — and had run its bluff past the "blue ribbon" panel.

The inescapable next step in the logical progression in the Commission's report was that *I* was directly responsible for the president's death. If the Commission concluded that the FBI had been unduly restrictive in not providing Oswald's identity to the Secret Service as a potential assassin, and I was the only FBI agent who could have done this, then I was derelict in my duties. Because of this the Secret Service did not have advance warning, and Oswald had been free to kill Kennedy. The logical conclusion was that I was negligent, and the president had lost his life because of this.

I played back everything about the Oswald file in my head like a movie. I saw myself at the meeting with all the agents and Shanklin on the morning of November 22, 1963. Was there *anything* at the time about Oswald that would merit a spot on the Secret Service's list of potential assassins? I carefully reviewed everything, just as I had on November 22, and again concluded I had nothing on Oswald to think he was even a *remote* threat to the president's life. Why then, had the Commission drawn this conclusion regarding the FBI and me?

How could Hoover had been so wrong about the Commission? What had happened to his so-called reliable information that the Commission would clear the FBI by a 5-to-2 vote? Ford later told the FBI that the vote went 4-to-3 against the FBI. Cooper and Dulles had switched sides.

I had always been a Kennedy man, and I would have been the first to have jumped in front of the bullet if it could have saved his life. But now, my heart was breaking.

Tuesday, September 29, 1964

TIME: 10:30 A.M.

For weeks, before I knew the Commission's report was going to be released, I had planned to take my first vacation since the assassination. But today of all days I just couldn't take staying at home, so I decided to go into the office to check on things. My dad asked if he could tag along, since he wanted to see the FBI office and meet the agents. I said sure, and we headed in.

When we got there, I gave a little tour and introduced Dad to people. While we were talking to one of the agents, Shanklin met my eyes and, with a funny expression, waved me over. He scooted me into his office, shut the door, and immediately lit a cigarette and took a long drag. After I took a seat in front of him, he sat down and began to squirm in his chair. His eyes were shifty, and not looking at me. Then he let it rip. "Jim, headquarters is transferring you to Kansas City," he blurted. As hard as that may have been for him to get out, it was even harder for me to hear. It took me a few seconds to register what he had said.

"What do you mean, I'm being transferred? Why?"

"Jim, this is not a disciplinary transfer, I can't stress that enough," Shanklin said. "Here — I shouldn't do this, but take a look at my copy of the transfer order. It just came in this morning."

I read his copy and saw no mention that this was for discipline. If it had been for discipline, it would have been prominently noted on Shanklin's copy. Shanklin was not supposed to let me look at his copy, but I could tell he was upset about the transfer and wanted to reassure me.

"This transfer apparently is being done for your own good. With that Revill memo crap and the local press just eating you up, you would have had a tough time staying in Dallas working."

He was right, of course. An FBI agent has to have good liaisons with local law enforcement in order to be effective. My relations with the Dallas police were severely strained, and the Dallas newspapers had been particularly irresponsible and unfair. I learned years later that Hoover had actually made the decision to transfer me out of Dallas back in April, when the Revill memo broke in the press. It was at this point that my relations with the police and press had reached a level of irreconcilable differences, which made it impossible for me to do my job effectively. Hoover delayed my transfer until just before the Warren Commission report was due to come out.

I slumped in my chair, and for a few moments neither one of us said anything.

Then Shanklin spoke up. "Look, Jim, I know Janet's pregnant again. I think it's your ninth child and she's due in February, right?" I nodded.

"And your boy, Dick, he's what, four years old? And severely disabled?"

Again I nodded

"Well, why don't you just sit tight and let me see if I can either delay this transfer, or even get you a better office."

"You know, Janet's parents live in West Palm Beach, Florida. Miami would work."

"Yes, now that's a good idea. Okay, don't do anything or say anything to anyone, and let me see if I can either delay this, or maybe even get it switched to Miami." Shanklin was trying his best to sound upbeat.

When I stood to leave, he shook my hand warmly and looked me straight in the eye. "Hang in there," he said. "Hang in there."

Monday, October 5, 1964

TIME: 7:00 A.M.

When I got back to the office after my vacation, I discovered a copy of the Warren Commission's report on my desk. The Associated Press had rushed publication on a black-bound copy of the report for the American public. The AP compilation was 366 pages long, and I quickly flipped pages, looking for any mention about my name or my performance as an investigator. I found the first reference on page 189, under the subtitle "Evaluation of Presidential Protection at the Time of Assassination of President Kennedy." In its discussion of whether or not I should have warned the Secret Service about Oswald, the Commission pointed out that both Hoover and Belmont supported my not doing so. The report read: "After summarizing the Bureau's investigative interest in Oswald prior to the assassination, J. Edgar Hoover concluded that 'There was nothing up to the time of the assassination that gave any indication that this man was a dangerous character who might do harm to the President or to the Vice President.'" The report continued by saying that Belmont, the chief of all investigative units, agreed with Hoover that there were no indicators by which I could have alerted the Secret Service about Oswald.

At least the FBI was standing by me.

The report then came to its conclusion on this point: "The Commission believes, however, that the FBI took an unduly restrictive view of its responsibilities in preventive intelligence work, prior to the assassination. The Commission appreciates the large volume of cases handled by the FBI (636,371 investigative matters during fiscal year 1963). There were no Secret Service criteria which specifically required the referral of Oswald's case to the Secret Service; nor was there any requirement to report the names of defectors. However, there was much material in the hands of the FBI about Oswald: the knowledge of his defection, his arrogance and hostility to the United States, his pro-Castro tendencies, his lies when interrogated by the FBI, his trip to Mexico where he was in contact with Soviet authorities, his presence in the School Book Depository job and its location along the route of the motorcade. All this does seem to amount to enough to have induced an alert agency, such as the FBI, possessed of this information to list Oswald as a potential threat to the safety of the President."

What a bunch of illogical crap! Did the Commission really write this nonsense? If that were the case, we might as well arrest hundreds, maybe thousands, of people every time a president comes to town. The vast majority of FBI subjects *routinely* lie and act arrogant and hostile to agents. Also, a fair percentage of America is composed of both leftists and rightists — people not in the "political mainstream." Was this really the great defender of civil liberties Earl Warren speaking? Under the Warren Commission's logic, from this day forward, the Secret Service must now use the Commission's overly broad criteria and ferret out potential assassins even when there is absolutely no evidence that 1) this person presents any kind of threat against the president; and 2) this person has any history of violence, or capability of violence.

I read on: "This conclusion may be tinged with hindsight, but is stated primarily to direct the thought of those responsible for the future safety of our President to the need for a more imaginative and less narrow interpretation of their responsibilities."

Now the Commission zeroed in on me: "It is the conclusion of the Commission that, even in the absence of Secret Service criteria which specifically required the referral of such a case as Oswald's to the Secret Service, a more alert and carefully considered treatment of the Oswald case by the Bureau might have brought about such a referral. Had such a review been undertaken by the FBI, there might conceivably have been additional investigation of the Oswald case between November 5 and November 22. Agent Hosty testified that several matters brought to his attention in late October and early November, including the visit to the Soviet Embassy in Mexico City, required further attention. Under proper procedures, knowledge of the pending presidential visit might have prompted Hosty to have made more vigorous efforts to locate Oswald's rooming house address in Dallas and to interview him regarding these unresolved matters."

The Commission didn't even ask me about that. All the Commission had asked was had I done anything after the brief November 5 meeting with Ruth Paine. I said no, and that ended the line of questioning. Had I known they were interested in exactly why I did what I did, I would have told them. But it had been firmly established as a question-and-answer session, not a forum for me to I say whatever I wanted. If the Commission was so interested in this issue, then why didn't they go into more questions about it? Why did they change the subject?

If they had bothered to ask, I would have explained why I didn't dare interview Lee Oswald. I would have told them about the long-standing, firmly entrenched, never-excepted policy between the CIA, FBI, and other federal agencies. Under this policy, I would have never been allowed to interview Lee Oswald between November 5 and 22, 1963. Because the CIA had secretly and surreptitiously picked up and monitored Oswald at the Soviet and Cuban embassies in Mexico City in October 1963, I would first have had to ask the CIA and the FBI's permission to approach Oswald for an interview on these matters. There was a better chance of a Communist getting elected president in the 1964 election than either the CIA or FBI granting me this permission. The CIA had set up ultra-secret listening devices in a strategic location outside both embassies in Mexico City. The Soviets and Cubans thought they were being clever by using Mexico City as a meeting site for their American contacts, and we wanted them to keep thinking that. If I had approached Oswald with our knowledge of his activities in Mexico City, Oswald would have given me some nonsense answers and I would have run the not so minor risk that Oswald would have then informed both the Soviets and the Cubans that American intelligence agencies had incredible surveillance and listening capabilities in Mexico City focused on their embassies.

Did the Warren Commission not know all this? Were they that naive, or were they just ignoring the facts and taking vicious strikes at me? The Warren Commission was literally packed with CIA and intelligence experts.

Even if the CIA had permitted me to approach Oswald about his Mexico City visit, I probably wouldn't have. FBI agents Fain and Quigley between them had three interviews with Oswald, and all three times he had lied and been evasive with the facts. In my judgment, a fourth attempt at Lee Oswald would have been just as fruitless and unproductive as the others. What hadn't been done was an interview with the more intriguing and potentially more important Marina Oswald.

I finished reviewing the Warren report and flipped it back on the table. I had no respect for a report whose writers had made such obvious blunders in just the small part dealing with me. However, I also noticed that the report steered completely clear of the Soviets and Cubans. The report concluded that Oswald's visit to Mexico City was inconsequential and made no reference to the Soviets or Cubans being even remotely connected to the Kennedy assassination. I began to wonder if the report had been completely forthcoming on that issue after all. I also wondered how the Commission could use the term "inconsequential" and yet blame both me and the Bureau for not having reacted to the knowledge of Oswald's visit.

TIME: 10:00 A.M.

I was summoned into Shanklin's office. Kyle Clark, the ASAC, was already seated in one of the chairs in front of Shanklin's desk. I was asked to close the door. By their solemn mood, I felt as if I had walked in on someone's funeral.

Shanklin had one burning cigarette in his hand and another in a nearby ashtray. He was acting edgy again, his eyes darting back and forth, occasionally sneaking a quick peek at me. Clark was slumped in his chair, like a just-defeated middle-weight fighter on the corner stool, broken and sullen.

I took my seat apprehensively. I figured Shanklin and Clark had been unsuccessful in their attempts to delay or change my transfer. Finally, Shanklin mustered up the courage to speak, his eyes pleading. "Now listen to me carefully, Jim. Don't do anything rash or crazy, and don't quit or anything like that. You've just been suspended for thirty days without pay and placed back on probation."

I was so drained of emotion by the Warren Commission report that I was too stunned to react. I just sagged deeper in my chair, saying nothing, no longer feeling anything. All I could think was that I *had* to survive. I had a family to consider. They were all I cared for anymore.

Shanklin was still speaking, but it was as if he was coming to me in a vague, fuzzy dream. He said that this 30-day suspension, the most severe penalty possible, was effective at the close of business today. There was no appeal, and punishment was final. "Jim, I need to take your badge and your gun."

I gazed at him for a moment, not having understood what he

said. Shanklin repeated, "Jim, I need to take your badge and gun." I removed my FBI badge from my belt and my FBI credential from my pocket, unbuckled my .38 revolver, and handed them to Shanklin.

"Jim, listen, why don't you stick it out today, and then just keep coming into the office as usual. I won't take your key to the office, and we don't have to tell anyone about your suspension. We'll just pretend as if nothing happened, okay?"

"Yeah, whatever," I mumbled.

Then Shanklin cleared his throat and said, "Jim, whatever you do, don't talk to the press about any of this. But I know I don't have to remind you about that."

I rose to leave and as I started for the door I felt a sudden surge of anger at my mandated silence, at my inability to defend myself. I turned around abruptly and, looking right at Shanklin, I pointed my finger at him and said, "I just want you to know one thing. I'll be damned if I quit, because that would be admitting guilt, and I've done nothing wrong." Then I walked out the office and back to my desk.

I soon learned that this had all been Hoover's doing. When Hoover saw the Warren Commission's criticism of the FBI, he'd hit the roof. In his hysteria he struck out blindly and wildly. As the main target of the Commission's criticism, I became one of those who sustained much of his wrath. Initially, Hoover wanted me summarily fired. Shanklin told me later that morning that all twelve assistant directors — including Jim Gale, who handled the internal investigation — tried to talk Hoover not only out of firing me but out of suspending me. I am sure that some of them may have felt I didn't deserve such treatment, but they also knew that as a World War II Army veteran I had a right to a full hearing and appeal if I was fired. The FBI leadership must have feared that if they had no more control over my fate and I had nothing left to lose, I might demand such a hearing in order to air the FBI's dirty laundry. Hoover's decision to fire me could have backfired on him in a big way. The 30-day suspension without pay was the most severe punishment they could mete out without being forced to grant me a right to a hearing and appeal.

I also learned that the Civil Service Commission told Hoover that even the 30-day suspension would not stand, since Hoover had already disciplined me for the same matters by a letter of censure and 90-day probation in December 1963. This constituted double jeopardy, but Shanklin strongly discouraged me from rocking the boat about it. In 1964, Hoover was at the pinnacle of his godlike respect from the American public. He had the respect of most of his agents, too, but he was feared, not loved. Field agents knew all too well the stories of what had happened to those agents who incurred Hoover's wrath. One of Hoover's favorite acts of terrorism on field agents was "bicycling." Hoover would order the out-of-favor agent transferred to some outback city. Then, once the agent had moved his family and enrolled his kids in school, Hoover would transfer him again. He would repeat this until the agent broke and quit. At this time, my only option was to not "rock the boat."

After I had received my letter of suspension and probation from Hoover, I wanted nothing to do with the man. But Clark insisted I had to respond. Not just respond, but grovel for Hoover's mercy. If I didn't, I would never get off probation. Clark typed up a letter. When I read it, and especially when I signed it, I became, literally, sick to my stomach.

PERSONAL

Mr. J. Edgar Hoover
Director
Federal Bureau of Investigation
Washington, D.C.

Dear Mr. Hoover:

I am in receipt of your letter dated October 5th wherein you found it necessary to take severe administrative action concerning my handling of an investigative matter.

It is with deep regret that you found it necessary to take such action; however, I wish to advise you of continued devotion to duty. In line with my high esteem for you and your direction of the Bureau and its operations, I wish to offer my services during the thirty day period I will be on leave without pay status. If at all possible, I would appreciate your allowing me to continue my services to you and the Bureau.

Sincerely,

James P. Hosty, Jr.

A few days later, Hoover wrote back to tell me two things. First, he thanked me for groveling, but he wanted me out of the office for my 30-day suspension. Second, he told me that he had read my letter in which I pleaded for a delay or change of location of my transfer because my wife's doctor had advised her not to leave Dallas until the baby was born, and because my son Dick had surgery scheduled in December. In cavalier fashion, Hoover brushed aside my family matters and told me to report to my Kansas City office at once.

So why had he testified to the Warren Commission back in May that in his view I had handled the Oswald cases properly?

In addition to my punishment, seventeen other agents were given disciplinary actions. Ken Howe, who had been demoted from supervisor to field agent in April 1964, was now transferred to Seattle. Howe was so angry when he learned he was being disciplined he stormed out of Shanklin's office, got in his car, and drove from Dallas straight to Washington without stopping. He stormed into FBI headquarters and demanded to talk to Hoover about his disciplinary action. Hoover refused to see him. When Howe returned, he initially talked of retiring, since he had reached retirement age, but several other agents, including me, pointed out that this would be tantamount to admitting guilt, and talked him out of it. So he packed up and sadly shipped out to Seattle.

Also disciplined was Milton Kaack, the field agent in New Orleans, who briefly had control over the files on Lee and Marina Oswald. Rather than take his disciplinary transfer, Kaack retired.

Marvin Gheesling, an FBI supervisor in the Soviet espionage section at headquarters in Washington, was transferred to Detroit, but because he was a war veteran he could not be penalized with a pay reduction without a Civil Service hearing and appeal. Instead, Hoover busted him to field agent and allowed him to keep his supervisor's rate of pay. Gheesling's crime? He had the unfortunate luck of authorizing the closing of the Oswald case in October 1962.

Elbert "Burt" Turner, a unit chief supervisor in the Soviet espionage section at FBI headquarters, lost two grades of pay and was ordered transferred to Milwaukee simply for having failed to ask for the file on Oswald before November 22, 1963. Assistant Director Bill Sullivan and Belmont got the transfer changed to the Washington, D.C., field office instead, thereby eliminating any need for him to pack up and move. His neighbors probably didn't even notice anything different. Turner would go on to become one of the top espionage agents in the Bureau, and ultimately served the country better as a "working agent" than as a paper-pusher at headquarters.

Belmont, Sullivan, Jim Malley, and other agents at headquarters only got letters of censure, what we agents laughingly referred to as "Ah, shucks" letters. Hoover gave out so many of these types of letters that they had lost any meaning. Practically everyone involved in any degree with the assassination got at least an "Ah, shucks" letter, even the relief supervisor who had routed mail to John Fain. Fain, down in his retirement home in Houston, was, of course, untouchable by Hoover, although I am sure Hoover must have thought long and hard about a way to reach him.

In the end, only five agents really took the brunt of Hoover's wrath: Howe, Kaack, Gheesling, Turner, and me. Shanklin escaped with only an "Ah, shucks" letter.

The Warren Commission's anti-FBI report had been like a poisonous pill Hoover had been forced to swallow. By disciplining so many agents, it was as if Hoover had purged himself of the poison and guilt.

TIME: 11:30 A.M.

"Janet? I'm in trouble." I cleared my throat nervously on the phone. "I'll explain when I get home."

Her voice sounded anxious. "Jim, are you all right?"

"I think so. I'll explain when I get home."

I hung up and, in a daze, left the office. To this day I still don't know how I got home. When I walked in the front door, my five-year-old daughter Maureen squealed with delight, "Daddy's home!" She came running up to me and hugged my leg. I touched my hand to her head, and then I saw my wife come around the corner.

I peeled Maureen off my leg, and Janet and I retreated to the living room. I took a chair across from Janet and fidgeted in my seat. I didn't know how to begin, and finally I just blurted it out in a rush. "I've been suspended without pay for thirty days, and we've been transferred to Kansas City. I had to turn in my badge and gun."

I didn't look for Janet's reaction, but I knew how she was feeling.

Finally she spoke. "Jim, how are you doing? Are you okay?"

I nodded, still not looking at her. I felt I had let her down. I knew things weren't going to be easy. Our four-year-old, Dick, had settled into a nice, comfortable routine with his therapists four days a week, and we had come to respect and appreciate his pediatrician and orthopedist. It was going to be difficult to pull him out of his environs.

Then there were the rest of the kids. They were all enjoying themselves at their grade school; tearing them away from their friends was going to be heart-wrenching.

And there was Janet. She had a lot of friends in Dallas, but more important, she was very pregnant with our ninth child. She had already suffered through three miscarriages. The strain of having to pack up all of our belongings and move to Kansas City was going to exact an incredible strain on her.

My own professional despair was only made worse when I thought of all the problems Hoover's "administrative actions" had caused my family.

Tuesday, October 13, 1964

TIME: 3:00 P.M.

Janet handed me the *Dallas Times Herald.* I had been warned that the paper was going to break a story about my suspension. I unrolled the paper. There on the front page was an article about Howe and me, explaining how we had been disciplined by Hoover. The details of my 30-day suspension and transfer were laid out for all the world to read. I felt totally humiliated. Now all my friends, family, and neighbors knew all the gory details. I later learned that a bunch of the Dallas police officers gloated. I went into the den and sat down in the recliner.

As it turned out, a couple of Dallas FBI agents were actually trying to help Howe and me, and leaked the entire story to the Dallas newspapers on purpose. Even after he had harshly disciplined us, Hoover was quoted time and again in the media protesting the Warren Commission's unfair criticism of the FBI and its agents. These hypocritical comments by Hoover were not lost on the agents in the field. If Hoover felt the Commission had been so wrong, why had he felt the need to discipline any of his agents? Several people wrote letters to Hoover protesting his unfair disciplinary actions. Each time Hoover responded that he was forced to take such actions because the Warren Commission had criticized the FBI. Hoover was making absolutely no sense, and in their frustration, some Dallas FBI agents leaked the story to the Dallas newspapers. The intention was to demonstrate to the public Hoover's hypocrisy and his unjust treatment of Howe and me. That isn't how it turned out.

I had devoted practically my entire adult life to serving my country, first in World War II, and then with the FBI, and now I was being held up for public ridicule. Look, everyone. That's Jim Hosty, the FBI agent who let Lee Harvey Oswald kill our beloved president.

I set the paper down quietly, leaned back in my recliner, closed my eyes, and tried to take myself away from all of it. The pain had become unbearable; I didn't know how much more I could take.

Then I turned and looked at the picture of my wife and children. At that very moment, I knew that somehow I would survive.

Part II:

The Truth Emerges

13

Other than the blasting of the guns, it was a peaceful, glorious June morning. The sun was out in all its splendor, and I was basking in its warm glow on a bench at the firing range at Fort Leavenworth, an army post just a short drive from the Kansas City FBI office. All of the Kansas City agents were using Fort Leavenworth's facilities to requalify with a handgun and shotgun, something we had to do four times a year, and I was waiting my turn. It was very springlike, with green pastures, full trees, blue skies, and gentle breezes. I had low expectations of Kansas when I had transferred there in 1964, but I was pleasantly surprised to discover how beautiful the state was and how congenial and warm the people.

When I arrived by myself at the Kansas City Municipal Airport on November 12, 1964, Kansas City agents Jim Laughlin and Roy Klager had driven out to meet me at my gate. I was grateful for their kind greeting and hospitality, and they told me that I would be well received in the Kansas City office. They drove me downtown where I met the agents, who greeted me with sympathy and open arms. They all knew a bum rap when they saw one. My new SAC, Henry Fitzgibbons, or "Fitz," had been my first supervisor in the Bureau when I was given my first office assignment in Louisville, Kentucky, in 1952. Fitz was a kind man who was truly sympathetic to my situation and tried to help me through the transition. He warned me not to buy a house in Kansas City yet, since one couldn't be sure whether or not Hoover was going to "bicycle" me.

I later learned that the Bureau had actually carefully chosen Kansas City for me. Although Kansas City had a history in the Bureau as being Hoover's Siberia for disavowed agents — Hoover found other cities to serve this purpose once Roy Roberts, the publisher of the Kansas City newspapers, got wind of the city's status and flew out to confront Hoover personally about this — it was a very friendly city to the Bureau. A reporter for the *Kansas City Star*, Joe Henderson, told me that shortly after I arrived in town, Roberts told all his reporters to lay off me. Also, the three major police departments in the area — Kansas City, Missouri; Kansas City, Kansas; and Independence, Missouri — all had former FBI agents as chiefs. Most notable among these was the chief of police of the largest of the three cities, Kansas City, Missouri: Clarence Kelley, a 20-year FBI man.

Fitz assigned me to work criminal cases, and I didn't argue. I was walking on eggshells in the Bureau, and it was best not to rock the boat and ask for a reassignment to the security squad. A few weeks after settling into the office, I flew back to Dallas to bring my wife and children to Kansas City.

Following Hoover's "October Massacre," Janet and I were astounded by the incredible support that sprang up. When the Dallas FBI agents learned of my suspension, they passed the hat and came up with almost enough money to make up for my lost pay. Then when our neighbors, parishioners, and the Knights of Columbus learned we were being transferred, they also passed the hat and bought our house from us, allowing us to make a quick, clean break from Dallas. A fellow agent, Bob Barrett, then bought our house from the others. The support was endless — another friend, Harry Kelly, who was also moving to Kansas City, allowed us to pack some of our belongings in his moving van. The FBI was pretty stingy back then on moving expenses, so this support was not just emotionally invaluable.

A few weeks later, we had a modest little Christmas in our rental house in Kansas City. The kids all thought the house was great because it had a fireplace, something no one in Dallas had. My son, Bobby, later told me that Christmas had been the best ever, because the family was all together and things were beginning to settle down again. On February 10, 1965, our ninth (and last) child, Cathy, was born safely.

I waited for my turn on the Fort Leavenworth firing range next to a young agent, Joe Holtzslag, who was stationed just up the road in St.

Joseph, Missouri. He and I chatted casually, enjoying this chance to bask in the sun. After a bit, Holtzslag figured out who I was: "Oh, I know you. You're that agent who had the Oswald case in Dallas. I heard about you."

Holtzslag told me that he had been going through his initial training at the FBI Academy in Quantico when the Warren Commission report was released. One evening after a day of training, one of the instructors, Simon Tulai, joined him and a group of young "new agents" for drinks at the bar on the Academy campus. One of the new agents remarked to Tulai that he didn't care what the Commission said about Oswald being a lone nut, he thought the Soviets were somehow involved. Tulai, who had worked in the Russian espionage section of Division 5, blurted out that the new agent was right. The Warren Commission had swept under the rug all the information about the Soviets; Tulai said the Commission had steered completely away from the fact that when Oswald was in Mexico City in October 1963, he had met with Kostikov, who, he explained, was a KGB agent from Division 13, the KGB department in charge of terrorism, sabotage, and assassinations.

What! Headquarters knew this and didn't tell *me*, the field agent in Dallas monitoring Oswald. Although I was churning inside, I tried my hardest not to let Holtzslag know how I was feeling. I didn't want this young agent to know that I had no clue about Kostikov. With the best poker face I could muster, I just nodded and said, "Yeah, that's incredible, isn't it?"

The conversation casually changed subjects, but I was thinking only about Kostikov. Now everything made sense. I now understood what Malley's aide, Dick Rogge, meant when he said that I had the case on Oswald but that I didn't know he was dangerous. It also made sense why Clark told me that Bill Sullivan, the man in charge of Division 5 and the Russian espionage section, was supporting me — Sullivan and Division 5 knew I didn't know about Kostikov's role in the KGB prior to the assassination. This also explained Shanklin's meltdown during those dark days in Dallas. Some tough calls had obviously been made on how to handle this information. Apparently, the top men at headquarters had made some determinations on need-to-know eligibility immediately following the assassination. When the wagons circled, I was left on the outside. Now it made sense why Howe pulled from my Oswald file the communiqués from headquarters about Oswald's Mexico City visit and his contact with the Soviet Embassy in Washington. It was also clear why everyone got so upset when they learned Belmont had ordered me to take part in his interrogation and to tell the police "everything the FBI had on Oswald." There was no way for Belmont to have known, in that first frantic hour following the assassination, that Oswald had secretly met with a KGB assassination expert. Some Division 5 man probably had this information, and there was a natural lag time before it got to Belmont. The FBI was trying to keep from the public the fact that Oswald had met with a KGB assassination expert six weeks before President Kennedy's assassination.

If the American public had known this, I probably wouldn't be sitting here on this glorious morning in Fort Leavenworth. We, as a nation, might well have gone to war with the Soviets, a war that could have ended in a rain of nuclear missiles.

The FBI was not operating independently. The FBI would not be concealing this information on its own. The Warren Commission was involved, and it was logical to assume that the CIA — who may have been able to listen in on all of Oswald's conversations in the Soviet and Cuban embassies in Mexico City — and the White House were as well. A cover-up of this scope had to have been ordered at the highest levels, which meant President Johnson.

I just prayed that those involved in this cover-up knew what they were doing. If the Soviets were behind Kennedy's death, I couldn't deny my own instinct to retaliate.

Someone over by the firing range yelled out my name. It was my turn. I got up and walked over to the station. I prepared to fire. I checked my revolver and saw the five rounds loaded and ready. I raised my arm, pointing the gun at the silhouette of a man on the target paper, and steadied my aim. Concentrating, I squeezed the trigger hard, five straight times. All five of my shots hit their mark in the silhouette. Kill shots.

14

I unlocked the door to the Kansas City FBI office and eased myself in. I moved around the receptionist's counter and strolled back to where the agents had their desks. A light was on in a back corner office, so I went over there first. Night clerks were stationed in all the major FBI offices in the country so that if any hot information came in, someone could notify the SAC or the proper agent. Night clerks were always young people, in their early twenties, either in school or just out, something like apprentice agents. I ducked my head in and said hello to the night clerk, telling him I forgot to do something during the day. I assured him I'd just be a little while. Then I turned and walked away. Looking over my shoulder, I noticed he had gone back to his filing. Good, I thought, he's going to stay in place while I get down to the dirty work.

About a year before, I had been turned down for a relief supervisor's position. Surprised, I had asked why, and was told I had the "Big T" on my personnel file. The "Big T" stood for Clyde Tolson, Hoover's right-hand man. If Tolson put his initial on your file, any promotion had first to be routed through him, which effectively blackballed you, and almost certainly prohibited any promotion in the Bureau. I was perplexed when I learned of the "Big T" on my file. According to federal government regulations, any censure lasted only three years, and since my discipline from Hoover in 1964, I had not only stayed completely clean but had earned letters of commendation.

The answer would definitely lie in my personnel file, so I decided I had to read it. It was here in Kansas City for my routine annual evaluation, but FBI personnel files are strictly off-limits to the agents. Only supervisors can access these files. If I was going to read my own personnel file, it would have to be on the sly.

So after leaving the clerk's office, I headed straight for my supervisor's safe, where the personnel files were kept for annual evaluations. Applying my hard-earned investigative skills, I had discreetly gleaned from normal conversation that the person who had programmed the combination to the safe had used the most obvious combination of all, his birthdate.

I found my file and pulled it out. I sat back in a chair, turned on a desk light, and opened it. I flipped through several items, seeing nothing that would warrant the blackballing. My file was jammed with all kinds of memos and items regarding my handling of the Oswald case. Not having seen many of these, I took my time reading them over. Eventually I came across my answers to the questions put to me formally by FBI headquarters in December 1963.

I read through the questions and answers, recalling everything as if it were yesterday. When I reached the end, I caught my breath. I read through them again, this time very closely. *Somebody had changed my answers.* And in this version, Special Agent James Hosty admitted to being negligent and derelict in his handling of the Oswald case.

When I was asked why I didn't follow up regarding Oswald's contacts with the Soviet and Cuban embassies, I had originally answered that I had received only sketchy information, nothing to mandate a quick follow-up. This response had been struck, leaving the impression that I had full, detailed knowledge of Oswald's contacts with the Soviets and Cubans, and therefore had been derelict in not interviewing him. Also, the changed answers specifically had me admitting that I delayed reporting information about Oswald to headquarters back in the summer of 1963. I had never admitted anything of the sort. I felt I had done everything I could have, and then some. If it hadn't been for me, the FBI wouldn't have had *any* files on the Oswalds. Our Fort Worth agent John Fain had shut down the Lee Oswald file, and my supervisor Ken Howe had only agreed to open the one on Marina Oswald after I practically begged him to.

I had been sold down the river. The expendable field agent, I was the classic scapegoat for J. Edgar Hoover. Following the assassination, Oswald had whined to the press that he was just the patsy. Now I knew who was the real patsy.

At least I still had my original answers. After Ken Howe had stormed out of that meeting in December 1963 with Shanklin and Inspector Jim Malley and, cryptically, shoved a copy of my original answers in my hand, I had heeded his advice to hang on to them. They had been safely stowed in a safe deposit box at my bank for the last nine years.

Shanklin and Malley had changed my answers, probably under pressure from the notorious Jim Gale, popularly known as "Barracuda." Gale was the assistant director of the inspection division, otherwise known as Division 10, which handled all personnel investigations, and he was in charge of an internal review on the Bureau's handling of the Oswald cases. When Malley and Shanklin first read my answers to the Bureau's questions on how I had handled the pre-assassination investigation, they probably could not believe I was not admitting any fault. I guess everyone expected me voluntarily to fall on my sword, even if I wasn't at fault. Hoover would have accepted nothing less.

I surmised that Shanklin and Malley changed my answers, had them retyped, and forwarded them to headquarters. This all made sense, because I had never understood the language in my letter of censure from Hoover dated December 13, 1963. In this letter, Hoover had referred to my delayed reporting and to my not having interviewed someone. Now it was clear to me that these changed answers were the basis for the censure and probation.

As I sat here with my changed answers in my hands, I thought back to 1965, when one of my fellow Kansas City agents, Joe Kissiah, showed me a letter dated September 23, 1965, which he had received from Victor Turyn. Turyn, one of the FBI's leading experts on counter-espionage matters, eventually attained the prestigious SAC position in New York City. In fact, he had just retired from it in 1972, having turned down the job of assistant director of Division 5. In the letter, Turyn explained how, shortly after the assassination, Hoover wanted an analysis done on my pre-assassination handling of the Oswald cases. Ordinarily, Jim Gale would have performed this analysis, but having no expertise in counter-espionage, he asked Turyn to do it. Turyn concluded that I had done nothing wrong, and that it would be in the best interests of the FBI not to find me at fault. When he told Gale, Gale told him, "That isn't what the director [Hoover] wants," suggesting to Turyn that he instead find me derelict in my duties.

But Turyn held his ground and told Gale, "Why don't you tell the director what would be in the best interests of the Bureau?"

"Why don't *you* tell the director?" Gale replied.

Turyn shot back that if Hoover had given him the assignment, he would. But Hoover didn't, so Gale would have to do it. In the end, of course, Gale reported that I was indeed derelict in my duties, which resulted in the October Massacre.

I got up and walked over to the photocopy machine and powered it up. I photocopied each page of the changed answers. Making these copies was technically against Bureau policy, but at this point I didn't give a damn — Bureau policy had screwed me far too many times. Someday I would find a way to set the record straight.

On the morning of Tuesday, May 2, 1972, Hoover's house staff found his lifeless body lying in his bed. He had passed away in his sleep from a coronary attack.

The Nixon White House wanted to make the announcement of his death at noon. They were stalling for time so that they could announce the FBI's new interim director at the same time.

Meanwhile, Hoover's body was wrapped in a blanket and driven straight to a Washington funeral home to avoid attention. Later, his casket would be closed for viewing — his dead body had apparently lost its commanding presence.

The following Sunday, as I exited Sunday services at my church in Kansas City, two neighbors, Don and Joan Carlton, asked me what I thought of Hoover's death.

"Ding, dong. The witch is dead," I said. Not very kind, I know, but that's how I really felt. If it hadn't been Sunday, I probably would have phrased it in more earthy terms.

15

Saturday, August 30, 1975

TIME: 7:30 P.M.

"Jim Hosty, please," the man on the phone requested.

"Speaking." I was standing in the kitchen by the table.

"This is Bob Dudney. I'm a reporter with the *Dallas Times Herald,* and I have Hugh Aynesworth on the line with me," Dudney said.

"Hello, Jim," Aynesworth said.

Great. My old buddy Aynesworth. This call had to be nothing but trouble.

"What do you want?" I asked, controlling my inner feelings.

"We're running an article tomorrow and I would like to read you the story and then ask for your comments." Dudney sounded young and nervous. He proceeded:

> Lee Harvey Oswald personally carried a "threatening" letter to the Federal Bureau of Investigation office here several days prior to the assassination of President John F. Kennedy, The Dallas Times Herald has learned.
>
> The letter, which apparently did not mention President Kennedy, was destroyed by FBI personnel shortly after the assassination and its existence never was revealed during intensive investigation

by the Warren Commission, according to sources within the FBI.

The FBI has launched a full internal inquiry into the Oswald visit and possible criminal violations in connection with the destruction of the note and failure to report its existence.

Dudney continued, citing various sources, including Hoover's successor, Clarence Kelley, acknowledging the note's existence and destruction, as well as an unnamed source who had been assigned to the Dallas FBI office at the time of the assassination.

Apparently those personnel in Dallas FBI offices at the time who knew of Oswald's visit and his letter have kept the incident secret for almost 12 years, sources told the Times Herald. . . .

"I honestly don't believe that Mr. [J. Edgar] Hoover or Mr. [J. Gordon] Shanklin ever knew of the existence of the letter. They would have gone through the roof," the source said.

Contacted by the Times Herald Saturday, Shanklin said: "I am cooperating with the FBI internal investigation on this. I never knew of it. If Oswald came by (the Dallas FBI office), I didn't know. . . ."

The Times Herald was told by a source within the FBI that following the assassination the note was destroyed. "After the assassination, they destroyed it," he said.

Asked to identify who "they" were, the FBI source only would state: "other personnel in the Dallas offices . . . you'll have to ask Hosty or Howe about that. I've told you all I'm going to say on that."

When he finished reading, Dudney asked for my comments regarding the note's destruction.

Caught off guard, I stuttered into the phone, "I don't know anything about that. Not that I — I'm sorry, I'm afraid I can't make any comment on this. I don't know what you're talking about." I was under strict orders not to comment on these matters, yet here were Kelley and an FBI source talking with the press. No one told me that the FBI was releasing this information to the press, and no one had given me any kind of instructions on how to respond to their inevitable call.

Dudney and Aynesworth persisted, begging me to make any kind of comment. I told them I couldn't and steered them to Director Kelley. "Well, like I say, you can see my position. I'm not in a position to say anything on that," I said. "I think I'm right, so I'll just go along and take orders." That ended the call.

I was again teetering on the edge of disaster. This article, however inaccurate, could very likely be the final catalyst to end my FBI career. I had committed the greatest crime an agent ever could: publicly disgracing the FBI. Shanklin and I had brought this misery on ourselves; he had made the foolish decision to destroy the note, and I had been a fool to obey his order to do it. Now Shanklin had blatantly lied. The slant of the story was that I had destroyed the note on my own initiative, perhaps with Howe's complicity.

Why had I gone along so willingly back in 1963? Why hadn't I questioned Shanklin harder before I destroyed the Oswald note? In many ways in those days immediately following the assassination, all reason had been wrenched from us. We were flat-out exhausted, emotionally drained, and not always thinking straight. But still, why didn't I hold off and think about the note's destruction more carefully?

I remembered thinking Shanklin wouldn't have ordered the note's destruction without the approval of his mentor, one of Hoover's top aides, Johnnie Mohr. If this were true, Shanklin was now protecting Mohr from any backlash by denying any knowledge of the note. I guess people figured I was expendable, free to twist in the wind alone. I felt certain that I would be fired on Monday morning. I was fifty-one years old, and with my twenty-three years in the Bureau, I knew I had the right to take early retirement. I admit my complicity in the destruction of the note, but a forced retirement at this point would imply my admission to a larger responsibility for Kennedy's assassination.

Still sitting at the kitchen table, I decided to call my Kansas City SAC, Bill Williams, at home to tell him about the phone call. Without going into my whole history with Aynesworth, I explained the *Times Herald* article to him. He told me to sit tight while he tried to help sort things out.

The article was a fitting climax to a remarkable summer. On July 17, Williams had called me into his office. Harry Bassett, an assistant director in charge of internal affairs, wanted to interview me about the assassination. I assumed he wanted to ask me about the matter of the changed answers.

When Hoover died, President Nixon had appointed Pat Gray as the new director of the FBI. Gray, however, got wrapped up in the Watergate matter, never gained Senate approval, and had to step down. Then former FBI agent and Kansas City police chief Clarence Kelley was appointed and approved for the director's job. Kelley took it on the condition that he could fly back from Washington to Kansas City every Friday because his wife was dying of cancer and couldn't leave Kansas City. Kelley opened an auxiliary office in the same U.S. Courthouse where the Kansas City FBI office was located. While we were all down on the third floor, Kelley kept a private office up on the eighth floor. I had patiently waited for a chance to rectify the injustice of the changed answers, and this arrangement provided me with an unbelievably fortuitous opportunity. So in 1973, a bit after Kelley had assumed the directorship, I requested an emergency private meeting with him. Emergency meetings were available to field agents, but they had to be for some very good reason. I figured I had a pretty damn good reason.

Kelley agreed to meet with me one Friday afternoon in the fall of 1973 in Kansas City, so at the appointed time I caught the elevator up to his office. I got straight to the point. I told him how I had been screwed when someone changed my answers, and I told him that I thought that someone included Shanklin, Malley, and perhaps Jim Gale. I gave Kelley a copy of my original answers and told him he would find the changed answers in my personnel file. I didn't elaborate as to how I had seen the changed answers, and fortunately, he didn't ask.

Kelley seemed genuinely shocked at my news, and vowed to get to the bottom of it. He told me to hold tight and let him investigate.

Several weeks later, Kelley delivered something I hadn't expected. He could do nothing for me, and so sent me a letter reaffirming Hoover's 1963 discipline. However, shortly after I received this bad news, my Kansas City supervisor, Jim Graham, asked me out of the blue what it would take to make me happy. He offered me a transfer to Florida, but my family was not prepared to be uprooted again. Instead I asked to be named our office's "Happy Warrior of the Year." The title was an inside joke, but it was a substantial meritorious raise that elevated me to the highest step in pay for a field agent and helped increase my pension. The Bureau quickly obliged. At the same time, Ken Howe was transferred to his office of preference, San Diego, and Marvin Gheesling got re-promoted to supervisor.

In 1985, when he was at work on his book *Kelley: The Story of an FBI Director* (Andrews, McMeel and Parker/Universal Press Syndicate, 1987), Kelley told me what had really happened in 1973. When he got back to Washington and told his aides — many of whom were Hoover's old cronies — about my discovery, they all advised him to drop it. If he reversed Hoover's 1963 discipline of me, he would "open a can of worms" that could lead to the unraveling of a much bigger and much dirtier secret. So Kelley took the safe course.

So now, there I was on July 17, 1975, two years later, and one of the top internal affairs men, Bassett, had come to Kansas City to talk to me about the assassination. Maybe Kelley had felt guilty and decided to investigate the issue after all? I sat down in Williams's office with him and Bassett, the door shut. Bassett handed me two sworn statements and asked me to read them. They were from Ken Howe and the Dallas receptionist, Nannie Lee Fenner. Howe's statement had been taken at his new office in San Diego on July 16. Fenner's statement had been taken in Dallas, and was dated July 15, 1975.

Subsequently I learned that this was Howe's second statement about the destroyed Oswald note. Apparently he had furnished an earlier statement, denying any knowledge, but then furnished a new one that reported he only remembered removing a note from Oswald from my file drawer on the day of the assassination, but couldn't recall its contents. Howe said he gave the note to either Shanklin or the ASAC, Kyle Clark. After that, Howe claimed that he never knew what happened to the note. He was either having a hard time remembering or was only being half-truthful. Howe had read the note and, further, knew damn well Shanklin had ordered the note's destruction.

I read through Fenner's statement next and saw that the entire statement was about Oswald delivering a note to me about ten days before the assassination. Fenner said she remembered reading a part of the note in which Oswald threatened to blow up the Dallas police station or the FBI office if I didn't stop interviewing his wife. She said the note was signed by Lee Harvey Oswald. She said that when Oswald dropped the note off at her desk in the Dallas office, he had a wild look in his eyes. I noticed she had told Basset that she was giving this statement while she was seriously sick and under the influence of powerful tranquilizers. Fenner was wrong about the note's contents. Oswald had written only that he wanted me to stop harassing his wife, or else he would take some kind of action against the FBI; I assumed he meant some kind of legal action. Also contrary to Fenner's testimony, Oswald had not signed the note.

For just a moment, Bassett tried to size me up. Then he began asking me questions about the note. How did I get it? What did it say? What did I do with it initially? Did I destroy it? I confessed everything to Bassett. The game was over, and we had been caught. When Bassett asked me who ordered the note's destruction, I told him Shanklin had, within hours of Oswald's death. Bassett did a double-take.

"No, no, no. You mean Kyle Clark ordered it destroyed," Bassett demanded.

"No, Shanklin did," I answered, miffed at his suggestion.

"Are you sure you don't mean Clark?" Bassett was now aggravated with me.

"Absolutely not, it was Shanklin," I retorted stubbornly.

Bassett harrumphed loudly, twisted in his chair, and shook his head in disgust. We had apparently finished this preliminary interview, since he asked that a steno be brought in so he could run me through a formal question-and-answer statement for the record. At the end of my testimony, Bassett ordered me not to talk with anyone about these matters. Headquarters would handle everything. I nodded. Business as usual.

Bassett got up quickly and left Williams's office. Williams came around his desk and stood beside me. Standing together, we watched Bassett stomp through our office. When he saw that Bassett was out of earshot, Williams said, "Well, it looks like Bassett has to go back to Dallas, 'cause it looks like old Shanklin has a lot of explaining to do."

"A *lot* of explaining," I echoed.

I was friendly with the night clerk in our office, and I learned from him that later that evening, after everyone else had gone home, he was sitting near the office from which Bassett was calling headquarters. The clerk told me that Bassett was clearly unglued and frustrated by my statement. Bassett told someone back at headquarters that I had screwed up their whole strategy. They had been convinced Clark was the culprit, and Bassett had been all set to fly out to New York City the next day to interview Clark in a hotel room. Bassett said he had it all planned: first he would get Clark talking, then once Clark broke, he would rush in a stenographer, who would be waiting in an adjacent room. But now my testimony had thrown a kink into all these well-laid plans to trap Clark.

But there was something bigger here. It wasn't just Clark and me they were after; they were after Bill Sullivan, a former top aide to Hoover. Sullivan had had a major falling out with Hoover in 1972, and now that he was out of the Bureau he was running his mouth, trashing Hoover in the press. Quite justifiably, I might add. After Nixon developed a case of weak knees, just like President Johnson, and had decided not to force Hoover to retire, Hoover became convinced that Sullivan had been the driving force to retire him, since Sullivan had advanced to a position where he was a logical heir apparent to the directorship. Hoover confronted Sullivan, and reportedly called him his Judas Iscariot.

Sullivan angrily retorted, "Well, I'm no Judas Iscariot, and you're no Jesus Christ!"

Hoover shot back, "You're sick!"

That evening, after Sullivan went home for the day, Hoover changed the locks on Sullivan's office door and had his name scratched off his door. The next day, Sullivan promptly retired.

With Hoover dead and Sullivan insulting the deceased, Hoover's old cronies were raging. This was where the Johnnie Mohr faction in the FBI came into the picture. Mohr and Sullivan had been bitter enemies when they served in Hoover's top team of aides. It is easy to identify Mohr's lackeys by perusing the invitation lists to the legendary poker parties at his home in Virginia. The regular group of players — which never included Sullivan — formed a kind of exclusive fraternity. It was this same group of agents that set out to avenge Hoover's honor.

Clark had always been clearly aligned with Sullivan. He had been stationed at headquarters in the early 1960s and had worked for him. Bassett was a Mohr loyalist, as was Bassett's immediate supervisor, Jim Adams, who was now Kelley's top aide as associate director. Apparently Adams and Bassett, on behalf of the Mohr faction, were gunning for Clark and hoping he would hang the whole note destruction business around Sullivan's neck. The Mohr faction would have loved nothing more.

Now I had dashed their plans, because I was pointing the finger directly at Shanklin, a prominent member of the Mohr faction. I can imagine Adams's and Bassett's consternation. Bassett had practically demanded I implicate Clark, not Shanklin; nevertheless, the day after he interviewed me, Bassett went ahead and flew to New York City to talk with Clark about the Oswald note. Naturally, Clark told Bassett he had no idea what he was talking about.

I learned from a newspaper reporter several years later that some weeks before Bassett arrived in Dallas in June 1975, a Dallas FBI agent had thrown a party. The host had committed the cardinal sin of inviting a reporter from the *Dallas Times Herald,* an old fraternity brother named Bob Dudney. One of the topics of the party was the rumor floating around the country that Congress was considering re-opening the inquiry into the Kennedy assassination. During this con-versation, one of the agent's wives blurted out, in the presence of Dudney, "Well, I wonder if they'll look into Oswald's visit to the FBI of-fice before the assassination."

Of course Dudney began asking more questions. The next day Dudney took his raw information to his editor-in-chief, Tom Johnson. Word got back to Shanklin. At first, Shanklin tried to kill the story, but when he couldn't, he immediately flew to Kansas City for a meeting with Kelley. I was on vacation at the time, and only learned later that Shanklin had been in town and had come by the office looking for me, without giving any specific reason. In his meeting with Kelley, Shanklin asked permission to take emergency early retirement. Although it made no sense for Shanklin to retire early — he had just gained a big pay in-crease and wouldn't face mandatory retirement for three more years, after which time he could retire with significantly more money — Kel-ley granted Shanklin's request. Shanklin went back to Dallas, immedi-ately packed up his things, and retired on June 28, 1975.

On July 3, 1975, Tom Johnson met with Kelley and Adams in Washington. Johnson confronted Kelley with the story the *Times Herald* had developed about Oswald's visit to the Dallas office before the assas-sination and wanted to know what it was all about. Kelley told Johnson this was all new to him and persuaded him to hold off running the story until he had a chance to conduct an internal investigation. John-son agreed, and Adams sent Bassett around the country interviewing Fenner, Howe, Clark, Shanklin, and me. The now retired Shanklin de-nied any knowledge of the note or the visit by Oswald.

FBI headquarters then spoon-fed the final story to Johnson and the *Times Herald* that I had destroyed the note from Oswald without making my supervisors aware of my actions. When the front-page story actually ran on August 31, 1975, the byline was given only to Tom John-son. The nation's newspapers picked up the story and ran it on their own front pages. On the evening news all the networks led off their newscasts with the story: Agent Hosty, on his own, had destroyed the Oswald note.

The day after the story broke I went into the office and braced myself for the worst. I was afraid I would be fired on the spot, and had resigned myself to taking early retirement instead. Williams and my fellow Kansas City agents kept a vigil. But nothing happened. Tues-day went by, again nothing. Then Wednesday, and finally the whole week went by. No one from headquarters called with anything about me. If an agent was going to be fired, the Bureau always acted swiftly.

Although I didn't hear a word out of headquarters, I heard plenty from the press. The nightmare of 1963 was back. I spurned every media request.

I later learned from Kelley that Adams and Bassett had screamed for my head. But Kelley had dug in and refused to comply. He knew I had been set up, and he also knew about the treachery of the changed answers. Kelley swung a big stick as the director, and he swatted down any talk of firing me.

When Bassett eventually sent a platoon of internal investigators to Dallas, it became apparent that they had been duped by Shanklin. Of course, neither Bassett nor Adams ever so much as hinted that Shanklin was the real snake in the whole matter. As a Mohr protégé, Shanklin was one of theirs, and as such he would be protected. The investigators tore the Dallas office apart about the note, interviewing everyone who worked in the office at the time. In the end, two-thirds of the Dallas FBI employees reported they knew about the note, and most of them said Shanklin knew about it as well. The other third denied any knowledge of it, something I found hard to believe. Although I had kept my mouth shut about the note and was surprised to learn so many knew about it, if two-thirds of them knew, *everyone* had to know. Agents shared everything with one another, especially something as juicy as this.

In typical Hooveristic fashion, Adams and Bassett wanted to censure all the agents who confessed they had known about the note, allowing the third who kept their mouths shut to go scot free. But Kelley was no Hoover, and he refused.

Saturday, September 6, 1975

When my brother-in-law, Jim Perry, a topflight criminal defense attorney in Cincinnati, read the news reports about my destruction of the Oswald note, he called immediately to advise us that there was a real possibility I could be criminally prosecuted. He saw me as a vulnerable lamb, surrounded by hidden and lurking wolves. He was astonished at my naïveté concerning the possible criminal ramifications and flew out to Kansas City as quickly he could.

As I waited outside the Delta gate, I cursed myself for not seeing the setup. Adams and Bassett had quietly and calmly collected their evidence, all the while probably keeping their eyes on criminal charges. Fear and anger: these were the two emotions of an FBI agent in the

Hoover FBI, and though Hoover was dead, his ghost lived on in his cronies, who still clung to their power positions.

From the airport, Jim and I drove straight to the Holiday Inn near my house. He told me he didn't want to go by the house since we had too much work to do and too little time. He wanted to catch a flight out the next afternoon. This visit would be all business; we agreed Janet would come over to the hotel later to catch a few minutes with her brother.

Jim and I settled into the two chairs in his hotel room, and without wasting any time, Jim took charge and began to pepper me with questions. He focused primarily on the note destruction, since that was the clearest way I could be prosecuted. I described everything to him, and he decided that the Justice Department probably couldn't prosecute me on this. His uncertainty, however, was unsettling. He was more certain about the lack of legal credibility of the allegations made in the Revill memo.

Late into the night and the next day, we discussed all my legal vulnerabilities, and concluded that I had good defenses on all fronts. What bothered Jim the most was the Bureau. His greatest fear was that I could lose my entire pension. Although I was fifty-one and completely vested in my pension rights, he still felt that, given the FBI's past actions, anything was possible. In his mind, Hoover's cronies posed my greatest threat. When Jim insisted with deadly precision that this was a real possibility, it was as if a cold steel knife had been pressed tight against my heart. Financial security and conservative savings had always been my mantle. I still had children in grade school. The fear of losing my job and my life savings hit me in my most sensitive spot.

Jim figured the Bureau would ask me to testify again on these matters. He repeatedly told me to tell the full truth and not hold back. I was now so bitter about how I had been treated and misjudged, I knew that the truth would be my only savior. He didn't have to remind me not to pull my punches.

After Janet and I dropped Jim off for his flight back to Cincinnati, I told Janet about Jim's last advice to me: Tell the truth and hope for the best. "Hope for the best," Janet repeated, almost to herself. We both shared a weary little laugh, looking at each other with the cynical wisdom of two battle-tested and badly scarred soldiers.

Tuesday, September 23, 1975

On September 22, 1975, I was called to Washington to give a second statement to Bassett. In it I told Bassett something I hadn't recalled the first time: Shanklin's order to destroy the handwritten letter from Oswald to the Soviet Embassy in Washington, written in November 1963. This letter became Warren Commission Exhibit #103. I received a silly letter of censure nine months later for not having recalled these facts in my first statement, since the second interview had cost the Bureau additional airline expenses.

While sitting on the plane back to Kansas City the next morning, I casually opened up the *New York Times*. Hoping for a good relaxing read, I instead learned how prophetic my brother-in-law had been. I was stunned to see a front page article under the headline "F.B.I. Focus of Inquiry on Oswald Note":

> The Justice Department has begun a criminal investigation of the circumstances surrounding the destruction of a letter threatening the Dallas police that was delivered by Lee Harvey Oswald to the Dallas office of the Federal Bureau of Investigation shortly before the assassination of John F. Kennedy.
>
> The investigation, which is being conducted by lawyers in the department's Criminal Division, was said by authoritative sources to be focusing on "conflicting statements" given by present and former F.B.I. agents and officials about their roles in, or knowledge of, the decision to destroy the letter following President Kennedy's assassination on Nov. 22, 1963. . . .
>
> Mr. Hosty, who is now assigned to the bureau's Kansas City, Mo., office, did not return a reporter's telephone call today. But sources said that he had conceded to the F.B.I. investigators that he had destroyed the Oswald letter, although on orders from his superiors in the bureau. The conflicting statements in question apparently concern the responses given to some of his assertions by others.

Despite my legal preparations, my heart rate jumped from an easy stroll to a full sprint. My mouth went dry. I could go to prison, I thought. After all this, I may spend some of my retirement years in a federal penitentiary. As somebody's scapegoat, but in prison nonetheless.

After this announcement, it took the Justice Department two months to conclude that it could not prosecute me for anything, because I had broken no laws. Although I was incredibly relieved to hear this, I was bitter at having been subjected to such a review in the first place. Justice had considered no one but me for prosecution. Shanklin's name was never even mentioned.

The Justice Department had considered three laws under which it was possible to prosecute me. The first was obstruction of justice. The Justice Department ruled just as Shanklin had on November 24, 1963: because Lee Oswald was dead, there could be no trial. But more important, President Johnson had announced on November 25 that there were to be no public hearings, only an investigation by the FBI. It wasn't until November 30 that he decided to form the Warren Commission. No one could be prosecuted for obstruction of justice because there was a possibility of a hearing; because there was no pending trial or hearing when I destroyed the note, there could be no obstruction of justice.

The Justice Department next reviewed the law on destruction of government documents. Oswald's letter had been personally addressed to me, making it a personal letter. Once an agent receives a letter such as this and decides to enter it into the official record by filing and cataloging it in the case file, the letter then becomes government property. But not until then. When I received the letter, it was unsigned, and I hadn't a clue who sent it. I placed it in my in-box. When Oswald was arrested, Howe removed the letter from my in-box and gave it to Shanklin. Shanklin then placed the letter in his "Do Not File" drawer. Because of the particular handling of the Oswald letter, it was never entered into the official record, and thus never became government property. I had simply destroyed a personal letter and was not guilty of destroying government documents.

The third issue involved perjury laws. When I testified before the Warren Commission, I was never asked anything about the note; despite the fact that both Marina Oswald and Ruth Paine testified to the Commission that Lee Oswald had delivered a note to me at the FBI office. Because no one asked, I gave no response; therefore there was nothing to perjure. I hadn't lied about anything while under oath. I had not volunteered the information, but I had not perjured myself.

Besides which, the statute of limitations on perjury had been exceeded, which would prevent a prosecution — it had been twelve years.

I had, in fact, been wrong to destroy the note. Although I had broken no laws, it was more relevant that the note was of no significance to the assassination. This is why justice was served when the decision was made not to prosecute me.

16

Thursday, December 11, 1975

TIME: 1:00 P.M.

I strode into the conference room for my pre-testimony briefing with the congressional staffers, flanked on both sides by two of the best hired guns anyone could find, attorneys Jack Bray and Frank Lilly. For the first time on Capitol Hill, I felt confident.

When I was summoned to Washington to testify before the House Judiciary Committee and the Senate Select Committee, I told the Bureau I wanted to have appointed counsel. I swore I would not be denied the right to counsel as the Warren Commission had done to me in 1964. Fortunately, Congress had recently passed a law requiring that a private attorney be hired for any FBI or CIA agent who faced criminal penalties for carrying out an order.

I had spent the whole morning trying to tell Bray and Lilly the inside story of the president's assassination and my part in the investigation. I explained the note destruction and other highlights of the last twelve years. That afternoon I was to brief congressional staffers about what I would testify before the House Judiciary Subcommittee charged with overseeing the FBI.

While Bray and I went into the conference room for the briefing, Lilly took up a post in the hearing room, where the subcommittee was taking testimony from Jim Adams, Nannie Lee Fenner, and Gordon Shanklin. Lilly thought it might be a good idea to get a feel for what was happening before my testimony, scheduled for the following morning.

First to testify had been Fenner, who shared a very colorful version of what the note from Oswald said. According to Fenner, ten days before the assassination, Oswald had given me a note threatening to blow up the FBI building and the police station. To this day, many people still believe this is what the note said. The implication was that this note was clear and direct evidence of Oswald's violent tendencies, and the FBI, and specifically myself, had been extremely derelict in our duties. The question on many persons' lips, then and now, was why didn't Hosty and the FBI take Oswald's threat seriously and neutralize him before the president's trip to Dallas?

I am almost certain that Fenner had never even read the note. It is more likely that she had heard about it and embellished her knowledge for a captive audience. To understand Fenner, it's important to note that just prior to Oswald's visit to the FBI office, she had been demoted from chief stenographer to receptionist. When the chief stenographer's job had come open, Fenner had pressured Shanklin to promote her, since she had the most seniority. Shanklin caved in. But Fenner couldn't even take shorthand, which enraged the other stenos, who threatened to walk out unless Fenner was removed. Shanklin reversed himself and demoted Fenner to receptionist.

Fenner, who was now — in 1975 — close to fifty, faced the House Judiciary Subcommittee dressed in her plain clothes and horn-rim eyeglasses. She came across to Lilly exactly as she usually had in the office — fussy and fidgety. To have her go first on Capitol Hill and in her nasal, Texan twang tell the entire nation what *my* letter said, well, it was maddening.

As much as Fenner's testimony irritated me, it was a reporter's dream come true. She provided all kinds of colorful quotes. She described how Oswald came into the office with "a wild look in his eye." After he gruffly asked if Hosty was in and was told by Fenner that I was out, Oswald "threw on the counter" the note in an envelope. Fenner said the note kind of slipped out of the envelope and she was just able to read the last portion. This was the part about "blowing up the FBI office and the police station." Seeing this, Fenner said she opened the rest of the note, which made some reference to my harassing Lee Oswald's wife. She said the note was signed "Lee Harvey Oswald." This despite the fact that it was well known that Oswald was known only as Lee Oswald and never signed anything with his full name.

Fenner said she then gave the note to the ASAC, Kyle Clark,

because of the ominous "bomb" threat. But then she testified that she wasn't alarmed or frightened, neither by the note nor by Oswald. She said after Clark read it, he walked back to her desk and gave her the letter back. He told her there was nothing to it.

Fenner also said that she let Helen May, a steno, read the note in her presence, because May wanted to know who "that creep" was. Fenner said that when I got back from lunch, I picked up the note, read it in her presence, and told her it was from "some nut." After that, Fenner said she didn't hear anything about the note again.

Bray and Lilly felt no one would believe Fenner once they saw how easily her credibility could be impeached. Her testimony was rife with inconsistencies, contradictions, exaggerations, and outright lies. They kept assuring me there was nothing to worry about.

There were six fundamental shortcomings in the credibility of Fenner's testimony. First, she had given no less than five different statements about what the note said before testifying to the subcommittee. In one statement to a co-worker, she said the note was a simple threat to me to stop bothering Oswald's wife. In another statement to a different co-worker, she said Oswald had dropped off a letter bomb for me. To another co-worker, she said Oswald threatened to kill me if I didn't stop bothering Oswald's wife. To still another co-worker, she said the note from Oswald made reference to the police and how angry he was about his dishonorable discharge. By the time Bassett interviewed her, she had settled on what would be her final version.

Second, Fenner provided a series of inconsistent lists of who had read the note before she reached her final version. In her first statement to Bassett, she said that besides Clark, two office aides, Joe Pierce and Jim White, and stenographer Helen May had read it. After this statement, Fenner was confronted with documents and testimony that showed that White was not even in the city of Dallas when Fenner said he had read the Oswald note. Fenner quickly reversed herself and said that White didn't read it after all; she had been mistaken. Then she was confronted with the statement from Pierce in which he denied ever seeing or reading the note. Fenner again rescinded her earlier statement; now she was absolutely certain that Pierce had not read the note. She had, again, been mistaken. When confronted with May's testimony in which she, too, vehemently denied having read the note, Fenner took a different approach. She called May "flighty," and said May was mistaken. And even though Clark also denied having read the note, Fenner insisted he had too.

The third problem involved the factual improbabilities in Fenner's version, primarily that Lee Oswald never signed letters with his middle name. The only document on which he had done so was his passport, and that was because it was required by law.

Fenner's fourth problem involved obvious inconsistencies. She swore to Bassett and others in 1975 that she had never told a soul about the note from Oswald before her interview with Bassett. According to their official statements and testimony, two-thirds of the Dallas FBI personnel knew about the Oswald note, and the vast majority of these people had first learned all about it from the gossipy busybody Fenner.

The fifth problem area was Fenner's physical impairments when she gave her statement. By her own account, when Bassett came to her home for the first time on July 15, 1975, to take her statement, she was a very sick woman. Earlier that day she had almost passed out, and she talked about going into the hospital for treatment. Just days before she had come out of major surgery where the doctors had to "remove her sinuses." When Bassett came by, she was confined to her bed, on tranquilizing medication so strong it made her "numb from the eyeballs on down." She warned Bassett that she was so weak she wasn't sure she would be able to complete any statement he might want to take from her. Despite this, Bassett pushed on. Could these medical impairments have affected her recollection of events? Once an individual is nailed down to a story, it takes a lot to get them to come off that story when shown it is false. Was this the case with Fenner?

Finally, Fenner had maintained a distinct reputation for gross exaggeration. There are many examples. In FBI Agent Jim Anderton's statement about Fenner telling him about the Oswald note in 1969 or 1970, Anderton points out that she gave him the impression she had not read the letter but simply knew of it. Then Anderton says, "My immediate reaction was that this was possibly rumor or office gossip. I had this reaction because in the past, especially concerning health and medical matters, Mrs. Fenner had a tendency to exaggerate. In other words, I did not put one hundred percent credence in her remarks. Because of this feeling on my part, I did not pursue the remarks any further, and I actually dismissed the incident from my mind at that time." Another agent, Will Griffin, who was friendly with Fenner, reported in his statement, "Upon hearing this information related by Mrs. Fenner concerning Oswald and the note, I paid no particular attention to her comment, and I want to clarify this by stating that Mrs. Fenner and I have worked closely together for the past ten years in handling applicant and related matters in the Dallas office. Mrs. Fenner is a great talker, a hypochondriac, one who, in my opinion, tends to exaggerate many situations and, considering these facts, I did not regard her comments as being earthshaking. I simply had a doubt." Then there is Pierce's assessment of Fenner. In his statement, he explains how in May 1974 Fenner told a group of FBI people that Oswald had delivered to me a note relating to a bomb. Pierce said, "I felt that this statement was nothing more than an exaggeration on the part of Mrs. Fenner. I tended to disregard this statement inasmuch as Mrs. Fenner has a tendency to exaggerate, in my opinion. I believe the other employees in the group also had the same reaction as I had." From my own experience, the sentiments expressed about Fenner by Anderton, Griffin, and Pierce were shared by most of the personnel in the Dallas FBI office.

But Bray and Lilly miscalculated. Despite everything that was wrong with Fenner's testimony, Bray and Lilly didn't factor in the mentality of the media. All that the media reported were the dramatic sound-bites of Fenner's testimony. I had to admit, Fenner gave some dynamite quotes, and I'm sure they helped sell a few newspapers. Even 20 years after Fenner's dramatic performance before the House in 1975, the media and the assassination buffs still quote her version of what the note said. For many, it has become historical fact, not to be disputed.

When Lilly told me about Shanklin's testimony, I was dismayed to learn that Shanklin held back the full truth. Shanklin told the congressmen that he didn't recall Oswald visiting the office before the assassination and leaving a note for me. Shanklin also had no recollection that I had destroyed this note, and emphatically denied he had given the order to do so. He said he hadn't learned of this matter until he read it in the Dallas newspapers in September 1975. Virtually every other sentence out of his mouth was, "I don't recall." I guess Shanklin was really taken through the wringer by the congressmen and their staff. Apparently no one was buying his supposed memory losses. Of the two-thirds of Dallas FBI personnel who said they knew about the note, most of them also said that Shanklin was aware of it as well.

Shanklin did make some rather interesting and carefully worded statements: "I understand that Agents Hosty and Howe have stated that the Oswald visit and note were brought to my attention during the period immediately following the assassination of the president. Since at that particular time I was overwhelmed with innumerable major problems and duties, it is, of course, conceivable that their recollection is correct. I simply do not remember anything like that. . . . I understand that, in one version of the story, I am supposed to have ordered the destruction of the note. I can state here and now that I gave no such order. I would never have, and certainly did not, order the destruction of the note." And then, Shanklin went on to the subject of Nannie Lee Fenner: "I understand that there is a discrepancy in what Mrs. Fenner says about what was in the note, and what Mr. Hosty says. In Mrs. Fenner's version, there is a threat to blow up the Dallas office and the Dallas field office. Had I ever been shown such a note, I assure you I would have remembered."

Shanklin went on to explain why, beyond the obvious, he would have remembered. When Bobby Kennedy and other Washington insiders saw that the Dallas police had jurisdiction over the investigation of the assassination, they were desperate to wrest it away for the FBI. The Justice Department and the FBI were frantic to find any loophole to jerk jurisdiction away from the police, and Shanklin was largely responsible for these endeavors. If Oswald had threatened to blow up the FBI office and the police station as Fenner claimed, Shanklin would have snatched this note as evidence of a federal crime, enabling the FBI to assert jurisdiction over the police. As Shanklin said, a bomb threat against federal agents is the "equivalent of a red flag in front of a bull." He and other agents would have moved quickly to eliminate such a threat. Thus, because he didn't recall the note, Shanklin in essence endorsed my version of the note's contents.

What did the note say? Fenner's version is unreliable, and Howe and Shanklin, while not recalling the specifics of the note, were inclined to agree with my version. If it had been Fenner's version, they both said they would have remembered, but what about the note's author: What did Lee Oswald say the note said? In his November 9, 1963, letter to the Soviet Embassy in Washington, Oswald wrote about my visiting his wife and how "Agent Hasty" supposedly tried to get her to defect. Then he says, "I and my wife strongly protested these tactics by the notorious FBI." After the assassination, Marina Oswald told the Warren Commission that her husband visited the FBI office in response to my visiting her. Ruth Paine also testified that a few weeks before the assassination Oswald told her he had just dropped off a letter to the FBI, and though she couldn't recall what exactly Oswald said the letter was about, she did say that based upon what Oswald told her, she knew it had been "irritating" or "abrasive." These are not words to describe a bomb threat. Also, on the afternoon of November 22 in Captain Fritz's office, Oswald, upon learning my identity, protested with irritating language my having had contact with his wife. From Oswald's own words, therefore, we can piece together what the note said — he was protesting against my having interviewed his wife and he wanted me to stop.

Shanklin's secretary, Marion Roberts, who had her desk right outside Shanklin's door, also made a statement: "After the assassination, I heard from an unrecalled source that it was decided to destroy the note. I do not know who made this decision or who would have destroyed the note." Those appeared to be carefully chosen words. Roberts would be loyal to her boss, and would never pin the destruction orders on Shanklin directly. She probably also knew it was I who destroyed the note. In all likelihood, she was trying to be kind to us by not specifically identifying us to Bassett and his internal investigators. She knew all too well how the Bureau treated its out-of-favor agents.

Just as Roberts was doubtless protecting her boss, Shanklin was also probably protecting his boss and mentor, Johnny Mohr. Bill Sullivan, in his September 1975 statement to Bassett's men, said that shortly after the assassination he had spoken with Shanklin by phone. During this conversation, Shanklin told Sullivan he had internal personnel problems in the Oswald case because one of his agents (the name was not given to Sullivan, or if so he had forgotten) had received a threatening letter from Oswald while Oswald was still alive, a letter from Oswald prompted by the agent's investigation of him. Sullivan told Bassett's men that he tried to get more details from Shanklin, but that Shanklin seemed disinclined to discuss it further, other than to say he was handling it with Mohr as a personnel problem. Shanklin made no mention of anything being destroyed. Sullivan also told Bassett's men that later he had another phone conversation with Shanklin, during which he identified me as the agent who had received the threatening note, again failing to mention that the note had been destroyed. He also mentioned that Hoover was furious with me and was going to transfer me out of Dallas.

On September 15, 1975, *Time* magazine ran an article entitled "The Oswald Cover-up" that made reference to Oswald delivering the note to me. However, *Time* relied on sworn affidavits from as many as six high-ranking FBI men to assert, "Both current and former FBI agents have reported that [the letter] was burned and shredded in Dallas on orders from Mohr." The article also pointed out that Adams and Bassett were clearly aligned with Mohr's faction, and yet it was those very men who were being asked to investigate this issue, suggesting the strong possibility of a conflict of interest in the internal investigation. Both Adams and Mohr threatened to sue *Time* for libel, but Sandy Smith, the author of the *Time* article, essentially told them to go ahead, because he was standing by the veracity of his information. Mohr and Adams never sued.

Friday, December 12, 1975

TIME: 9:40 A.M.

Lilly held the door to the congressional hearing room open for me, and I walked in. I looked around the packed room, trying to orient myself. The press and public were crammed into the gallery section of the subcommittee's hearing room, room 2237 of the Rayburn House Office Building on Capitol Hill. Bray and Lilly guided me through the crowd and showed me to my seat at a large conference table placed front and center before the U-shaped panel for the congressmen. Bray and Lilly took chairs on either side of me. A staffer adjusted a microphone and placed it directly in front of me. There was a buzz of anticipation in the room. A couple of photographers were slinking about on the floor in front of my table trying to position themselves for a shot of me.

This was a very public hearing, very different from the Warren Commission.

As my attorneys and I were getting ourselves set at our table, a large, dark-bearded man elbowed his way in to get next to me. "Mark Lane, Mr. Hosty. I have a question: When you met with the Army intelligence officer the morning of the assassination, was this Agent Powell?" Before I could answer, Bray jabbed his arm between Lane and me. I was not going to answer any questions for him.

Lane, a well-known assassination buff, claimed to be a Communist and actually belonged to an organization called the National Guardian Club that followed the Communist party line. However, I do know that he was never a member of the U.S. Communist party. At any rate, he had written a book in 1967, *Rush to Judgment,* about the assassination in which he concluded that Oswald had not killed Kennedy. Lane was also trying to steer all public dialogue away from the Soviet and Cuban angles. It was easy to see his agenda.

That meeting Lane referred to on the morning of November 22, 1963, was utterly unrelated to the assassination, but by this time I learned that assassination buffs went by their own rules of logic. That morning, I had a prescheduled meeting to compare notes with Agent Ed Coyle of the Army Intelligence unit and Agent Jack Ellsworth of the Alcohol, Tobacco, and Firearms Bureau about a weapons case involving an Army ordinance officer at a nearby base who had been embezzling equipment, including guns and ammunition. This officer was then fencing the goods to an outside party, and we had discovered that a right-wing extremist group was trying to purchase the weaponry.

I later learned that Agent Powell was another Army Intelligence man who had been in downtown Dallas when the assassination occurred, doing some routine background checks at the Sheriff's Department across the street from the assassination site. When the call came over that shots may have come from the book depository building, Powell and about twenty sheriff's deputies dashed over to the building and volunteered their services in searching. Because Powell wasn't in a police uniform, he at first made people suspicious and was briefly detained by the police while they confirmed his identity.

After Bray's interjection prevented me from talking to him, Lane walked straight up to Congressman Christopher Dodd of Connecticut. Dodd leaned close to Lane. I watched as Lane mouthed some words to Dodd, who nodded in seeming agreement. Then they both looked directly at me. Dodd seemed to then say "thank you" to Lane.

Jack French, an agent from FBI headquarters who had once been stationed in Kansas City with me, came up and told me he had been sent by headquarters to observe my testimony. He was a good guy, and he wished me luck.

When Congressman Don Edwards called the hearing to order, the press came to attention: photographers began clicking away and television cameramen set their cameras to whirring. The court reporter began to tap away silently on his machine.

Edwards introduced me to the committee, then turned matters over to the subcommittee's lead staffer, Alan Parker. Parker got down to work and began questioning me, laying out the basic foundation of my testimony for the committee. I described how I came to receive the note, what the note said, what I did with it, and finally, how Shanklin ordered me to destroy it. Once Parker completed this task, the six congressmen on the subcommittee began their tag-team process of questioning me.

Then it was Dodd's turn. "OK, did you meet on the morning of November twenty-second with an Army Intelligence agent?"

"I did," I responded evenly, masking how disturbed I was knowing that Lane served as some type of an advisor to Dodd. I wondered if Dodd's late father, who had been an FBI agent himself, was turning over in his grave.

"Is his name James Powell?"

"No, sir."

Dodd couldn't hide his disappointment. "Would you give me his name?"

"Ed Coyle," I said, and then elaborated, "C-O-Y-L-E."

"Do you know James Powell?" Dodd persisted.

"Not — I don't think so, sir," I replied, bringing that line of questioning to an abrupt conclusion.

Although Congressman Robert Drinan, a Catholic priest, put me through a venomous, abusive, and accusatory third degree, most of the congressmen seemed sympathetic. They seemed to believe my story, to disbelieve Fenner's version, and to distrust Shanklin's supposed memory loss.

At 12:20 P.M., Chairman Edwards brought a halt to my testimony and excused me. As I stood up, Edwards came around the panel table and strode right up to me. He took my hand and shook it vigorously, thanking me for testifying and wishing me good luck. His face was warm and smiling. Pleasantly surprised, I thanked him. Edwards had been an FBI agent during the World War II era, but apparently got out of the Bureau because of Hoover. Maybe he could see how I had been left out to dry. I don't know, but I appreciated his public sign of support of me.

An hour later, Ken Howe, my old supervisor, took the stand. Howe was really starting to show his age, and the brief encounter I had with him in the hallway had been strained. He didn't want to relive those nightmarish days in Dallas. It was a bad dream for me as well, but it seemed worse for Howe.

Howe for the most part supported my version of events. He had no patience with Fenner's outrageous claims. He testified that on the afternoon of the assassination, he and Shanklin had confronted me about the Oswald note. Howe testified that I had kept insisting the note was no big deal and wondered why they were so upset. After Oswald was killed, Howe said that Shanklin had wanted to talk with me. Howe said that he accompanied me to Shanklin's office, and while I went in and talked to Shanklin, he stood in the doorway. He said he couldn't hear a word of what Shanklin was telling me, and had no idea the note had been destroyed.

I was still the only man with blood left on his hands.

17

Friday, December 12, 1975

TIME: 2:00 P.M.

Having wrapped up my House testimony, I now headed for the Church Committee, officially named the Senate Select Committee on Intelligence, to testify before one of its subcommittees. This committee, headed by Senator Frank Church, was conducting a broad investigation of the different intelligence agencies. The subcommittee I was to appear for was charged with probing intelligence aspects of the Kennedy assassination. While I was told that the subcommittee wanted to hear testimony about the note's destruction, I would learn during the hearing of their interest in much deeper issues, including the Soviet and Cuban angles of the assassination.

With my two attorneys in tow, I was allowed entrance to the hearing room. This hearing, like the Warren Commission hearing, and in stark contrast to the House hearing, was closed. In fact, the entire hearing was completely classified and top secret; the records of my testimony have been locked away and will never see the light of day. Because only Senators Walter Mondale, Gary Hart, and Richard Schweiker composed this subcommittee, I was to testify at a conference table in a conference room.

Mondale was the chairman, but I never saw him. The only senator present when I walked in was Schweiker. He deferred to the subcommittee's two key staffers to handle the majority of matters. Paul Wallach, the senior staffer, swore me in. Wallach looked like a Wall Street lawyer type, his hair neatly combed, dressed in a finely pressed shirt, a sharp dark suit, and polished shoes. A second staffer, Mike Epstein, was his clone. Wallach ran me through some initial foundation questions.

Early in this questioning, I made what I considered a passing remark. I said I felt the FBI and myself in particular had been unduly and harshly criticized by the Warren Commission. When I said this, Epstein leaned forward and, pointing his finger at me, said angrily, "How can you even say that when you and the FBI knew that Oswald had been in contact with KGB agent Kostikov, the Department 13 man for terrorism and assassinations?"

"I did not know this information in 1963," I retorted briskly.

"Oh yes, you did," Wallach shot back. He fished out a document from one of his files and slid it across the table to me. I picked it up and immediately recognized it. It was the October 18, 1963, FBI communiqué regarding Oswald's Mexico City contact with Kostikov.

"This says that Kostikov is a vice consul and says nothing about his being an assassination expert or a member of Department 13," I said as I flung it back across the table at Wallach.

Wallach snatched it back, and he and Epstein hunched over the communiqué, examining it. After a while, Wallach looked up at me sheepishly and said, "Oh, I see."

Schweiker, who had been leaning back, in his chair watching this testy exchange, decided it was probably best to call a quick recess. We had only been going for less than an hour, so I figured I had thrown Wallach and Epstein off balance. I later learned that during the break Wallach and Epstein conferred with FBI headquarters about my knowledge of Kostikov back in 1963. Headquarters admitted to Wallach and Epstein that in 1963 I had no notion of Kostikov's true identity.

When we resumed the hearing, I noticed a distinct difference in Wallach and Epstein's treatment of me. Now they were cordial and respectful. As the day wore on, I could tell I would be testifying over the long haul before this subcommittee. Schweiker, Wallach, and Epstein had an apparently inexhaustible supply of questions about the assassination as it related to the Soviet/Cuban angle, and I was a very cooperative witness for them. Any good investigator will tell you that when you want to pierce a cover-up, you usually learn the most from a disgruntled participant. To say I was disgruntled would be a fair statement.

Wallach, who was on loan to the Church Committee from the

Securities and Exchange Commission, put me through the most thorough and complete questioning I had ever seen, much less experienced. He was meticulous and detail oriented; I only wished he had been on the Warren Commission.

Senator Gary Hart interrupted us briefly at one point during the first day to ask some rather silly questions about whether right-wing Cuban exiles had anything to do with the killing of Kennedy. I suppose Hart was thinking back to the Bay of Pigs fiasco, and I couldn't help wondering if he had given any thought to the events since November 22, thirteen years ago. In any case, I told him I knew nothing to support such a far-fetched theory. Hart would not return during my four days of testimony. With Mondale never showing at all, the only other senator I saw was Schweiker. In the end, Schweiker, who was interested in my testimony, was only able to stay for just over half of it.

Although the subcommittee learned a lot from me, I must confess I learned more from its members' questions and responses. The Senate Select Committee on Intelligence had access to a lot more information than I did about what the CIA and FBI intelligence agents had learned about Lee Oswald's activities with the Soviets and Cubans.

The first of many revelations from Wallach and Epstein was that it was FBI headquarters that had neglected to notify me about Kostikov's true identity and the nature of his meetings with Lee Oswald in October 1963. In all these years, I had wrongly assumed it had been the CIA who had failed to pass this information on to the FBI. The revelation that it was my own agency stunned me. Wallach and Epstein also told me that the Warren Commission had assumed that I knew all about Kostikov's true identity, and that was why they had been so harsh with me. If the Warren Commission had been so interested in what I knew and when I knew it regarding Kostikov, why didn't they ask me about it?

Wallach asked me if I knew before the assassination that Oswald had been in regular contact with Vitaliy Gerasimov, the Soviet paymaster in Washington and the contact for deep-cover Soviet espionage agents in the United States. I told them no, and again, Wallach and Epstein told me that the Warren Commission had assumed I knew all about this prior to the assassination, which again meant that FBI headquarters had virtually set me up.

Wallach pressed on, asking me if I knew before the assassination that in the summer of 1963 it was an FBI office in the Southwest that discovered Kostikov's true identity. Again, I told them no, I was unaware of any of this. When I got back to Kansas City a few days later, one of the first things I did was locate this highly classified file and read it cover to cover. I cannot reveal specifics, but part of Kostikov's trade involved sabotage, and he was a very dangerous man.

This round of testimony lasted two days, and after a week's break in Kansas City, I flew back to Washington for two more days. Throughout all four days of testimony, the staffers persisted in trying to get me to criticize FBI Agents John Fain and Milton Kaack. Fain had the Oswald case in Fort Worth just before me, and Kaack had the Oswald case in New Orleans for a good part of 1963. I told the staffers they ought to talk to Fain and Kaack themselves, and offered no comment.

As I was leaving, the staffers told me I might be recalled in January or February of 1976. While I never was, I learned some of my fellow Kansas City agents were called to Washington. Agents Ray Howe (no relation to Ken Howe), Joe Kissiah, and Tom Trettis were all asked if I had ever told them that Oswald had been my informant; each one of them said no, I had not. Wallach and Company were double-checking my credibility.

I later learned what territory Wallach was exploring. Back in May or June 1965, former Kansas City FBI agent Carver Gayton, then a new young agent, had come forward with a story about Oswald being my informant. I think I know where Gayton got his information — or misinformation. One morning, Kissiah, Trettis, and I — but not Ray Howe — were sitting at a long table in a coffee shop near the Kansas City office talking about the Kennedy assassination. Gayton was sitting at the opposite end of the table talking with several other agents. Kissiah asked me if the rumor that Oswald was an FBI informant was true. I laughed and said, "No," but that Jack Ruby had been one. Trettis, who was an out-of-town agent called into Dallas back in 1963, nodded in confirmation. Then Kissiah asked why in the world Ruby was an informant. "Probably for organized crime matters," I said. I had my back to Gayton, and I think it likely Gayton missed the key words, namely, that the informant was Ruby. Instead, he probably heard only Kissiah's questions, part of my answers, my laughing, and Trettis nodding and saying, "Yes, that's true."

The next thing I knew, Gayton was claiming I had confirmed that Oswald was an organized crime informant for me in Dallas. This, despite the fact I never worked organized crime cases in Dallas. To this day Kissiah and Trettis say that it was all a big misunderstanding on Gayton's part. Gayton, who had been one of the few Kansas City agents to act aloof toward me when I first transferred to Kansas City, stuck to his story, which somehow got to a reporter. I don't know if Gayton leaked the story to the press or not. I only wish he had come to me.

Thursday, April 6, 1976

TIME: 10:00 A.M.

I was in Washington for an FBI school on terrorism. This was my day off, so I received permission to run over to Capitol Hill to review my testimony from the Senate subcommittee proceedings. I ran into Wallach and asked him why the subcommittee had never recalled me. With a genuine smile, he told me that everything I had reported had checked out one hundred percent, so they saw no reason to recall me.

Relieved, I sat down in the Church Committee's staff room and spent the rest of the day reading my four days of testimony. Because it was classified I was not allowed to take any notes or make any copies. While I was sitting in the little screened-off cubicle, three Church Committee staffers had a brief conversation on the other side of my partition. I could easily hear everything they were talking about. Two of them were saying they had just came from a closed-door meeting of the full committee and were telling the third staffer how the committee had just decided to "delete it" and that "it would not appear in the final report," much to the staffers' frustration.

I cannot say what exactly they were talking about, but a short time after this, the Church Committee on Intelligence released its final report on the Kennedy assassination. According to press accounts, the final report had originally been 166 pages long, but the committee had released a 106-page report. In this abridged version, the committee, like the Warren Commission, steered totally clear of all the Soviet and Cuban information — information that again had been deliberately kept from the American people. In 1976, the United States was still locked in the cold war, so maybe the reasoning went that this information could still lead to an international confrontation, thirteen years after the fact.

My more cynical side speculated that the Senate committee was packed with Soviet/Cuban apologists. In 1976, there were many people who wanted to negotiate peace with the Soviets and the Cubans, which they hoped would include nuclear arms limitation treaties. I also suspected that Senator Church, who was gearing up for a run for the presidency in 1976, may not have wanted to stir the pot, especially since letting everything come out would have forced him to acknowledge that John and Bobby Kennedy were two of the driving forces to overthrow Castro. This kind of admission would have embarrassed and angered many in the Kennedy faction, whose support he desperately needed.

One of the more significant things to come out of the final report was the Church Committee's criticism of the CIA. The committee falsely alleged that the CIA had failed to follow up on obvious leads that could have implicated Castro in Kennedy's death. When the 1963 U.S. ambassador to Mexico, Thomas Mann — who became President Johnson's undersecretary of state — read this, he blew his stack. He struck back in the press, explaining that CIA agents in Mexico City had tried to run out all information about Oswald's dealings with the Cubans, but they had been ordered by Bobby Kennedy to cease and desist their investigation just days after the assassination. As Mann told the *Chicago Sun-Times* (June 24, 1976), "If the President's brother thought Oswald did it entirely on his own, I didn't see why I should be more Catholic than the Pope." Because of the cease-and-desist order, the investigation into the Soviet/Cuban angles of the president's assassination was left incomplete.

18

September 11, 1977

TIME: 9:30 A.M.

In the newspaper, I saw yet another article about the final formation of the House of Representatives Select Committee on Assassinations. This committee was going to reexamine the evidence of the assassinations of Kennedy and Dr. Martin Luther King, Jr., supposedly with an objective eye toward settling those cases once and for all.

This morning I couldn't help but ask myself if the Kennedy side of the committee would have the guts to face the truth. I had my doubts, for it seemed to be a pattern in Washington to maintain a veil of secrecy over some key aspects of the president's assassination.

Over the years, understandably, I had spent a great deal of time examining every detail of this "crime of the century." I had a personal, vested interest in the subject. Patiently, painfully, I had reconstructed those days leading up to the assassination and immediately following, in an effort to understand and appreciate why certain things happened as they did. To understand things the way I saw them, let me start from the beginning, even at the risk of repeating some things I have already said at various places throughout the book.

At age seventeen, Lee Oswald convinced his mother to allow him to enlist in the Marines, where he qualified for the prestigious title "Sharpshooter" by hitting targets 200, 300, and 500 yards away. In 1958, while he was stationed in Japan, it is believed he had contact with a Soviet KGB or military intelligence (GRU) intermediary. The next year, before his term was up with the Marines, he took an emergency discharge, claiming his mother was sick. (In 1962, because of Oswald's defection, this was changed to a dishonorable discharge.) Oswald gathered his things and headed for Finland. At the time, it was not commonly known that Finland had the most lax process for someone to enter the Soviet Union. Once Oswald arrived in Helsinki, all he needed to do was stop by the Soviet Embassy to apply for a tourist visa, which was granted in a few days. Any other European country would have made Oswald go through a much more rigorous process.

Once in the Soviet Union, Oswald told the authorities he wanted to defect. For several years now, Oswald had been an avid reader of Communist literature and a strong Marxist ideologue. Many in the U.S. intelligence field bristle at any suggestion that Oswald was actually a CIA spy sent to Russia — the United States had years before stopped trying to infiltrate the Soviet Union in such a simplistic manner. When Oswald was temporarily placed in the psychiatric ward in Moscow, it is safe to assume that the KGB subjected him to a battery of truth detection methods, including sodium pentothal and other chemical "truth serums." There is no way Oswald could have resisted the KGB's methods. If Oswald had been an American spy, he would never have left that Moscow hospital alive.

But Oswald was sent to Minsk, a city our intelligence agencies had identified as the city to which the Soviets sent many of their Western immigrants, and, less positively, as one of the KGB's training schools for foreign spies. While in Minsk, Oswald was set up in a nice apartment and given a KGB/Red Cross supplemental salary.

In Minsk, Oswald married Marina, she of the very suspicious KGB/MVD connections. That Oswald and his bride were granted an easy exit by the Soviets and the KGB is also highly suspect. Once back in the United States, Oswald's passion for Communist politics burned ever stronger. In New Orleans he was head of the Fair Play for Cuba Committee, handing out pro-Castro literature. Of course, there was no one else to become head, since the committee had a membership of one, Lee Oswald.

While in Fort Worth, then in New Orleans, and then in Dallas, Oswald maintained a correspondence with Second Secretary Vitaliy Gerasimov, the KGB agent in the Soviet Embassy in Washington with the job of paying and maintaining contact with KGB deep-cover or "sleeper" agents in the United States. When the Oswalds' baby, Rachel, was born, and when they changed residences, Lee informed Gerasimov. The contacts with Gerasimov meant that Marina met another important FBI criterion to be a suspected KGB plant.

On June 19, 1963, when the Oswalds were living in New Orleans, President Kennedy secretly granted the CIA the authority to engage in several attempts to overthrow Castro. In one of the attempts documented in the material made public by the Church Committee, the CIA made contact with Rolando Cubela (code name AMLASH), a political rival of Castro's who had led the urban half of the revolution against Batista while Castro led his armed rebels through the hills and countryside of Cuba. As a hero of the revolution, Cubela was given many privileges, one of which was the freedom to travel out of the country. The CIA met with Cubela on the sly in Brazil and enlisted him to help overthrow Castro. The plan was for Cubela, who despised the Soviets and their presence in Cuba, to take control of Cuba and to kick out the Soviets and their troops.

After Cubela returned from Brazil, it is widely believed in the intelligence field that Castro caught wind of Cubela's treason and had him arrested. Rather than execute him, it is believed Castro decided to turn Cubela into a double agent. Castro wanted Cubela to go on working with the CIA, but to report back to him. After a few years, when Cubela's usefulness had been exhausted, Castro decided to imprison him. After a trial for treason, Cubela was sentenced to die, but just before he was to be executed, Castro commuted his sentence to life imprisonment. Castro later released Cubela, who took up exile in Spain.

In early September 1963, Castro went to a party at the Brazilian Embassy in Havana, where he knew Western journalists would be, and sought out the Associated Press reporter, Canadian Daniel Harker. Without warning, Castro strode up to Harker and denounced American attempts to assassinate him and overthrow his regime, finally threatening, "United States leaders should think that if they are aiding terrorist plans to eliminate Cuban leaders, they themselves will not be safe." Castro was getting word back to Washington that two can play this deadly game.

Harker ran these quotes in a story published on September 9, 1963. The Oswalds were living in New Orleans, and while many newspapers and magazines, including the ones I read in Dallas, did not run the story, the *New Orleans Times-Picayune* did, under the headline CASTRO BLASTS RAIDS ON CUBA. Oswald was an avid newspaper reader and, especially considering his involvement with Cuban-American issues, I have to believe he read Castro's quotes.

Six days later, on September 15, Oswald took his first overt step on his mysterious Mexico City trip. He obtained his Mexican transit visa.

On September 25, Oswald put his pregnant wife and infant daughter in Ruth Paine's car bound for Dallas. The next day, Oswald caught a bus for the Mexican border at Laredo, Texas.

On September 26, we know from U.S. and Mexican border records that Oswald crossed the border and climbed on a bus bound for Mexico City. Oswald had been identified as a passenger on this bus by the bus manifest and by several of his fellow passengers, including an older English couple and two Australian girls who were touring Mexico. The latter pair shared a casual conversation with Oswald, in which he told the girls he had been to Mexico City before, and recommended a cheap but clean hotel.

CIA agents later confirmed this hotel existed and even found a maid who "thought" she recalled Oswald as having stayed there earlier. But because there had been a change of ownership just before the assassination, register records had been destroyed. Also, U.S. and Mexican border records were then preserved for only six months. While there is no documentation to support Oswald's claims of being familiar with Mexico City, we do know that the KGB liked to meet there with their American agents on a six-month basis. There were two time periods in which Oswald's movements were unaccounted for. During one full week in the fall of 1962, no one can account for Oswald; during two to three weeks in April 1963, only Marina can vouch for Oswald's presence in the United States.

On the morning of Friday, September 27, the bus arrived in Mexico City. The Australian girls watched Oswald disembark and walk away into the depths of Mexico City. Then the CIA picked him up, within the Soviet Embassy. The CIA was able to bug both the Soviet and Cuban embassies and set up visual surveillance outside the Cuban Embassy and outside the Soviet Embassy's front entrance — where they were also able to photograph comings and goings — but not the side entrances.

The CIA heard Oswald talk with Soviet Embassy officials about obtaining entrance visas for himself and his family. Oswald told the Soviets that he had information so hot that they would allow the Oswalds to settle in a city of their choice. Oswald wanted the Miami of Russia, the warm climate of Odessa on the Black Sea. After the assassination, Marina told us that the one thing her husband hated about Russia was its bitter cold winters.

While no one is sure — or no one will reveal — what this "hot information" was, it is reasonable to assume, given his contact with the Cuban community, that Oswald had learned about a group of right-wing Cuban exiles in outlying areas of New Orleans who were preparing a paramilitary invasion of Cuba.

As could be expected in the intelligence world, they took all this information from Oswald, then sent him to the Cuban Embassy, where he needed to obtain a transit visa allowing him to fly from Mexico City to Havana, and there board a plane for the Soviet Union. The CIA next picked up Oswald's presence inside the Cuban Embassy, where he asked the Cubans for a transit visa. The Cubans informed Oswald that he could only get a transit visa once he had received his entrance visa from the Soviets, though he was able to fill out an application for a transit visa and even posed for a visa photo. The Warren Commission later got this application and photo from the Cubans — the photo was clearly of Oswald, and the signature was conclusively determined to be his.

Oswald then went back to the Soviet Embassy and explained his quandary to them. They apologized, but insisted that he still had to get a transit visa from the Cubans before he could get his entrance visa from them.

To understand the situation Oswald found himself in, it's interesting to study a similar story about another American, John George Gessner, who tried to trade secrets for a comfortable life in the Soviet Union. In 1962, Gessner, a young Army soldier who had been stationed at the Los Alamos atomic weapons base in New Mexico, traveled to Mexico City and met with the Soviets in their embassy, where he spilled his knowledge of American atomic secrets. He then asked permission to defect to the Soviet Union as his reward. Once the Soviets had his information, he was of no further use to them, but he could be extraordinarily useful if he returned to Los Alamos and acted as their spy. To give an appearance that they were trying to help Gessner defect, the Soviets sent him to the Cuban Embassy to get his transit visa, assuring him they would grant him his entrance visa. The CIA listened while this American soldier scurried back and forth between the two embassies, just like Oswald, with each embassy blaming the other. The CIA taped all his conversations and photographed him repeatedly.

Finally realizing he was trapped with nowhere to go, the American soldier went back to America. He was arrested as soon as he crossed the border. He was imprisoned at Fort Leavenworth, Kansas, and was eventually tried in federal court in Kansas City, Kansas. Although he was convicted, the appellate court reversed the decision, concluding his confession had been improperly obtained. It turned out that the soldier had been wavering on whether to confess or not and had asked the prison chaplain for advice. The chaplain told him "to get right with the Lord." He then decided to confess.

The CIA refused to allow the prosecution to use their photo and wiretap evidence because the Soviets and Cubans would have discovered the CIA's sources and methods in Mexico City. The CIA wanted to keep fishing for more traitors and didn't want its cover blown. With the confession invalidated, the court set the soldier free. He stood legally unconvicted, but the entire nation had read his confession to treason in the newspapers, and in the hearts of many, he was as good as convicted. A short time after he left prison, he committed suicide.

Oswald, however, had no access to American military secrets to bargain with. When Oswald returned to the Cuban Embassy to ask for his transit visa again, he told Cuban intelligence officers stationed there that he was going to kill "that son of a bitch" John Kennedy. The next day Oswald met with KGB Colonel Kostikov.

In Mexico City, Kostikov was frequently seen by the CIA running around with a group of burly Mexican thugs who fancied carrying clubs wrapped in newspapers. According to Michael DeGuire, an FBI agent stationed in Mexico City at the time, they were strongly believed to carry out Kostikov's dirty jobs. One such job, believed to have been orchestrated by Kostikov, was the bludgeoning murder of an American. This particular American, the CIA learned, went to Kostikov with some "classified" information he had stolen from the U.S. government. Kostikov paid the American for the information, but soon discovered he had been duped: the information was not really classified. A day or so after selling Kostikov the phony secret information, the American was found dead in his Mexico City hotel, his head smashed like a pumpkin. No one was able to definitively pin this murder on Kostikov, but it certainly carried his signature. He was well known to the CIA as a highly dangerous man.

From what I have been able to learn from my source, Oswald had a clandestine meeting with Kostikov at an undisclosed restaurant near a water fountain in Mexico City. We do not know, and will never know, what Kostikov and Oswald talked about, but I find it more than disturbing that the day after Oswald offered to kill the president for the Cubans, he was seen meeting with the KGB's chief assassination expert for the Western hemisphere.

The rest of that weekend and the following Monday, Oswald was observed hanging around town socializing with some Mexican college

215

students. He was also seen in the company of a female Cuban Embassy official. Many people make the mistake of thinking it was Sylvia Duran, the Mexican woman who was acting as the embassy receptionist. I believe it was Luisa Calderon, who has been identified as a Cuban intelligence official, because Calderon was later heard to say that she knew Kennedy was going to be killed.

On Tuesday, October 1, the CIA picked up Oswald's voice again in the Cuban Embassy. While there, Oswald telephoned the Soviet Embassy. With their tape recorders routinely running, the CIA heard Oswald talk on the phone to KGB security guard Ivan Obeykov. Oswald explained that he still wanted to get his entrance visa. When Obeykov asked Oswald who he was working with in the Soviet Embassy, Oswald told him Kostikov. Obeykov then told Oswald to go ahead and come over.

After the assassination, the CIA learned from eyewitnesses that shortly after hanging up with Obeykov, Oswald left the embassy and got in a car with two Cuban men, tentatively identified as Manuel Vega y Perez and Rogelio Rodriguez y Lopez, both of whom had also been identified as Cuban intelligence agents. The car carrying Oswald and these two men was seen driving off in the direction of the Soviet Embassy. The CIA agents staking out the Soviet Embassy scrambled to get their cameras ready for Oswald's entrance, but Oswald apparently used the side entrance to the embassy, the entrance for Russian-speaking persons.

The CIA agents still waited patiently, hoping Oswald would exit from the front door. Eventually they saw a Western-looking white man of stocky build exit the front door, stuffing some papers in his wallet. Thinking it could be Oswald carrying his visa papers, the agents started furiously snapping pictures of him as he walked away.

A copy of one of these photos would end up in Dallas FBI Agent Bardwell Odum's hands on the morning of November 23, 1963. Odum showed it to me, and I told him it wasn't Oswald. Then I would help Odum crop the photo, eliminating the front door to the Soviet Embassy so that no one would know the CIA had been staking it out. To this day this man has never been identified. My guess is that he was some Soviet seaman routinely getting his papers in proper order. Oswald probably slipped undetected out the same side door he had entered. Odum figured as much.

In my mind, with all this evidence, there was absolutely no question that it was Oswald who had killed the president. We knew what his motivation was. Oswald, desperately trying to go back to the Soviet Union, was having his chain jerked by both the Soviets and the Cubans. Perhaps Oswald felt the Soviets and Cubans weren't taking him seriously. If he was trying to find a way to prove his loyalty and worth to his fellow Communists, killing the leader of the Western world had to be the ultimate proof on both points.

A short time later, the CIA would give FBI headquarters all its information about Oswald's activities in Mexico City. Tragically, headquarters failed to relay the critical parts of this information to me. I only discovered why in 1994. When Agent John Fain had the Oswald case, it was considered a Soviet defector case. Therefore, the Russian section of Division 5 in the Bureau had responsibility to disseminate relevant information to the field. When I reactivated the case, it was placed in the Nationalities section, under the subgrouping "Cuban Affairs," because of Oswald's Fair Play for Cuba activities. When the CIA notified the FBI of Oswald's contact with Kostikov, and later when Oswald's letter to the Soviets explaining he had been in contact with Kostikov was intercepted, the information was routed to the Cuban section of Division 5. The Cuban section knew nothing about Kostikov's true identity; consequently they had nothing to pass on to me. The Russian section did know of Kostikov's significance, but because they tightly guarded their information on the need-to-know basis, the Cuban section never caught on. I learned that a Russian section agent stumbled across the information concerning Oswald's meeting with the Soviets in Mexico City on November 21. On that day he requested to see it, and it was not until the afternoon of November 22 that he finally received the file and discovered that Oswald had met with the notorious Kostikov.

After the assassination, three KGB colonels — Kostikov, Yatskov, and Nechiprenko — would confirm what the CIA already knew: that they had been in contact with Oswald at their embassy in Mexico City. Of course, they said that Oswald had simply sought an entrance visa and nothing more. Marina Oswald would also confirm only that her husband had been in Mexico City.

On Wednesday, October 2, the day after his last visit to the Soviet Embassy, Oswald boarded a bus bound for the Texas border. On October 4, Oswald was back in Dallas — we retrieved his room check-in records at a local YMCA. Several weeks later, Ruth Paine would tell a friend that Oswald was looking for work; the friend suggested Oswald apply for a laborer's job at the Texas School Book Depository.

On November 19, the *Dallas Times Herald* ran a front-page story, under the headline KENNEDY VIRTUALLY INVITES CUBAN COUP, about a speech President Kennedy gave to a group of Cuban exiles in Miami, in which he essentially told them to overthrow Castro, saying that "it would be a happy day if the Castro government is ousted." Again, the avid newspaper reader Oswald would doubtless have been infuriated by Kennedy's comments.

On the same day, the Dallas newspapers published the president's motorcade route, showing how the president would drive directly past the book depository. On November 21, Oswald's co-workers were buzzing with excitement about how close the president would be. That night Oswald broke his routine and went home in the middle of the week. The next morning, he retrieved his rifle and left a lump of cash for his wife while she was still asleep. He took off his wedding ring and left it with the cash.

In Mexico City, the Cubans had done the unbelievable: they had actually granted him his transit visa to Havana. All Oswald had to do was make it to Mexico City and pick it up. Then he could jump on a plane to Havana.

On November 22, shortly before the president's motorcade was due to pass by, Oswald was seen by a co-worker on the sixth floor of the depository. As shots rang out, a newspaper reporter saw a rifle poking out of the sixth-floor window. More important, Howard Brennan, a spectator standing across the street from the book depository, saw a man resembling Oswald firing a rifle at the president. Several minutes after the shooting, Oswald was spotted on the second floor.

Oswald escaped from the building only to be stopped by Officer J. D. Tippit. The entire Dallas police force had heard the all-points bulletin giving Brennan's description of Oswald, so it was natural that Tippit should decide to check out the fast-walking, nervous-acting Oswald on the streets of Oak Cliff. Witnesses saw Oswald lean into the front passenger window of Tippit's patrol car as Oswald and Tippit talked briefly. Tippit probably asked to see some ID, because the first thing an officer does on a stop such as this is ask for the person's identification. I figure Oswald handed over his wallet, and Tippit then saw the two identifications, one in the name Oswald and the other in the name Alek Hidell. If this were the case, then it is understandable for Tippit's suspicions to have been aroused and to have motivated him to step out of the patrol car to check out Oswald further. Oswald probably knew he would be detained, which would dash any plans of flight to Mexico, so he pulled out his revolver and shot Tippit. As Tippit fell to the ground, it is possible he dropped Oswald's wallet, just as Agent Barrett described.

When he was finally apprehended in the movie theater, he tried to get off a shot at another officer.

Upon Oswald's arrest, his identity was immediately flashed to Washington. The Division 5 men in the Bureau then told their chief, Bill Sullivan, about Oswald's background. The lower-ranking CIA agents were probably telling their chiefs at the same time, and between Sullivan and the CIA, the newly sworn-in president and his National Security Council learned this disturbing information.

At about the same time as Oswald's arrest and identification, I learned after the assassination from two independent sources, fully armed warplanes were sent screaming toward Cuba. Just before they entered Cuban airspace, they were hastily called back. With the launching of warplanes, the entire U.S. military went on alert. The Pentagon ordered us to Defense Condition 3, more commonly known as Def Con 3 — the equivalent of loading and locking your weapon, and then placing your finger on the trigger. The power cells within Washington's Beltway were in a panic.

Meanwhile, back at FBI headquarters, Belmont had unwittingly ordered me to go down to the police station and share with the police "everything the FBI had in its file on Oswald." When Sullivan heard this, he instantly saw how catastrophically wrong this order was. Despite lacking proper authority, he immediately countermanded Belmont's order. With what I had originally assumed to be Hoover's order, he told Clark to get me out of the police station.

In Dallas, Shanklin must have been briefed on the full scale of Oswald's Soviet and Cuban contacts. I am sure he was under tremendous strain, and this may partly explain his actions regarding me during the days following the assassination.

In Mexico City, still within hours of the president's death, a CIA telephone wiretap picked up Cuban intelligence official Luisa Calderon telling someone that she had known beforehand that Kennedy was going to be killed.

A transcript had been sent up with the photos on the night of the assassination. Was it of this conversation? Or was it of a telephone conversation that Kostikov had with a fellow KGB agent in Washington just after his meeting with Oswald (a fact I learned later)?

When the CIA heard the president had just been killed by Oswald, then heard Calderon saying that the Cubans knew this was going to happen, they went into a full-court press, cover or no cover. The Mexican authorities immediately arrested Sylvia Duran, the receptionist at the Cuban Embassy. A Mexican citizen, she had no diplomatic cover. Duran confirmed for the Mexican authorities that it was in fact Oswald who had been in the Cuban Embassy talking with Calderon, Vega, and Rodriguez. She didn't know, however, what they had talked about.

On November 27, 1963, Castro, in one of his typical long-winded speeches, mentioned Oswald making a "provocative statement" when he visited the Cuban Embassy in Mexico City. A few months later, the FBI sent Jack Childs to Havana to try to follow up on Castro's passing comment. Jack Childs, the U.S. Communist party's financial advisor, and his brother Morris, former editor of the *Daily Worker*, comprised one of the FBI's most valuable intelligence sources, known collectively as SOLO source. The Childs brothers had been two of the first members of the U.S. Communist party, but when Stalin ordered the demotion of Jews throughout all Communist parties worldwide, the Childs, themselves Soviet-born Jews, became disillusioned. The FBI recruited them as counter-intelligence agents. Not only did the Childs brothers, as part of their party duties, fly to Moscow once a year to pick up the party's annual $2–3 million dollar subsidy from the Kremlin (the Soviet support of the U.S. Communist party has been corroborated by Russian president Boris Yeltsin), but they also had the confidence of Castro. During his audience with Castro, Jack Childs asked him what he meant by "provocative statement." Castro, thinking he was talking with confidants, told him of Oswald's announcement that he was going to kill Kennedy. SOLO source had proven to be reliable in every other instance, and I had absolutely no reason to doubt the veracity of this report.

The CIA also discovered something else intriguing. When Oswald left his rooming house in the Oak Cliff area of Dallas immediately after the assassination, his path led straight to a bus stop. It was determined that this bus went by the Red Bird Airport in the Oak Cliff area. Shortly after Oswald's arrest was announced, a plane took off from this airport. Per usual procedure at such a small airport, no flight records were made for the plane; no one knows whose plane it was, who was flying it, where it came from, or, most important, where it was going. Several hours later, after a time period consistent with a flight time from Dallas to Mexico City, a small plane consistent with the mysterious Red Bird plane touched down at the Mexico City International Airport. This plane improperly bypassed the normal pattern of being inspected by Mexican airport authorities. Instead, it taxied straight up to a Cuban plane, which was already revving its engines. As the smaller plane pulled up next to the Cuban plane, an unidentified man jumped out and sprinted across the tarmac and jumped into the Cuban plane. The Cuban plane, which had already delayed its regularly scheduled departure time by five hours, gunned its engines and took off for Havana.

In Washington, the response to the assassination needed to develop instantaneously. President Johnson was getting quick, rapid-fire briefings on all this information. To him and the National Security Council, things were looking very grim. Some time shortly after the assassination, Johnson was on the hot-line with Moscow and Premier Nikita Khrushchev. Given the circumstances, this was not in itself remarkable, but Johnson's professionally discreet press secretary Pierre Salinger has said publicly that if these conversations were ever released, they would prove compelling.

It is unlikely that Moscow knew Oswald was going to kill Kennedy, because after the assassination the Russians never went on a military alert. If they had been behind his death, they most certainly would have been braced for possible retaliation. Besides which, they never would have used someone with such obvious ties to the Soviet Union.

The Cubans, however, were giving ominous signs of a country bracing for a conflict. Officials in the Cuban Embassy in Mexico City scrambled to destroy their sensitive documents, apparently anticipating that Americans might burst into their embassy. Within hours of her disturbing comments about knowing Kennedy was going to be killed, Calderon was ordered back to Havana at once. U.S. Ambassador Mann wanted the Mexican government to question her, but to this day Castro has kept her under wraps, never letting anyone get near her. She was the only person Castro would not let the House Select Committee on Assassinations speak with.

Meanwhile, back in Washington, while it was becoming clear that Oswald had many serious dealings with both the Soviets and the Cubans, a decision was made that there was simply no conclusive proof that either country had actively participated in the president's death. The evidence was just too sketchy. It was very likely that Oswald had killed Kennedy on his own, perhaps in an effort to impress the Soviets and Cubans. Or perhaps to secure the dubious but prominent place in history Oswald so craved.

In short order, Johnson ordered the CIA to cease its investigation in Mexico City. According to CIA Assistant Deputy Director Thomas Karamessines, the White House did not want the Cubans implicated as accessories, because if they were, the White House would be forced to do something it didn't want to do: retaliate against Cuba. And any retaliation against the Cubans would have entangled the

Soviets. They would have been forced to respond in kind, which could easily have escalated to a full-scale war, with all the nuclear risk nobody wanted.

As Johnson later told Earl Warren when he persuaded him to head the Commission, if certain information wasn't properly handled — that is, covered up convincingly — millions could be killed in a nuclear war. The Mafia didn't have any nuclear weapons; in 1963, only the Soviets and Americans did.

The National Security Council and Johnson must have concluded it was pointless to subject the nation to the risks of war simply on the *possibility* that the Cubans knew beforehand that Oswald intended to kill Kennedy. Based on information I have reviewed, I seriously doubt the Cubans were more deeply involved than having prior knowledge of Oswald's intent. Assuming this, I had to agree with the assessment I presumed the White House made. It infuriates me to think the Cubans had prior knowledge of Oswald's intentions, but it was not feasible to take any kind of meaningful revenge.

Besides, when Oswald made the offer to kill Kennedy, neither Oswald nor the Cubans could have known that the president would pass right in front of Oswald's place of employment just a month and a half later, although there had been reports in the newspapers in early September that Kennedy intended to visit Texas to shore up support for the upcoming 1964 elections. Perhaps Oswald had also read these reports.

When Johnson ordered the CIA to shut down its Mexico City investigation, the CIA agents went into near mutiny: they had been going gangbusters on some very hot leads. The CIA station chief, Winston Scott, had to threaten to fire his agents and send them back to the States if they did not stop their investigations. It really wasn't until Bobby Kennedy seconded Johnson's order that the agents finally settled down. The U.S. ambassador to Mexico, Thomas Mann, has also come out publicly saying he, too, was furious about Johnson's orders to cease and desist.

As it turned out, Johnson gave the Warren Commission its priorities. The Commission was to reassure the public and calm everyone down, and to disclose as much evidence to the public as it could.

The cover-up was on. The American public would not be told of Oswald's dealings with the Soviets and Cubans. It would be for their own good. World War I had been ignited when Austria's crown prince was assassinated by a Bosnian-Serb nationalist, and this time even more was at stake. We had just come out of the Cuban Missile Crisis, and if the full extent of Oswald's contact with the Soviets and Cubans had been disclosed in 1963, it was quite logical to expect the United States, as an enraged collective body, to abandon reason, to ignore the lack of evidence of direct complicity, and to demand revenge on the Cubans and the Soviets.

While this sort of conspiracy of the powers-that-be to lie to the American people may be offensive to many, it is important to consider the official mindset regarding the threat of nuclear war. In early 1963, in the wake of the Cuban Missile Crisis, Assistant Secretary of Defense Arthur Sylvester, one of Kennedy's most trusted aides, commented publicly, "The U.S. government not only has the right but has the obligation to lie if it means the prevention of an atomic war." While Sylvester caught some flak from the press, Kennedy was quick to back up Sylvester on his comments. When Kennedy was killed, his advisors instantly became Johnson's advisors, and I am sure Sylvester's public sentiments were shared by his colleagues.

In the end, it is easy to see how the Warren Commission drew its conclusion that Oswald had killed the president as a "lone assassin." It is also easy now to understand what Warren meant when he said that the full truth of the assassination would not be released for another generation. I suppose the Commission figured that with the passage of thirty to forty years, time would heal the wounds and allow cooler heads to prevail.

The cover-up was not completely confined to government officials; it also involved some of the most powerful, respected media figures in America. Late in his presidential term, during an interview with Walter Cronkite, Johnson made some inadvertent comments implying that the Cubans had prior knowledge of Oswald's assassination plans. Immediately after the interview, Cronkite complied with Johnson's top aides' entreaties to delete those comments. Also in early 1964, Isaac Don Levine, an expert on the KGB's assassination of Trotsky, conducted an in-depth interview with Marina Oswald. His long article was all set to run in *Life* magazine when Warren Commission member John J. McCloy caught wind of the fact that Levine was going to all but accuse Marina Oswald of being a KGB agent. During one of the Commission's executive sessions, McCloy declared that Levine's article "could blow the lid off." Allen Dulles, however, calmly interjected that he was a good friend of *Life*'s publisher, Henry Luce, and assured everyone he would get the story spiked. In his memoirs, Levine mentions a "no notes, off-the-record" talk with Dulles, after which the story was indeed spiked.

From an insider's point-of-view, the most intriguing piece of suppressed Warren Commission evidence is Secret Service Supervisor

Robert Bouck's list of eighteen derogatory items that collectively should have placed Oswald on the Secret Service's watch list and effectively prevented the assassination. But, as Bouck explained, no one agency had all of these items — they were spread across the FBI, CIA, Secret Service, State Department, and Navy Intelligence — and therefore it is understandable that Oswald had not been placed on this list prior to Kennedy's visit to Dallas. I have never seen this list, but having appraised all the evidence, and having become intimately familiar with the Secret Service's criteria, it is possible to surmise its general contents. Here is my educated guess:

1. Oswald's two court-martials in the Marines, once for assaulting a non-commissioned officer and another for possession of an illegal pistol.
2. Oswald's contacts with a female KGB intermediary in Japan.
3. Oswald's knowledge of the U-2 spy plane while stationed in Japan, and his possible divulging of same to the Soviets.
4. Oswald's reported contacts with Cuban officers in California.
5. Oswald's defection to the Soviet Union with the aid of the KGB.
6. The KGB's "hospitalization" and interrogation of Oswald in Moscow.
7. Oswald's marriage to Marina in light of the Mintkenbaugh information.
8. Oswald's subscription to the *Daily Worker.*
9. The CIA's use of the Mafia to try to kill Castro, and Oswald's possible awareness of this.
10. Oswald's awareness of U.S. attempts to overthrow Castro.
11. Oswald's trip to Mexico City.
12. Oswald's contact with Kostikov, the KGB assassination expert.
13. Oswald's contact with KGB agents Yatskov (Kostikov's boss) and Obeytov.
14. Oswald's contact with Calderon and other Cuban intelligence officers.
15. Oswald's contact with Gerasimov, the confirmed Soviet paymaster of deep-cover spies in the United States.
16. Kostikov's contact with the Soviet Embassy in Washington, possibly with Gerasimov, about Oswald.
17. The Cubans granting a transit visa to Oswald *prior* to the assassination.

18. Oswald's intimate knowledge about the Mexico City Cuban consulate's removal.

In January 1964, Yuriy Nosenko, a KGB captain, defected to the United States. One of the first things he said was that he knew for a fact Oswald was not in any way connected to the KGB. There were, however, several serious flaws and inconsistencies in Nosenko's story. First, the timing of his defection seemed too convenient. Second, Nosenko told the FBI that he held the rank of lieutenant colonel in the KGB, while in fact he was only a captain. Third, he claimed that he had access to Oswald's KGB file, and from reading it, knew that the KGB had only monitored Oswald, not recruited him. This was a factual impossibility: Nosenko was from Second Chief Directorate (the SCD), the internal security, or counter-intelligence, arm of the KGB. It was the First Chief Directorate (FCD) of the KGB, the external arm, that recruited and used foreigners as spies. The SCD was equivalent to the FBI, the FCD to the CIA; the SCD and FCD operated separately, and we knew the FCD didn't show its files to the SCD. When Nosenko told us that he knew for a fact that Oswald had never been developed as a KGB agent, it was equivalent to an FBI agent telling the Soviets he knew who the CIA used as foreign spies. Fact is, we don't.

The conclusive bit of evidence needed to undermine Nosenko's claims has only recently come to light. Nosenko told the FBI and the CIA that Oswald had never been interviewed by the KGB; in the spirit of glasnost, the Russian government has now acknowledged that the KGB had in fact done so. This was the first piece of evidence that did not simply attack Nosenko's trustworthiness as a source, but actually contradicted a vital piece of the information he presented. Nosenko fed us a story that was just too good to be true. He had to be a plant.

The FBI men who bought Nosenko's story were the same ones who didn't take the Oswald information seriously prior to the assassination. To buy into Nosenko's story justified their failure to catch the significance of Oswald's Mexico City visit, his contact with KGB paymaster Gerasimov, and the parallels to James Mintkenbaugh's proposal from the KGB to take back to America a young Soviet wife. Bobby Kennedy, who authorized Nosenko's confinement and interrogation, became one of Nosenko's biggest skeptics.

That leaves us with only two conclusions. First, there is dramatic, but insufficient, evidence that would directly implicate the Soviets or Cubans in the president's death. Second, it is abundantly clear why Oswald killed the president. Whether or not he was a KGB sleeper agent, Oswald was without question a Communist and Castro loyalist. He saw Kennedy's killing as a means to demonstrate his ideological commitment. We know, too, that Oswald, a basically unstable, barely literate man (read his letters and notes), had an almost insane desire to be "in the news." Ironically, if he had succeeded in assassinating General Edwin Walker, chances are that: 1) he would have been caught, and 2) that act would have satisfied his thirst for fame and notoriety. Oswald's motives were as old as mankind's political systems. Men have proven time and again that they are willing to kill for their own political beliefs and purposes. Such was the case with Oswald.

19

An afternoon in November 1977

TIME: 3:30 P.M.

I was sitting at my desk going over one of my cases when my supervisor, Jim Graham, interrupted to tell me to drop everything, go home, and start packing — the House Select Committee on Assassinations in Washington wanted to me to testify first thing the next morning. I had been expecting to be called for a while, but in order to get there on time, I knew I would have to catch a red-eye to Washington that night. If I were lucky, that might get me into a hotel bed by midnight.

I immediately called my old Washington attorney, Jack Bray, and told him about the committee's extraordinarily short notice. I asked him if he would be able to represent me at tomorrow morning's hearing; not surprisingly, he said it was impossible for him to break his previously scheduled matters. Bray then put me on hold to check with his associate, Frank Lilly, who came on the line and told me the earliest he would be available would be next week. I told Bray and Lilly that I refused to testify tomorrow without counsel. Lilly promised to call the committee immediately to reschedule my appearance and explain my position on legal counsel.

I had been following the developments of the House Select Committee on Assassinations in the news, and I could see how seriously flawed its approach was. The way the committee was set up and operating, it was readily apparent that it had begun its investigation with the conviction that the Mafia had been behind Kennedy's death. The Soviet and Cuban connections, perhaps by design, since we were still in the throes of the cold war — or perhaps due to simple ignorance — would have no place in this committee's investigation.

The history of the House Select Committee on Assassinations shows how far things had gone astray from the beginning. Following the Church Committee's final report on the assassination in June 1976, the Senate voted to make it a full-fledged, permanent committee, rechristening it the Senate Intelligence Committee. Because Senator Church was also the chairman of the Foreign Relations Committee, he was forced to give up his chairmanship of the Intelligence Committee, passing it on to Senator Dan Inouye of Hawaii. One of the Inouye's first acts as chairman was to repudiate Senator Church's "rogue elephant" comment about the CIA, a not-so-veiled suggestion that the CIA routinely acted on its own initiative and was out of control. Inouye, who was trying to soothe the CIA's ruffled feathers, announced that he could find no evidence that the CIA had ever acted without a presidential order. Inouye and the Intelligence Committee ultimately decided to drop plans to follow up on the Church Committee's final report, effectively eliminating the committee's role in the investigation of the Kennedy assassination.

This withdrawal prompted Representative Henry Gonzalez of Texas to initiate the formation of a House committee to look into the assassination. Gonzalez had been a part of the presidential motorcade on November 22, 1963. In the years following, Gonzalez had been the target of right-wing extremists and had developed a bias that one of these extremists had killed Kennedy. In late 1976, Gonzalez was able to get the House Select Committee on Assassinations formed, with himself as chairman. Gonzalez selected as his chief-of-staff a tough Pennsylvania prosecutor, Richard Sprague, who exerted a take-charge attitude, immediately declaring his intention to use wiretaps, polygraphs, and a get-tough attitude with the FBI and CIA. Soon Gonzalez and Sprague were fighting over who was really in charge. Amid this bickering, Congress voted to cut off the funding for the House Select Committee on Assassinations.

Largely controlling the spigot of funds was the chairman of the House Rules Committee, Representative Dick Bolling of the Kansas City, Missouri, area. Bolling had a branch office in the U.S. Courthouse in downtown Kansas City, the same building that housed the Kansas City FBI. Assuming that when and if the House Select Committee on Assassinations got off the ground I would be called to testify, I went and talked with one of Bolling's senior aides in the courthouse office. When I asked him about the committee's status, Bolling's aide told me that per the direct request of Ethel Kennedy, Bobby Kennedy's widow and a close friend of Bolling's, Bolling was holding up funding for House Select Committee on Assassinations indefinitely.

But just months later, Bolling reversed himself when the Congressional Black Caucus demanded that the House Select Committee on Assassinations get its funding so it could investigate the assassination of Martin Luther King, Jr. This caucus was curious if any group had provided support to James Earl Ray.

Now that the House Select Committee on Assassinations was fully funded and charged with the dual mission of looking into both the Kennedy and King deaths, a new chairman was appointed. Both Representative Gonzalez and Sprague were ejected, and Representative Louis Stokes of Ohio was appointed chair. Stokes, acting as overall chairman, also took specific oversight of the King investigation and let Representative Richardson Pryor of North Carolina oversee the Kennedy investigation.

The House Select Committee on Assassinations chose Professor Robert Blakey of Cornell University Law School to be the top aide on both investigations. Blakey had previously served in the Kennedy Justice Department as an organized crime–Mafia attorney. Gary Cornwell, another Kennedy Justice Department organized crime–Mafia attorney, became Blakey's first assistant counsel on the Kennedy investigation. Cornwell had worked a stint for the Justice Department in Kansas City on the Organized Crime Strike Force. Blakey stocked the Kennedy assassination staff full of organized crime–Mafia experts. There were no experts on the staff from the field of Soviet and Cuban espionage and intelligence; the only link to Castro was through a few staffers who were virulently suspicious of Cuban exiles. It was clear Blakey was convinced from the outset that the Mafia had killed Kennedy, and his choice of staff left no hope that the committee would explore any other angles, except perhaps a joint venture by the Mafia and the Cuban exiles. Apparently the theory was that the Cuban exiles were so furious with Kennedy because of the Bay of Pigs fiasco, they decided to kill him. The fact that there was no evidence to support these theories didn't seem to bother the House committee in the least. Even before the committee had called its first witness, Blakey negotiated with a major publishing house to publish his book on the committee's investigation and findings. Blakey was now bound by a lucrative contract to prove that the Mafia had killed Kennedy. Objectivity had been dismissed immediately, and it was already apparent that both Blakey's book deal and his professional pride would be serious obstacles on the way to the truth, especially if Blakey discovered that the Mafia had no role in Kennedy's death.

It wasn't until the fall of 1977 that the House Select Committee on Assassinations finally sorted things out and got down to the business at hand. When I read about the different witnesses being called to Washington to testify, I figured I would be called soon.

I was instructed by the Bureau that my only liaison with the committee was the ASAC in the Kansas City office, Jack Lawn. Lawn had been transferred to Kansas City shortly after the Oswald note destruction furor in 1975. Before coming to Kansas City, he had been one of FBI Associate Director Jim Adams's protégés in Washington and had been heavily involved in Adams's investigation of the note destruction. I figured Adams had sent Lawn down to Kansas City to keep an eye on me. As a practical matter, any information I had regarding the Kennedy assassination had to first go through Lawn. So as soon as the first witnesses were called, I went to Lawn to ask him when I would be called to testify before the House Select Committee on Assassinations.

A generally friendly and congenial New York Irishman, Lawn kept putting me off. He said he'd let me know when something came up concerning me. Now, without even twenty-four hours' notice, Graham, not Lawn, was sending me to Washington.

Over the years quite a few authors and commentators have developed their own theories on Kennedy's death, and more than a few people have accused me of some rather outrageous things. Among the less serious accusations was that Oswald was my informant, and that I had tried to cover up this embarrassing fact. Some of the weightier accusations were that I was directly involved in killing President Kennedy, as a facilitator or handler of Lee Oswald. With the House Select Committee on Assassinations on the (false) scent of Mafia issues, I couldn't trust them. When an investigation was this misguided, I feared it might come up with its own outrageous claims about me. Therefore there was no chance I was going to testify without preparation and legal representation.

When Bray and Lilly told me they couldn't clear their calendars to assist me the next day, I asked Lilly to call the House Select Committee on Assassinations and convey my regrets. I wouldn't be able to testify under these circumstances. I told Lilly to reschedule me for the next week when it was convenient for both of us.

Jim Graham was astounded that I was disobeying the committee's instructions — he found it "audacious." Cornwell and the committee staff were furious with me for refusing to fly to Washington at once; Cornwell threatened to treat me as a hostile witness. When I heard that, I laughed. But they caved in and agreed to reschedule me.

While Lilly was in touch with the committee, I shot off an urgent teletype to FBI headquarters telling them that I would not be coming to Washington as instructed. I explained I had not been given adequate notice, and therefore my attorneys were not available. I told headquarters that unless they told me otherwise, I would come to Washington the next week, when it was convenient for my attorneys and me. Officially, headquarters never responded to my teletype, so I took that as an affirmation to delay my trip to Washington until the following week. Unofficially, I heard that everyone at headquarters was irate.

I learned later that shortly before my arrival in Washington, FBI headquarters showed Cornwell part of my highly classified testimony before the Senate's Church Committee. By so doing, the FBI violated all kinds of national security rules, but headquarters was trying to calm Cornwell and show him I was, indeed, a very knowledgeable witness on all aspects of the Kennedy assassination.

The next week, November 1977
TIME: 9:00 A.M.

Lilly and I were escorted to the conference room where I would have a pre-testimony briefing with Cornwell and other members of the committee staff. This was standard operating procedure with congressional committees, which wanted to know ahead of time what the witness would report so that there would be no — or at least few — surprises.

Lilly and I took our seats on one side of the long wood-veneered table in the rather bland-looking conference room. Cornwell took a chair opposite me. Despite the previous week's altercation, and the fact that I knew Cornwell and Blakey were heading down the wrong path with their Mafia suspicions, I was impressed by Gary Cornwell. He was sharp and articulate, and when it came to organized crime issues he knew his stuff. I knew he had been a big asset at Justice to the Organized Crime Strike Force.

So, big cigar clenched in his teeth, Cornwell absently ran his hand through his sandy-colored hair and began to question me. He started off with the usual introductory questions, such as how long had I been in the FBI, when did I get the Oswald assignment, etc. I was pleasantly surprised by Cornwell's polite demeanor. He told me that FBI headquarters had let him read my testimony from the Church subcommittee and that he had been very impressed with the breadth of my knowledge.

Then, as I had suspected it would, Cornwell's questioning took an inevitable turn down the Mafia path. Cornwell wanted to know about some Mafia matters in New Orleans and whether Lee Oswald had any connections with any or all of them. At first I was polite and told Cornwell that while I did not work the Oswald case in New Orleans, I was privy to all the information developed both before and after the assassination involving Oswald's time in New Orleans. I assured Cornwell that there was not even a remote connection between any Mafia group and Oswald.

But Cornwell persisted. Finally, when Cornwell asked me if I knew of any evidence of a conspiracy between Oswald and the New Orleans Mafia to kill Kennedy, I lost my cool: "That's pure rubbish! If there had been a conspiracy, and I'm not saying there was, it took place in Mexico City, not in New Orleans."

A female staffer sitting just down the table from Cornwell let out a gasp. Cornwell, taken aback, chomped down on his cigar. With everyone at the table frozen in surprise, I decided to press on. I began reciting all the evidence I knew regarding the Soviet and Cuban angles. I explained that Oswald had gone down to Mexico City where he had said he was going to kill Kennedy. I talked about Oswald's clandestine meeting with the KGB hitman Kostikov and I explained how Oswald had maintained contact with Gerasimov in Washington, adding that Gerasimov had been identified as the KGB's man in charge of Soviet spies and sleeper agents.

Five minutes later, having finished my monologue, I looked around the table and could see the young staffers' heads spinning. Although Cornwell had seen my Senate testimony and was at least aware of this evidence, none of the staffers had a clue about anything I had just said. They were all organized crime experts; not one of them had any expertise in espionage or intelligence work.

Cornwell regained his composure and tried to switch gears on me. His face broadcast just how loaded his next question would be. "Okay, Mr. Hosty. Tell us, who authorized the wiretap on Marina Oswald in February and March of 1964?" Cornwell leaned forward with his pointed question, but couldn't resist turning his head to the staffer next to him, smiling at his clever trap, since he fully expected me to tell him that J. Edgar Hoover and the FBI had ordered it.

Instead I began to softly chuckle, imagining my face broadening into a big Cheshire cat grin, which it surely did to the best of its ability. Cornwell turned to look at me, his face distressed, as I responded. "Well, Mr. Cornwell, I'm sorry to disappoint you, but Earl Warren and the Warren Commission ordered that wiretap. And furthermore, it was against the FBI's advice."

"What! Earl Warren ordered it! I don't believe that." Cornwell was half out of his chair, his face red with indignation.

"I sure as hell am right, and the FBI has it in writing!" I shot back. If these people weren't interested in the truth, I might as well enjoy myself at the expense of their ignorance.

By now Cornwell had lost his composure — and his interview. He stood up sharply and announced, "All right, that's it, Mr. Hosty, we are stopping this interview. I'm taking you down to Mr. Blakey's office and I want you to tell him what you just told me."

"Fine, let's go."

With that Lilly gathered up his files, and he and I followed Cornwell out of the conference room and down the hall to Blakey's office. Cornwell rapped on the door and then, without waiting for a reply, opened it. After belatedly asking if he could interrupt for just a moment, Cornwell waved Lilly and me into Blakey's spartan little office. Seated behind his desk, Blakey furrowed his thick, dark eyebrows, and in his professorlike demeanor, asked Cornwell what this was all about. Cornwell told me to repeat what I said about the wiretap on Marina Oswald. After I finished, Blakey leaned forward in his chair, his forehead creased in disbelief.

"But that can't be true," Blakey reflected with the patience of a scholar when faced with the unexpected. "Earl Warren couldn't have done that, because when I worked organized crime cases he always gave us such a hard time on our use of wiretaps."

"Well, Warren and the Commission authorized it this time," I replied.

"But why?" Blakey asked.

"Obviously the Warren Commission didn't believe Marina was telling them the full truth," I reasoned.

Blakey leaned back in his chair and considered me for a moment. He rubbed his chin, as if in deep thought. After a moment, he sat up straight, with the confidence of a man who had just solved a dilemma. He said, in carefully measured words, "Mr. Cornwell, we aren't ready for Mr. Hosty to testify yet. Mr. Hosty, we need to check into what you've reported, and once we have finished our research we'll recall you to testify." He was clearly frustrated with me, the monkey wrench in their Mafia-driven investigation.

The next day, I took my seat in the committee's hearing room with Lilly at my side. Today's hearing was closed to the public. When Representative Pryor asked Cornwell to swear me in to testify, Cornwell stood and announced that the staff was not ready to receive my testimony since new information had come up. Pryor gave Cornwell the obligatory admonishment for not being ready, then instructed me that I was still under subpoena and would be recalled at some future date.

Immediately after I left the hearing room, the testimony of two of my old Dallas FBI buddies, Bob Gemberling and John Kesler, was taken in a closed hearing before the committee. Later I learned that I was supposed to have been lumped in with them. The reason the committee called Gemberling and Kesler had nothing to do with the Kennedy assassination; the committee only wanted details of some rather embarrassing omissions on the FBI's part.

Back on November 22, 1963, the Dallas police had searched Oswald's rooming house and discovered, among other things, Oswald's little black address book. It was in this book that Oswald had written my name, office phone number, Bureau auto license tag number, and the date I first visited Marina Oswald and Ruth Paine. After Warren DeBrueys and I had cataloged it, Gemberling and Kesler were given the task of recording each of the entries in Oswald's address book. When they saw the entry about me, they intentionally omitted it from their report.

Now the House Select Committee on Assassinations wanted to know what the meaning was behind all of this. On the surface, I am sure their action looked sinister, as if there had been some dark purpose behind the omission. But Gemberling and Kesler said they were interested only in possible leads and knew the entry regarding me was not a lead. Because of this, they considered it unnecessary to include it in their report.

Kesler added one other point. He said he felt sorry for me, because he knew the entry in Oswald's book would be embarrassing to me. Kesler had simply been trying to save me from Hoover's wrath, nothing more. I appreciated Kesler's show of mercy, but in hindsight, he would have done me a greater favor by including my entry in the first place. The irony of all this was that Kesler was later appointed to the FBI's Office of Professional Responsibility, or "Goon Squad," which investigated agent misconduct.

It was abundantly clear to me that this committee was seriously misguided. They had their minds made up, and above all didn't want to be confused with the facts.

Wednesday, August 23, 1978

TIME: 10:30 A.M.

I had returned to Kansas City and impatiently waited ten months for the committee to recall me. It never did. Earlier in the month, I had read in the newspaper that the committee was about to wind down witness testimonies. Today, with ASAC Jack Lawn on vacation, I decided to take matters into my own hands. I called the committee. When I was placed on hold while the clerk on the end of the line searched for a staffer, I mulled things over.

When I returned from my briefing with Cornwell and company, Jack Lawn told me the entire staff investigating Kennedy's assassination wanted to read my classified Church subcommittee testimony. The Senate Intelligence Committee wouldn't let the House staffers read it because none of them had security clearance; when background checks were done, only five staffers were cleared to read my testimony.

In the testimony before the Church subcommittee, I had explained how many of the answers to the Soviet and Cuban angles could be found in the CIA's files. When the eligible House staffers read this, they went to the CIA asking for this information. I have learned that the CIA showed the House staffers only what the CIA wanted to show them. Furthermore, because the House staffers were all organized crime experts, they had no background in deciphering what they were being shown by the CIA.

In response to my testimony, the House committee initiated a wholly inadequate and misguided review of the Cuban connections. They interviewed Fidel Castro and several other Cuban officials about their contacts with Oswald. But many of the staffers conducting these interviews were actually Castro apologists: they felt that, while Castro was a Communist, considering all the great things he had done for his people, he wasn't such a bad guy once you got to know him.

Yeah, right. And where were you during the Cuban Missile Crisis?

The Cubans wouldn't admit to anything. But what could you expect? The House staffers interviewed the CIA's AMLASH source, Rolando Cubela, while he was behind bars in a Cuban jail cell, his Cuban jailers looking over his shoulder. When a staffer asked Cubela if it was true that he had had agreed to overthrow Castro for the CIA before the assassination, of course Cubela denied it. One of the House staffers present told me this years later, and when I responded that that was what I would have expected Cubela to say in front of his jailers, the staffer shook his head, and explained, "No, you don't understand, Cubela was very sincere when he denied it."

One House staffer wrote a report concluding that an impostor had contacted the Soviet and Cuban embassies in Mexico City posing as Oswald, in an effort to frame the real Oswald. When he showed his report to Blakey, Blakey took one look at it and reportedly asked the staffer if he also believed in the tooth fairy. Blakey promptly spiked the report.

The committee also reviewed the FBI's SOLO source (the Childs brothers) and the information they provided about their meeting with Castro. Unbelievably, the committee concluded that even though SOLO source had proved reliable in every other instance over their twenty-year relationship with the FBI and was one of the FBI's best intelligence sources ever, SOLO source was not reliable in this case. A year or so later, in his book *Plot to Kill the President,* Blakey said that he personally believed SOLO source, but that the congressmen did not.

One possible reason the committee refused to believe SOLO source was that it probably realized that if it confirmed SOLO source's information, it would be tantamount to declaring war on Cuba. If this congressional committee acknowledged that Castro and the Cuban officials knew, *ahead of time,* Oswald's intentions, and if it ever came out that the Cubans actually encouraged Oswald to do it, Congress would have no choice but to go to war with Cuba.

Just as President Johnson wasn't prepared to risk being forced into war in 1963, Congress wasn't ready in 1978. Among the reasons: the Soviet military was still enmeshed in Cuba with the Cuban military.

I suppose it was okay for Blakey to conclude as much, for he was not a member of Congress. But when I read that, I also asked myself, if Blakey believes that Oswald offered to kill Kennedy for the Cubans in Mexico City in September of 1963, why then did he still tenaciously cling to his unfounded theory that it was the Mafia who killed Kennedy?

After I had been waiting on hold for several minutes, a young staffer named Thomas Genzman came on the line and asked what he could do for me. I identified myself and asked when the committee intended to recall me.

Caught off guard, he fumbled around before finally telling me he was a little confused, but to be on the safe side I had better come to Washington at once.

I made arrangements with Frank Lilly to accompany me to Capitol Hill. Then on August 25, I caught a flight to D.C. When I arrived, I decided to stop by FBI headquarters — it was always a good idea to check in with the Bureau. I found the FBI's liaison office to the House committee. When I walked in, the FBI supervisors were floored. I was the last person they were expecting to see. They demanded to know what I was doing there.

I told them I had been recalled by the House committee to testify. The Bureau didn't know what to do, so I decided to call Lilly and see if he was ready. Lilly broke the news: he had just gotten off the phone with a senior staffer on the committee, he said, and apparently Genzman had made a mistake. I was not to be recalled. Ever. The committee staff had read my Church subcommittee testimony and did not want to hear from me.

As a compromise, the House committee decided to let Genzman take a statement from me. When I was first called by this committee, I was interviewed by Cornwell, the first assistant counsel, in a large conference room, around a large table surrounded by several staffers. Now I was put in a tiny room in front of a small, square table. I was to give my statement to Genzman, a junior staffer. No hearing room, no congressman, no public record. Then Genzman informed me that, even though he was taking what was called a staff deposition, my statement would never be entered into the official record, and furthermore, no congressmen would ever read it. For all practical purposes, my statement was to be treated as if it never existed.

Although I realized this was all an exercise in futility, I decided to go ahead and give the statement. I'd do my part, and if the committee chose to ignore my testimony that was its call.

Meanwhile the committee plowed ahead, calling a second group of expert witnesses — the first group had failed — to verify the presence of a second gunman on the grassy knoll and another group of witnesses who explained how the Mafia had hired Oswald and/or this second gunman to kill Kennedy.

Friday, September 8, 1978

TIME: 6:00 P.M.

My daughter Cathy told me I had a phone call from a Dallas reporter. Now what?

"Jim Hosty," I said into the phone, in as neutral a tone as I could muster.

"This is Earl Golz of the *Dallas Morning News*," the caller said. "I've been following the House Select Committee on Assassinations hearings, and I notice you haven't been called yet. I just wanted to know when you would be, as I see the last of the public testimony is about to begin."

I knew of Golz — he was a real assassination buff. He had previously called me about some crazy assassination theory, and fortunately, I had been able to persuade him he was on the wrong track. I really didn't want to talk with Golz again, but decided I probably should.

"The committee isn't going to call me," I explained. "If they are going to contain their investigation like the Church Committee and the Warren Commission, then they don't want me up there."

Golz asked me to explain.

Despite the Bureau's policy of not speaking to the press, I was sufficiently ticked off — and close enough to retirement age — that I decided "the hell with it" and spoke my piece.

"I was called last November and I started telling them the real story. The committee members apparently didn't want to hear it, so they sent me home. They said, 'We'll get in touch with you.'" I told Golz I thought the committee was trying to avoid me, and explained how I had forced their hand a few weeks ago and how Genzman had taken a meaningless, off-the-record statement from me on August 25.

Golz pressed me for details on what information I had that the committee was seeking to avoid. As I was still in the Bureau, and bound by regulations, I declined further comment.

Two days later, the headline of the *Dallas Morning News* screamed in bold print, MAN'S 'BOMBS' REPORTEDLY INSTILL FEAR. Its first paragraph began, "The FBI agent who monitored Lee Harvey Oswald in Dallas before the assassination of President John F. Kennedy told the *News* the House Select Committee on Assassinations fears he will 'drop bombs' if called to testify publicly."

Golz had badly misquoted me about "dropping bombs," but I wasn't too upset. Maybe it would help rattle the House committee. The committee deserved it.

Wednesday, September 20, 1978

In the end, the committee called only two FBI officials, Jim Malley and Jim Gale. The now-retired Malley had been the senior FBI official in Dallas during the post-assassination investigation, and the committee asked him to testify about these matters. Gale, also retired, the agent who conducted an inspection division investigation on how the FBI agents in the field had performed prior to the assassination, was called to testify about all the pre-assassination investigative issues.

Their hearings were going to be broadcast live on National Public Radio. Just a month or so away from retiring, and having plenty of leave left, I decided to take the day off and hole up in the basement with my little clock radio. While the kids were at school and Janet was at work, I had a nice, quiet house in which to listen.

At the appointed hour, Malley and Gale were sworn in and run through the routine questioning by a young staffer. From the sound of them, both Malley and Gale had turned into cranky old men. They both repeatedly berated the young staffers questioning them, at times practically shouting at them. One of Malley's favorite phrases of the day was, "Now that's a stupid question." The chairman finally had to admonish him to behave himself.

Nevertheless, it was Gale's testimony that proved the more interesting. The committee was questioning him about how Oswald had seemingly slipped through the FBI's net and killed the president. Gale said that even if all the FBI field agents had done everything that Gale had in hindsight wished they had done, the assassination still could not have been prevented. For the first time in all these years, Gale had finally admitted that there was nothing I, or anyone else, could have done to prevent Kennedy's assassination.

When the House Select Committee on Assassinations finished its report, of the twelve members on the committee, only seven would sign it, a bare majority. Five other congressman refused to sign, and two of them filed minority reports. After two years of work and six and a half million taxpayers' dollars, the House Select Committee on Assassinations in the end did a pretty good imitation of the Warren Report: the conclusion then and now was that Oswald killed the president. But there was a new twist.

At the tail end of its investigation in the fall of 1978, the staff called a few last-minute witnesses to the stand. A Dallas policeman who had been in close proximity to Kennedy's car when the fatal shots were fired reluctantly testified that he had left the microphone on his motorcycle open. The committee discovered a tape from the archives of the Dallas police dispatcher that they believed included a recording of the fatal shots on the officer's open microphone. A committee-appointed audio expert concluded with "95 percent" certainty that, based on this tape, a second gunman had fired one shot from the grassy knoll. The committee warmly embraced this opinion, and its final report stated that Oswald and a second gunman simultaneously fired their guns at Kennedy. While two of Oswald's three shots hit their mark, the second gunman's single shot missed.

I found it hard to believe that this phantom gunman was able to set up on the grassy knoll, with dozens of people within yards of him, including amateur filmmaker Abraham Zapruder, fire one shot, and miss the president. Why didn't anyone see him? Why is there no physical evidence to support this — a spent shell casing or the remains of the missed bullet? And if the phantom gunman missed, why didn't his shot hit any of the dozens of bystanders stationed directly across the street and in his line of fire? It didn't take long for a whole slew of other audio experts to annihilate the committee's findings, effectively proving the committee an ill-motivated — and very expensive — waste of time.

20

The technician adjusted the lights in the Fort Myers, Florida, hotel room. He was seeking optimum lighting for his television camera. I straightened my tie and cleared my throat.

Larry Woods of CNN was busy with some last-minute note scribbling. Both of us were seated in the two customary chairs in front of the curtained window found in any hotel room in America. The cameraman was right in front of us, with two cameras set up. One was angled so it was facing me, the other was set up facing Woods.

CNN was interviewing me for a special called, "Thirty Years Later: Reflections of the FBI." It was set to air on November 22, as a thirtieth-anniversary special on the president's assassination. CNN's chief of staff, Tom Johnson, had been the one to orchestrate this interview and special program. This was the same Tom Johnson who wrote the 1975 *Dallas Times Herald* article that portrayed me as a renegade agent who destroyed the Oswald note without any supervisor's knowledge. Apparently Johnson had subsequently figured out that Shanklin had duped him.

For this program, Woods interviewed two other FBI men: Hoover's assistant director of public relations and later his number-three man, Cartha DeLoach, and my fellow Dallas agent, Vince Drain. CNN wanted DeLoach, Drain, and me to tell it like it was, no holds barred. Johnson and Woods were trying to let the nation understand how things looked from the FBI's perspective.

One startling fact came out. When Larry Woods asked former Deputy Associate Director DeLoach if Hoover knew about the note from Oswald to Hosty, he promptly answered, "Yes, he did." He then quickly added, "After the fact, that is."

So Hoover did know. I was shocked. I always thought the note was ordered destroyed to keep Hoover from finding out about it and "blowing up."

Later I called DeLoach and asked him what he meant. He told me when he was promoted to number-three man in the FBI after Belmont retired in early 1965, he reviewed Belmont's files and saw a memo from Hoover to Belmont. Hoover had heard Oswald had visited the Dallas office of the FBI and wanted Belmont to check it out. De-Loach said Belmont's file disclosed no reply, which indicated that it had been an oral reply only.

I can only speculate that Hoover may have read Marina Oswald's and Ruth Paine's Warren Commission testimony, in which they told of Oswald's visits to the Dallas office shortly before the assassination.

Another point of conjecture is this: If DeLoach knew "after the fact" about my destruction of the Oswald note, when he saw the Hoover memo, did he tell President Johnson? DeLoach was close to Johnson. He was in line to be the next FBI director. My guess is that he would not take a chance and would protect himself by telling Johnson.

When President Kennedy was gunned down on the streets of downtown Dallas, I was thirty-nine years old. As I neared my seventieth birthday, I found myself still choking up when I thought about November 22, 1963.

After the House Select Committee on Assassinations debacle, I decided I had had enough. The mandatory retirement age of fifty-five was upon me. So on January 14, 1979, on my own terms, I finally stepped down from the Bureau. All things considered, my 27-year career with the FBI had been a good one.

After I was transferred to Kansas City, I spent three years working criminal cases. In this capacity, I twice found myself in highly tense situations with bullets whizzing over my head. In one of these, in the summer of 1966, I was part of a joint police-FBI effort to arrest a ring of bank robbers in Kansas City. After they fled the bank, one of the robbers had been cornered in an apartment complex — with dozens of innocent bystanders trapped in the building with the fugitive. The police and FBI surrounded the building, and because the criminal had opened fire from within the building, many of the police officers panicked and began returning fire. An already serious problem had now just gotten worse. We could hear the screams of panic from the innocents still trapped in the building. Along with several other agents, I crawled up to the building, bullets flying overhead, to evacuate these people. Sweat poring down my face, I slammed my body up tight against the building's wall. Only then could I distinctly hear a baby's wailing. About six feet down from me along the wall was an open window. Inching my way down to the window, I quickly peeked in. Seeing only a terrified young mother clutching her little baby girl and no bad guy, I hurled myself inside. I hit the floor with a thud. Within a second, I was at her side. She began sobbing uncontrollably when I placed my hand on her shoulder. Though the gunfire erupting all around us was deafening, I still didn't know the exact position of the fugitive, so I hoarsely whispered to the young mother to get on the ground and crawl with me back to the window. Once we got to this open window, I took a quick peek while holding up my FBI badge as high as I dared. I didn't want any cops to think I was the criminal trying to make a break for freedom. Then I helped boost the young woman, who was still clutching her baby, out the window. I hurriedly followed, and the three of us hastily scurried to safety. Later, after a state trooper had been killed and the fugitive had been wounded and apprehended, I walked back through the room where I had found the young mother. The room and baby crib were riddled with bullet holes.

I am not telling this story to cite my own heroism, but get to its twisted ending. Hoover gave letters of commendation and pay bonuses to my fellow agents for their similar actions, yet refused to extend the same to me. I was still in the Hoover doghouse.

It's funny, but in a way Hoover's irrational behavior actually helped pull all of us field agents closer together. As soon as I retired, I really did miss my fellow agents. They were a bunch of hardworking, honest men, trying to do the right thing. We stuck together and helped one another out in order to survive. I considered it an honor to have had the opportunity to work with those men.

Despite these positive feelings, I did retire with two pieces of business still unresolved: Hoover's second disciplinary action against me based upon the Warren report's criticism — which left many with the impression that I had somehow been negligent regarding President Kennedy's death — and the changed answers attributed to me in the Bureau's internal investigation following the assassination.

Both FBI Director Clarence Kelley and his successor, William Webster ruled that I was not to be considered, in any fashion, responsible for the president's death. Both directors recognized the fact that Lee Oswald had only been considered a possible espionage risk, but in no measure a risk to the president. They also recognized that I had not been provided with full and accurate information regarding Oswald's Mexico City trip and his contact with KGB assassination expert Kostikov.

On the issue of Hoover's disciplinary action against me, Webster addressed those concerns to me in an October 25, 1979 letter issued after my retirement. He wrote, in part:

> While I am unwilling to look behind and interfere with former Director Hoover's discretion in the December 13, 1963 disciplinary action taken against you, I believe that corrective action is both warranted and desirable as to the October 5, 1964 disciplinary action since that action constituted a second punishment for the same basic conduct.
>
> Accordingly, I have determined, as a matter of grace, that you should be compensated for the calculable salary and annual leave benefits you lost as a direct result of the 1964 disciplinary action.
>
> A copy of this letter, which is being made a part of your permanent personnel records at FBI headquarters, will constitute documentation of the corrective action taken by me in this matter.
>
> I wish you well in your retirement years ahead.
>
> Sincerely yours,
>
> William H. Webster, Director

Although the changed-answers issue had been largely ignored, I appreciated Webster's letter, and felt a token of justice had been served. In this, I felt some vindication.

• • • •

More than thirty years afterward, people still ask me if the assassination could have been prevented. The practical answer is no. The CIA, FBI, Secret Service, State Department, and the Navy Intelligence Unit would have needed to cooperate absolutely so that Bouck's eighteen pieces of derogatory information about Oswald could have been compiled, thus initiating the neutralization of Oswald days before Kennedy arrived in Dallas. Bureaucratically speaking, I doubt this sort of cooperation will ever occur.

The net of security surrounding a president will never be absolutely effective. Sadly, it is not that hard to breach the Secret Service's protective bubble around the president and vice president. My wife did it twice without even trying. In the late 1960s, at the height of America's assassination fears following the shootings of Bobby Kennedy and Martin Luther King, my wife got very close to President Nixon and Vice President Hubert Humphrey. Both times she had been just another face in the crowd, excited to get up close to both men. Perfectly innocent acts. But she could have been someone else, someone with a motive — and with a gun: the Secret Service had done nothing to check her or any other person.

There is also the example of John Hinckley firing a whole series of shots at President Ronald Reagan in a supposedly closed and secure area. But the most telling example involved President Gerald Ford, a member of the Warren Commission who had sharply criticized lapses in presidential protection and sought to offer solutions to these problems. When Ford was president, he barely escaped two assassination attempts. In a crowd, "Squeaky" Fromm came right up to Ford, pointed her pistol at him at point-blank range, and pulled the trigger of her loaded gun. Unbelievably, she did not know to cock the pistol first, and the gun did not fire. The Secret Service pounced on her, but not before she had demonstrated how easily she could have killed the president. In another crowd, Sara Jane Moore was actually able to fire her gun at Ford. Because she was just a little too far away, she missed, hitting an innocent bystander instead. The FBI had warned the Secret Service about both Fromm and Moore. The Secret Service had even interviewed Moore the day before her assassination attempt, but released her as harmless.

Through the years following the assassination, I have yet to meet anyone who is completely satisfied with the Warren report's conclusions. The vast majority of Americans suspect there is much more to the story than the conclusion that Oswald had acted as a "lone nut." The problem, of course, is that the U.S. government has yet to uncork the rest of its evidence. It's high time it did.

For this country to find a satisfactory resolution of this national tragedy, two fundamental questions must be answered: 1) Who exactly killed the president? and 2) Why did he do it? The public must be given full and accurate information on both questions before we can put this painful part of our history to rest.

The first question has been effectively answered. A close, thorough, and honest examination of the available evidence proves beyond a reasonable doubt that Lee Oswald, and Oswald alone, killed President Kennedy. The evidence is all out there in the Warren Commission's findings. Over the years, two books have done a commendable job of explaining this evidence, Gerald Posner's *Case Closed* and David Belin's *You Are the Jury*.

The answer to the second question, *why* Oswald killed Kennedy, has never been satisfactorily answered, certainly not by the Warren Commission. After examining the evidence available to me, I think it is safe to assume, at a minimum, that Oswald killed Kennedy for ideological/political reasons. Perhaps he was trying to impress the Soviets and Cubans. We don't know how the Cubans reacted to Oswald's threat to kill Kennedy, and perhaps we never will. Or perhaps we will when Castro is dead.

I am frequently confronted with all types of wild assassination theories expounded by the seemingly endless line of buffs and pundits. In almost every case, I find that they have conducted their "investigations" ass-backward. The fundamental rule in conducting any investigation is that you must always start from the beginning and work your case forward. As you follow the evidence, it will eventually lead you to the suspect. It is only then, at the end of the investigation, that it becomes clear who the guilty party is. But these buffs always start from the end — from their preconceived conviction or theory — and work back to the beginning. They first decide who the guilty party is — the Mafia, right-wing fanatics, the military-industrial complex, the Castro Cubans — and then they go about proving this theory, using only the evidence that supports it. What these people fail to understand is that just because a particular person or group might have a reason to kill Kennedy, that doesn't mean they did.

Politically motivated conspiracy theories are still popular. Immediately after the assassination, the Kremlin put out the story that right-wing extremists in America were behind Kennedy's death, not the Communist Oswald. Recent release of top secret information on the Soviets shows that the Soviet Union, Castro, and the American Communists, almost from the day of the assassination, tried to deflect suspicion that the left wing was responsible for the act, and tried to focus on the right wing. Several of the early writers on the subject had clear left-wing leanings and backgrounds, and it would appear that their intent was either to mislead the American public or to steer its thinking away from any possible connection to the left. Looking back from the perspective of today — and taking into account not only those early books but the immensely successful, immensely misleading movie *JFK* — I'd have to conclude that they largely succeeded. Oliver Stone's *JFK* is one of the most outrageous examples of misdirection I have ever seen. I don't doubt for a second that Stone has every reason in the world to be bitter about his Vietnam War experience, and I could appreciate his anger at the U.S. government and the military-industrial complex. But disinformation is a major tool in the espionage wars, and the Cubans and Soviets are masters of it. Stone, on a visit to Cuba to receive an award for one of his films, seems to have swallowed the Cuban version — Jim Garrison's story — hook, line, and sinker. In Stone's theory the pro-Castro Oswald is the innocent patsy. Stone decides that (surprise!) the military-industrial complex killed Kennedy, with the assistance of the CIA, the FBI, and the Dallas police. In fact, Stone says that I played an integral part in the plot. I do hope *JFK* helped Stone exorcise some demons from his Vietnam experience.

In my retirement, Janet and I are quite happy. We ended up making it down to Florida after all. From our new home we now spend our evenings watching the sun set peacefully and gloriously.

As much as the assassination has haunted much of my life, I must say that life has largely treated me kindly. Our nine kids all ended up with college degrees. Three of them have masters', another a doctorate. Our son Dick is now a professional in a social agency working for other people with disabilities. And there are the grandchildren. Lots of them.

It gives Janet and me great pride and joy to see our adult children, their spouses, and their children.

I believe history will be kind to President Johnson, the Warren Commission, the FBI, the CIA, and all the other parties involved in perhaps the greatest cover-up this nation has experienced. The bottom line is that the correct guilty party was identified and this nation's peace was preserved. In 1963, those were the two most important things.

Unfortunately, a consequence of these decisions was the

sacrifice of the U.S. government's credibility. The people know their government has lied to them, held back something momentous regarding the assassination. Even if the cover-up was well intended from an international viewpoint, the fact remains that the people of the United States — We the People — were lied to and betrayed. When a government — any government — makes a willful decision to lie, or obfuscate what the elected leaders know to be the truth, a momentary political objective may have been served. But by the same token, a basic underpinning of the democratic process has been destroyed. Sadly, many Americans today have no faith in anything a governmental official tells them. And that probably includes me.

It is time to disclose the truth, no matter how ugly. America is ready for it. The risks are minimal. It is time for our nation's collective soul to find an inner peace with President Kennedy's tragic assassination.

Back in the Fort Myers hotel room, the CNN camera crew signaled to Woods that they were ready to roll. Woods turned to me and asked if I was ready to "let it all hang out and to tell the truth."

"Absolutely," I said. "Let's do it."

Postscript

In this book, I think I have made it abundantly clear that I believe that Lee Oswald killed President Kennedy. I am convinced Oswald acted alone. I arrive at my conclusions based solely upon the readily available evidence. It's all there for anyone to examine.

What isn't readily available to the public is the highly classified material regarding the Soviets and Cubans. The only issue left unresolved in my mind is whether the Soviets or Cubans were in any way involved in the assassination. This involvement could range from active involvement to tacit encouragement.

While I have already discussed the issues surrounding the Soviets and Cubans, I have not gone into any great detail about the actual evidence of the assassination, but at least two books have done a commendable job reviewing that evidence: David Belin's *You Are the Jury* and Gerald Posner's *Case Closed*. In this book, I simply told my story, how I saw the events unfold from my perspective.

Yet I cannot resist at least a short discussion of the evidence, because time and again I am confronted by people challenging my basic conclusion that Oswald acted alone.

A common objection to the conclusion that Oswald alone shot the president is that there is no way any person could have fired three shots in approximately six seconds. First, the six-second theory derives from the FBI's incorrect conclusions based on the Zapruder film. The Bureau decided that the first shot hit Kennedy; at this point, the clock begins ticking. The FBI then concluded that the second shot hit Governor John Connally, approximately three seconds later. The final shot — still according to the FBI — then hit the president in the head, some six seconds after the first.

What is more likely is that the first shot missed and the second hit Kennedy in the neck and then Connally in the back. Then, six seconds after the second shot, Oswald fired the third shot. Posner put forth an intriguing theory on this point in *Case Closed,* as he may have discovered evidence that the first shot did in fact miss, giving Oswald over nine seconds from the time the first shot was fired to the third. Posner discovered that Zapruder, while holding his camera in his hands, jiggled it about three seconds before conventional wisdom had the first shot being fired. This "jiggle" is consistent with an involuntary muscular reflex of a person filming an event when a gun is fired nearby, something which has been documented and accepted in the scientific community. Also, at the same instant Zapruder jiggled the camera, a little girl who is running in the film stops dead in her tracks, consistent with someone who has just heard a gunshot. Posner's theory is intriguing, and if true, then Oswald did indeed have over nine seconds — more than enough time for a Marine sharpshooter to have fired three shots.

Just as important, many people fail to realize that Oswald had perhaps ten to fifteen seconds to line up his first shot. Once he had it lined up, then he fired. Within the next six (according to the FBI) or nine seconds (according to Posner), Oswald had to fire only *two* more shots, not three. The FBI had an agent recreate this shooting sequence; he accomplished it easily. In short, Oswald had more than enough time to get off all three shots.

People also confront me with the "magic bullet" problem. I am no forensic scientist, but I think I can give a fair summary on why there is no magic to that bullet. Contrary to Oliver Stone's portrayal of the facts, Kennedy and Connally were not sitting in perfect, straight-back postures in a line. Kennedy's seat was slightly higher than Connally's and a few inches off to the right side. When the second shot was fired, the Zapruder film indicates Kennedy was leaning forward, perhaps in reaction to hearing the off-target first shot. Connally is twisting around in his seat to look behind him, also apparently reacting to the first shot. He is holding his hand down on his thigh.

The two men are in this position when the second shot is fired. The bullet goes into the back of Kennedy's neck at an angle and exits at the front through the knot of his tie. The threads of this tie were examined; they were blown outward, consistent with an exit wound. The bullet, still moving rapidly, now begins to tumble in the airspace between Kennedy's neck and Connally's back. This tumbling is consistent with ballistic studies of bullets that enter and then exit without striking any bone, as was the case with Kennedy. The tumbling bullet then enters Connally's upper back sideways, not front or back first. Connally's back wound is oblong, consistent with a sideways entry, not a normal entry wound. The bullet, now traveling through Connally's body, smashes sideways into one of his ribs. Deflected off the bone, the bullet's direction changes slightly and exits Connally's body a little lower, just below the nipple. The bullet, now traveling more slowly because of its impact with the rib and having traversed two bodies, continues its downward path; it has just enough speed to strike Connally's wrist, damaging the wrist bones. The slowed bullet now ricochets off Connally's wrist bone, penetrates his pant leg and barely embeds itself in the flesh of his thigh.

When Connally was placed on a stretcher at Parkland Hospital, his trousers were removed, he was placed on a second stretcher and urgently wheeled into emergency surgery. During the frenzied efforts to save Connally's life, medical personnel did not notice the bullet fall out of Connally's leg and onto the first stretcher. A short time later, a hospital attendant discovered this bullet and gave it to an FBI agent, who gave it to a Secret Service agent.

Despite Oliver Stone's claims, the bullet did not zig and zag; its path is easily understood when carefully examined. Again, it is important to remember that Kennedy was leaning forward and Connally had turned to look behind him.

People also take issue with the bullet's condition, which they describe as pristine. First, one should remember that no two bullets change condition in exactly the same way when fired into an object. Second, the bullet is *not* pristine; it is partially flattened on one side, consistent with the bullet hitting Connally's rib sideways when it was traveling at its highest speed. Prior to that, the bullet had only traveled through soft flesh. After striking the rib, it rapidly began to lose its velocity, so that when it hit its next hard object, Connally's wrist, it was traveling much more slowly, preventing any further damage to the bullet. There is also one inescapable bit of evidence many ignore: the traces of lead recovered from Connally's wrist conclusively match the so-called stretcher bullet. The bullet was copper-jacketed with a lead core. The core was exposed on the rear end only; a small amount of it was squeezed out like toothpaste from a tube and left in Connally's wrist.

People also attack the conclusion that Oswald acted alone by arguing that the final, and fatal, shot to Kennedy's head came from the front, not the rear from where Oswald was shooting. These people say that a second gunman had to have been positioned in front, in the area of the "grassy knoll." The answer to that argument: first, the evidence clearly indicates that the third shot came from the rear; second, there is simply no credible evidence to support the second gunman theory.

In the examination of the president's body, doctors found a small bullet hole in the back of his head. The front right-side of Kennedy's head was blown open. When a bullet enters a body, it leaves a small entry wound. When it exits, it either leaves a similarly small hole or it fragments when it enters the body and blows a bigger hole when it exits. The brutal fact is, Kennedy's brain matter was blown toward the front of the car, and some was recovered on the inside of the front windshield. Bullet fragments were found on the floorboards by the driver of the president's limo; consistent with the exit wound, this bullet apparently fragmented upon hitting Kennedy's skull. When the bullet fragments were recovered it was also discovered that the inside of the front windshield had dents or knicks in it, consistent with high-velocity bullet fragments hitting it. Prior to the assassination, the president's limo had been kept in pristine condition; the windshield had no knicks or dents. Clearly the bullet entered the rear of Kennedy's head and exploded out the front.

Still, people counter with the fact that with the third shot Kennedy's head rocketed backward and to his left. I blame the movies for this misconception, for on the screen people shot from the front are almost always flung backward. In real life, it is just as possible for a person to jerk in the opposite direction, due to the "jet effect." Forensic scientists have long ago discovered that when a person is shot in the back of the head, a jet effect could cause the head to jerk backward. This finding has been documented and recreated on film.

On the second point, that there must have been a second gunman, there is no credible evidence to support this theory. I know various people have come forward over the years, claiming to have *seen* this phantom gunman, but their stories simply do not hold water. In the evidence collected from witnesses who gave statements to officials in 1963 and 1964, of all the people standing in Dealey Plaza, only one described seeing a puff of smoke near the tree line along the grassy knoll at approximately the same time the first shot fired and missed. That's it. Nothing more. Over the years, many conspiracy theorists have taken this "puff" and either extrapolated a second gunman out of it or have distorted the evidence to prove there was a second gunman.

What would cause a puff of smoke? We know one of the three shots missed, and the evidence indicates that it was Oswald's first shot.

At the same time this shot missed, a man standing near the grassy knoll was struck by a high-speed object that grazed his face and caused slight bleeding. A portion of the curb a short distance in front of him was struck by a hard, high-speed object consistent with a bullet. The errant bullet was never found, consistent with a bullet shattering upon impact with a concrete curb. The curb was in the possible line of fire for Oswald's missed shot. It is my theory that the first shot missed the motorcade and hit the curb, causing fragments of both curb and bullet to fly through the air, one of which struck the man and another of which skidded into the dirt under the trees on the grassy knoll, causing a puff of dust.

No one in Dealey Plaza on November 22 ever said they saw a second gunman. If there had been a second gunman on the grassy knoll, he would have been seen. The area is small and close to the street. Zapruder and others would have been less than ten yards from this gunman. Dozens of people, including law enforcement officers, swarmed up to the grassy knoll within seconds of the shots being fired — no doubt confused by the unusual acoustics of Dealey Plaza — in their efforts to find where the shots came from. None of these people saw a second gunman. Furthermore, how could this second gunman leave no trace? There were no spent bullet casings or any other signs that anyone had fired shots from that area. Where did his fired bullets go? A shot from the grassy knoll would have gone smack into a crowd of bystanders waving at Kennedy, yet not one was hit, nor did anyone report hearing, feeling, or seeing any bullets fired in their direction.

People also take issue with the conclusion that Oswald shot the rifle from the sixth floor — where his rifle and his prints, all over a makeshift sniper's nest, were recovered — by pointing out that it would have been impossible for him to get from the sixth to second floor before a Dallas police officer and Roy Truely, the manager of the book depository, saw Oswald in the second-floor lunchroom. I suspect the police officer and Truely misjudged how quickly they got to the second-floor lunchroom. The officer, who was riding his motorcycle in the motorcade, dumped his motorcycle on Elm Street, ran up the stairs to the front door of the depository, identified himself to and briefly conversed with Truely, paused at the elevator, pushed the elevator button, then decided to abandon that effort and run up the flight of stairs to the second floor, all of which in my view had to take at least two minutes — more than enough time for Oswald to run down the stairs from the sixth to second floor. When my fellow agents Ike Lee and Bob Barrett reenacted Oswald's dash from the sixth-floor window to the second-floor lunchroom, each time they did it in less than a minute. There is no mystery to the fact that Oswald fired his rifle from the sixth floor, made his way down to the second-floor lunchroom, then fled the building altogether.

Anyone who has examined the evidence carefully as I have over many years cannot help but come to the conclusion that Oswald was the lone gunman. Most people have come to their conclusions about the assassination from short, partial readings of different theories; very few people have examined all the evidence. When they do, they follow step by step the actions Oswald took prior to the assassination — purchasing the rifle under an assumed name; trying to kill General Edwin Walker in April 1963; going to Mexico in September and October, where he contacted V. V. Kostikov, ostensibly a vice consul at the Soviet Embassy but in reality a high-ranking KGB member in charge of assassinations and sabotage in the Western hemisphere; coming to the Paines' home and retrieving his rifle the day before the assassination and carrying it disguised as curtain rods when he hitched a ride to work on November 22, 1963 — and they follow his post-assassination path to Oak Cliff, where he murdered Officer Tippit in cold blood — an act witnessed by five people — and then, in the movie theater, tried to take a second shot at an officer with the same gun he used to kill Tippit. With all this evidence and more, for the life of me, I don't understand why some people still don't think Oswald did it, or that there was a second gunman.

As I said, the evidence is there for anyone to examine.

Appendix

FD-302 (Rev. 3-3-59)   FEDERAL BUREAU OF INVESTIGATION

Date _____ 11/23/63

1

       LEE HARVEY OSWALD, 1026 North Beckley, Dallas,
Texas, was interviewed by Captain WILL FRITZ of the
Homicide Bureau, Dallas Police Department. Special
Agents JAMES P. HOSTY, JR. and JAMES W. BOOKHOUT were
present during this interview. When the Agents entered
the interview room at 3:15 p.m., Captain FRITZ had been
previously interviewing LEE HARVEY OSWALD for an undetermined
period of time. Both Agents identified themselves to
OSWALD and advised him they were law enforcement officers
and anything he said could be used against him. OSWALD
at this time adopted a violent attitude toward the FBI
and both Agents and made many uncomplimentary remarks
about the FBI. OSWALD requested that Captain FRITZ remove
the cuffs from him, it being noted that OSWALD was hand-
cuffed with his hands behind him. Captain FRITZ had one
of his detectives remove the handcuffs and handcuff
OSWALD with his hands in front of him.

       Captain FRITZ asked OSWALD if he ever owned a rifle
and OSWALD stated that he had observed a MR. TRUELY (phonetic),
a supervisor at the Texas Schoolbook Depository on November
20, 1963, display a rifle to some individuals in his office
on the first floor of the Texas Schoolbook Depository, but
denied ever owning a rifle himself. OSWALD stated that he
had never been in Mexico except to Tijuana on one occasion.
However, he admitted to Captain FRITZ to having resided in
the Soviet Union for three years where he has many friends
and relatives of his wife.

       OSWALD also admitted that he was the secretary
for the Fair Play for Cuba Committee in New Orleans,
Louisiana a few months ago. OSWALD stated that the Fair
Play for Cuba Committee has its headquarters in New York
City. OSWALD admitted to having received an award for
marksmanship while a member of the U.S. Marine Corps. He
further admitted that he was living at 1026 N. Beckley in
Dallas, Texas, under the name of O. H. LEE. OSWALD admitted
that he was present in the Texas Schoolbook Depository on
November 22, 1963, where he has been employed since October 15,
1963. OSWALD stated that as a laborer, he has access to
the entire building which has offices on the first and second

on ___11/22/63___ at ___Dallas, Texas___ / _____ File # ___DL 89-43-1707___

by Special Agent S ___JAMES P. HOSTY, JR. and___
___JAMES W. BOOKHOUT___/wvm _____ Date dictated ___11/23/63___

Agent Hosty's official report of the first post-assassination interview of Lee Harvey Oswald. Hosty was ordered out of the interview before he could pursue any of his most important questions because his FBI superiors became concerned that he would bring up information about which they had decided to deny any knowledge. (Document length: 2 pages) WARREN COMMISSION EXHIBIT NO. 832

floors and storage on the third and fourth, as well as the
fifth and sixth floors. OSWALD stated that he went to
lunch at approximately noon and he claimed he ate his lunch
on the first floor in the lunchroom; however he went to the
second floor where the Coca-Cola machine was located and
obtained a bottle of Coca-Cola for his lunch. OSWALD claimed
to be on the first floor when President JOHN F. KENNEDY
passed this building.

After hearing what had happened, he said that
because of all the confusion there would be no work performed that afternoon so he decided to go home. OSWALD
stated he then went home by bus and changed his clothes
and went to a movie. OSWALD admitted to carrying a pistol
with him to this movie stating he did this because he
felt like it, giving no other reason. OSWALD further
admitted attempting to fight the Dallas police officers
who arrested him in this movie theater when he received a
cut and a bump.

OSWALD frantically denied shooting Dallas police
officer TIPPETT or shooting President JOHN F. KENNEDY. The
interview was concluded at 4:05 p.m. when OSWALD was removed
for a lineup.

FD-302 (Rev. 3-3-59)

FEDERAL BUREAU OF INVESTIGATION

Date _____11/28/63_____

     Mrs. MARINA NIKOLAEVNA OSWALD was interviewed in the Russian language by SA LEON I. GOPADZE of the U. S. Secret Service, with SA MAX D. PHILLIPS of the U. S. Secret Service also present. SA GOPADZE introduced himself as Mr. LEE, an agent of the Government, and introduced the two interviewing FBI agents as agents of the Federal Bureau of Investigation.

     At the outset of the interview, before SA GOPADZE could advise MARINA OSWALD of her constitutional rights, she stated, "Do I have a right not to answer questions if I do not want to." MARINA OSWALD was advised she did not have to talk if she did not want to, that she had a right to an attorney, and anything she did say could be used against her.

     She was asked if she would mind answering questions that were to be asked. She replied that she did not wish to be asked anything, as anything she had to say she had said before and she had no further information.

     MARINA OSWALD was advised that there were many unanswered questions and would she care to be asked these questions. She replied that she was tired and worried about one of her children, who was slightly ill, and for this reason she did not care to be interviewed. She was told that her cooperation in this investigation was needed and she was asked whether she would consider an interview at a later date or on some other occasion. She indicated that she did not wish to be interviewed.

     MARINA OSWALD stated the Government knows all the facts and she has no further facts except what is known to the Government. MARINA OSWALD stated she did not have a friendly attitude toward the FBI because she felt the FBI had caused her husband to lose his job following his arrest in New Orleans for distributing pro-Castro literature and disturbing the peace.

     When asked if she intended to stay in the United States, MARINA OSWALD stated she would like to stay in the United States because of her children and to be near where her husband is buried. She then asked for assurance that she would be allowed to stay in the United States and she was advised that this was a matter coming under the jurisdiction of the Immigration and Naturalization

Commission Exhibit No. 1780

on __11/27/63__ at _____Arlington, Texas_____ File # ___DL 89-43___

          CHARLES T. BROWN, JR.,
by Special Agents and JAMES P. HOSTY, JR. / mac Date dictated ___11/28/63___

This document contains neither recommendations nor conclusions of the FBI. It is the property of the FBI and is loaned to your agency; it and its contents are not to be distributed outside your agency.

Agent Hosty's official report of the first post-assassination interview of Marina Oswald. It was difficult to get anything vital out of Marina because the INS had met with her minutes before to assure her that she would not be deported, leaving Hosty with no leverage or bargaining tools. (Document length: 3 pages) WARREN COMMISSION EXHIBIT No. 1780

2
DL 89-43

Service. She was advised that the Government needs her cooperation and this might help. MARINA OSWALD then stated if she was
not allowed to stay in the United States, then that was all right
also. When asked how she intended to live and support her
children, she stated she would find some type of work. She was
then advised that if she cooperated with the Government this
could be of some assistance to her.

MARINA OSWALD then stated she was tired of answering
questions. When told that the Government only wanted the facts,
she stated she had the same facts as everyone else and no other.
MARINA OSWALD was then asked if she ever had any conversations
with her husband about former President JOHN F. KENNEDY. MARINA
OSWALD stated "No." She was then asked if her husband, LEE
OSWALD, ever indicated in any way that he intended to kill former
President KENNEDY. She stated "No, I feel he did not do it
because he never spoke against President KENNEDY at any time."
When asked if he had ever said anything against Texas Governor
JOHN CONNALLY, she stated she could not recall any statements
that LEE OSWALD made against Texas Governor JOHN CONNALLY. When
asked if LEE OSWALD could have had a grudge against Texas Governor
CONNALLY, she stated she did not know. MARINA OSWALD then stated
"I swear before God that LEE OSWALD did not intend to kill President KENNEDY." When asked if she believed in God, MARINA OSWALD
stated she has believed in God since the death of her mother.
When asked if she was a Christian, she said "Yes." MARINA OSWALD
was then asked if she knew any of her husband's associates, and
she stated "No," that LEE OSWALD was a "loner" and was always by
himself. MARINA OSWALD also stated her husband never expressed
political views or opinions to her since he felt that women did
not belong in politics. When asked if LEE OSWALD had any friends
in Russia, she stated "No," as he was a "loner" in Russia also and
he was always reading Marxist books, such as "Das Kapital."
MARINA OSWALD stated that one time she became so exasperated
with LEE OSWALD she asked him "What are you trying to do, start
another revolution?" She stated that LEE OSWALD was strong-
willed and stubborn; he was hot-headed and had his own ideas
about everything. MARINA OSWALD was asked if she had ever seen
LEE OSWALD with a gun and she stated "No." When asked if she had
ever seen him go hunting, MARINA OSWALD stated there was no place
around Dallas or Fort Worth where he could hunt and he had no
transportation to go hunting and could not drive an automobile.

108

When asked if she would like to have another visit from the FBI , she stated that there is no reason for another visit. MARINA OSWALD stated that she was treated satisfactorily, however, she hoped she would not be bothered again, that the Government has all the facts and in her mind, due to what has been told her, she is satisfied that LEE OSWALD had killed President JOHN F. KENNEDY.

MARINA OSWALD was then asked if she would help furnish additional facts so that it might be possible to clear her husband, LEE OSWALD, if he had not killed the President. MARINA OSWALD stated if she knew any additional facts she would furnish them to clear up the case. She stated that "the Government knows more than I do".

The conversation was momentarily interrupted, at which time MARINA OSWALD snapped "Let's come to the business of this conversation". MARINA OSWALD then requested termination of the interview and it was discontinued immediately at this point.

109

Dear Sirs:

This is to inform you of recent events and my interviews with comrade Kostine in the Embassy of the Soviet Union, Mexico City, Mexico.

I was unable to remain in Mexico City indefinitely because of my Mexican visa restrictions which was for 15 days only. I could not apply for an extension unless I used my real name, so I returned to the U.S.

I and my wife Marina Nicholieva are now living in Dallas, Texas.

The FBI is not now interested in my activities in the progressive organization FPCC of which I was secretary in New Orleans, since I no longer live in that State.

The FBI has visited us here in Dallas on Nov. 1st. Agent of the FBI James P. Hosty warned me that if I attempted to engage in FPcc activities in Texas the FBI will again take an "interest" in me. Also, they "suggested" that my wife could "remain" in the U.S. under FBI "protection," that is, she could defect from the Soviet Union.

Of course I and my wife strongly protested

The rough draft of a letter, in Oswald's hand, that Oswald would later type up and send to the Soviet Embassy. In the letter Oswald mentions his interviews with "Comrade Kostine" and complains about Agent Hosty's November 1 meeting with Marina. (Document length: 2 pages) WARREN COMMISSION EXHIBIT No. 103

these tactics by the notorious F.B.I..

~~result. It was important that the Soviet Embassy~~ was unable to aid me in mexico city ~~so~~ I had not planned to contact the mexican city Embassy at all so of course they were unprepared for me. Had I been able to reach Havana as planned I ~~could have contacted~~ the Soviet Embassy there ~~for the completion of would have been able to they get the necessary documents its I required assist me.~~ would have had ~~the~~ time to assist me. but of course the ~~stupid~~ stupid cuban Consul was at fault here, I'm glad he has since been replaced by another.

Office of the Director

UNITED STATES DEPARTMENT OF JUSTICE

Federal Bureau of Investigation

Washington 25, D.C.

December 19, 1963

Mr. J. Gordon Shanklin
Federal Bureau of Investigation
Dallas, Texas

Dear Mr. Shanklin:

It is a pleasure to commend, through you, the personnel who contributed in such a splendid fashion to the investigation of the assassination of the President.

The devotion to duty, efficiency and competence everyone exhibited in carrying out his indivdual responsibilities were of the highest, caliber. The concerted efforts of those who took part were of material assistance in this involved and delicate investigation and I want you to convey my sincere appreciation to all.

Sincerely yours,

/s/   J. EDGAR HOOVER

1 - SAC, Dallas (Personal Attention)
Place a copy of this letter in files of personnel who participated in this matter but were not individually recognized.

1 - Personnel file of each employee on Special Assignment, Dallas, and each Dallas Div. employee who was not individually recognized.
JGS:mfr

Letter of December 19, 1963, from FBI director J. Edgar Hoover to Dallas SAC J. Gordon Shanklin, requesting that all personnel who worked with such devotion and duty on the Kennedy assassination be commended for their effort. FREEDOM OF INFORMATION/PRIVACY ACT

UNITED STATES DEPARTMENT OF JUSTICE

FEDERAL BUREAU OF INVESTIGATION

Dallas, Texas

'n Reply, Please Refer to
'ile No.

January 21, 1964

Mr. James P. Hosty, Jr.
Federal Bureau of Investigation
Dallas, Texas

Dear Jim:

    I desire to extend my personal appreciation to you for the splendid manner in which you conducted investigation in connection with the assassination of President Kennedy and related investigations.

    Your willingness to work long hours without relief and with complete disregard for your personal and family demands certainly reflected favorably upon you as an Agent of the FBI. You have a right to be proud of your many contributions in this involved and delicate investigation.

Sincerely,

J. GORDON SHANKLIN
Special Agent in Charge

Letter of personal appreciation of January 21, 1964, from Shanklin to Hosty on the splendid manner in which he conducted investigation in connection with the assassination of President Kennedy. FREEDOM OF INFORMATION/PRIVACY ACT

November 22, 1963

Captain W.P. Gannaway
Special Service Bureau

                    SUBJECT: Lee Harvey Oswald
                              605 Elsbeth Street

Sir:

On November 22, 1963, at approximately 2:50PM, the undersigned officer
met Special Agent James Hosty of the Federal Bureau of Investigation in
the basement of the City Hall.

At that time Special Agent Hosty related to this officer that the Subject
was a member of the Communist Party, and that he was residing in Dallas.

The Subject was arrested for the murder of Officer J.D. Tippit and is a
prime suspect in the assassination of President Kennedy.

The information regarding the Subject's affiliation with the Communist
Party is the first information this officer has received from the Federal
Bureau of Investigation regarding same.

Agent Hosty further stated that the Federal Bureau of Investigation was
aware of the Subject and that they had information that this Subject
was capable of committing the assassination of President Kennedy.

                              Respectfully submitted,

                              Jack Revill
                              Jack Revill, Lieutenant
                              Criminal Intelligence Section

Sworn to and subscribed before me, this the 7th day of April, 1964.

                              Frances Bock
                              FRANCES BOCK
                              Notary, Dallas County, Dallas, Texas

Sworn statement of Dallas police lieutenant Jack Revill, dated November 22,
1963, sworn to April 7, 1964. This memo is accurate until the incendiary last
paragraph. WARREN COMMISSION EXHIBIT NO. 709

FBI Knew Oswald Capable of Act, Reports Indicate

By HUGH AYNESWORTH

© The Dallas Morning News, 1964

A source close to the Warren Commission told The Dallas News Thursday that the commission has testimony from Dallas police that an FBI agent told them moments after the arrest and identification of Lee Harvey Oswald on Nov. 22, that "we knew he was capable of assassinating the president, but we didn't dream he would do it."

In a memorandum to superiors on Nov. 22, Lt. Jack Revill, head of the Dallas police criminal intelligence squad, reported that FBI special agent James (Joe) Hosty had acknowledged awareness of Oswald in the basement of the City Hall at 2:05 p.m. Nov. 22. His remark was made as five officers brought Oswald in from Oak Cliff, Revill reported.

LT. REVILL appeared before Warren Commission investigators here several weeks ago. Police Chief Jesse Curry testified before the commission in Washington Wednesday. Neither would comment on their appearance or their testimony.

Chief Curry was reported to have been questioned about the incident and was said to have given the commission a photostatic copy of Lt. Revill's 5-paragraph memo. He also was said to have given the commission the name of a second Dallas police officer who supported Revill's statement and filled in other parts of the conversation between Revill and Hosty.

The second officer, V. J. (Jackie) Bryan, a member of the criminal intelligence squad, also declined comment.

CHIEF CURRY had Lt. Revill's report in hand within hours of President Kennedy's death, even before all the facts and circumstances concerning Oswald were known.

Gordon Shanklin, special agent in charge of the Dallas FBI office, would make no comment.

The commission Thursday had not talked to agent Hosty, but The News' source said he anticipated that the agent would be called to testify.

CURRY WILL not show the report to reporters, nor will he comment on it or any other phase of the assassination.

"That's for the Warren Commission to talk about," the chief said.

Revill's memo is still in Chief Curry's possession.

In addition to mentioning that Hosty said the FBI knew Oswald was capable of such an act, the memo said Hosty told Revill other facts about the one-time Russia resident and admitted Marxist.

DALLAS POLICE officers watched several known extremists prior to the Kennedy visit and even sent representatives as far as 75 miles to interview others thought to be planning demonstrations.

Curry privately has told friends, "If we had known that a defector or a Communist was anywhere in this town, let alone on the parade route, we would have been sitting on his lap, you can bet on that." But he has refused public comment.

Dallas Morning News article of April 24, 1964, reporting, under the headline "FBI KNEW OSWALD CAPABLE OF ACTS, REPORTS INDICATE," Revill's testimony to the Warren Commission. WARREN COMMISSION EXHIBIT NO. 857A

AFFIDAVIT

I, JAMES P. HOSTY, JR., being duly sworn, depose as follows:

I am a Special Agent of the Federal Bureau of Investigation, U. S. Department of Justice, and have been so employed since January 21, 1952.

My attention has been called to an article appearing on the front page of the "Dallas Morning News," of April 24, 1964, captioned, "FBI KNEW OSWALD CAPABLE OF ACT, REPORTS INDICATE," written by HUGH AYNESWORTH, which reads in part as follows:

> "A source close to the Warren Commission told The Dallas News Thursday that the commission has testimony from Dallas police that an FBI agent told them moments after the arrest and identification of Lee Harvey Oswald on Nov. 22, that 'we knew he was capable of assassinating the president, but we didn't dream he would do it.'

> "In a memorandum to superiors on Nov. 22, Lt. Jack Revill, head of the Dallas police criminal intelligence squad, reported that FBI special agent James (Joe) Hosty had acknowledged awareness of Oswald in the basement of the City Hall at 2:05 p.m. Nov. 22. His remark was made as five officers brought Oswald in from Oak Cliff, Revill reported . . ."

> The article refers to "Lt. Revill's five-paragraph memo" concerning the above-mentioned incident and also stated

COMMISSION EXHIBIT 831—Continued

Agent Hosty's sworn statement of April 24, 1964, describing his memory of the meeting with Revill in the police garage the afternoon of November 22, 1963, and the conversation that followed. The Commission would ultimately ignore Revill's version. (Document length: 5 pages) WARREN COMMISSION EXHIBIT NO. 831.

that a second officer, V. J. (JACKIE) BRYAN, of the Dallas Police Department had "supported REVILL's statement and filled in other parts of the conversation between REVILL and HOSTY . . ."

The article continues that "in addition to mentioning that HOSTY said the FBI knew OSWALD was capable of such an act, the memo said HOSTY told REVILL other facts about the one-time Russia resident and admitted Marxist . . ."

On November 22, 1963, at approximately 3:00 PM, I arrived at the Dallas Police Department for the purpose of sitting in on an interview of LEE HARVEY OSWALD. When I arrived at the basement of the Dallas Police Department, I met Lieutenant JACK REVILL, whom I know to be the head of the Intelligence Unit of the Dallas Police Department. Lieutenant REVILL advised me that he "had a hot lead" on the assassination of President KENNEDY and that a man whose first name was LEE was the only employee of the Texas School Book Depository who had not been accounted for. I then told Lieutenant REVILL that LEE HARVEY OSWALD had already been arrested about one hour previously by the Dallas Police Department and was at that time in the office of Captain WILL FRITZ, Homicide Bureau, Dallas Police Department, being interrogated.

-2-

COMMISSION EXHIBIT 831—Continued

To my knowledge, this was the first time that
Lieutenant REVILL knew of OSWALD's arrest.

I further advised Lieutenant REVILL that OSWALD
had defected to Russia and had returned to this area in 1962,
and that OSWALD was employed at the Texas School Book Depository. I also advised Lieutenant REVILL that OSWALD was at
that time the main suspect in the assassination of President
KENNEDY.

The above constitutes the entire contents of my
conversation with Lieutenant REVILL which took place on the
stairway from the basement to the third floor at the Dallas
Police Department, during which time both Lieutenant REVILL
and myself were running up the stairs and not facing each
other. There were numerous people going up and down the
stairs at the time of my conversation with Lieutenant REVILL
and the noise level was very high, making it very difficult
to hear anything. Although I know Detective V. J. (JACKIE)
BRYAN, of the Dallas Police Department, by sight, I do not
recall seeing him on this occasion or ever having a conversation with Lieutenant REVILL in BRYAN's presence, or having a
conversation with Detective BRYAN.

-3-

COMMISSION EXHIBIT 831—Continued

I unequivocally deny ever having made a statement to Lieutenant REVILL or anyone else that the FBI knew OSWALD was capable of assassinating the President or that OSWALD possessed any potential for violence.

I specifically deny ever having made the statement as quoted in this article, "We knew he was capable of assassinating the President, but we didn't dream he would do it."

In fact, prior to the assassination of President JOHN FITZGERALD KENNEDY, I never had any information indicating potential violence on the part of LEE HARVEY OSWALD.

My conversation with Lieutenant REVILL on November 22, 1963, lasted not more than a minute and a half. Furthermore, I did not reach the Dallas Police Department until approximately 3:00 PM, November 22, which was after OSWALD had been brought to the Dallas Police Department, identified, and was in Captain WILL FRITZ's office. As stated above, my purpose in going to the Dallas Police Department was to sit in on an interview with LEE HARVEY OSWALD and I commenced this assignment at 3:15 PM, according to my wrist watch.

-4-

COMMISSION EXHIBIT 831—Continued

James P. Hosty, Jr.
JAMES P. HOSTY, JR.
Special Agent
Federal Bureau of Investigation

Sworn to and subscribed before me on this 2 day

of _Apr._, 1964.

Matt Harris
Notary Public
Dallas County, Texas

-5-

COMMISSION EXHIBIT 831—Continued

272

OFFICE OF THE DIRECTOR

UNITED STATES DEPARTMENT OF JUSTICE

FEDERAL BUREAU OF INVESTIGATION

WASHINGTON 25, D.C.

April 27, 1964

BY COURIER SERVICE

Honorable J. Lee Rankin
General Counsel
The President's Commission
200 Maryland Avenue, N. E.
Washington, D. C.

Dear Mr. Rankin:

The "Dallas Morning News," Dallas, Texas, had an article in its April 24, 1964, edition entitled "FBI Knew Oswald Capable of Act, Reports Indicate." The article, written by Hugh Aynesworth reported that "A source close to the Warren Commission told The Dallas News Thursday that the commission has testimony from Dallas police that an FBI agent told them moments after the arrest and identification of Lee Harvey Oswald on Nov. 22, that 'we knew he was capable of assassinating the president, but we didn't dream he would do it.'" A copy of the article in question is attached for the information of the Commission.

There is enclosed for the Commission an affidavit executed by Special Agent James P. Hosty, Jr., wherein Special Agent Hosty explains the purpose of his contact with the Dallas Police Department on November 22, 1963. Special Agent Hosty unequivocally denies ever having made a statement to Lieutenant Revill or anyone else that the FBI knew Oswald was capable of assassinating the President or that Oswald possessed any potential for violence. Special Agent Hosty specifically denies ever having made the statement as quoted in this article "We knew he was capable of assassinating the president, but we didn't dream he would do it." Special Agent Hosty points out that prior to the assassination of President John Fitzgerald Kennedy, he never had any information indicating potential violence on the part of Lee Harvey Oswald.

Sincerely yours,

J. Edgar Hoover

Enclosures - 2

Letter of April 27, 1964, from Hoover to J. Lee Rankin, General Counsel to the Commission, regarding the *Dallas Morning News* article of April 24, 1964. At this point, before the Commission had leveled its criticisms against the FBI, Hoover came out in complete support of Hosty. WARREN COMMISSION EXHIBIT NO. 831.

Mr. J. Gordon Shanklin
Special Agent in Charge
Federal Bureau of Investigation
U. S. Department of Justice
Room 200, Mercantile Continental Bldg.
Dallas, Texas

Dear Gordon:

      Having read in the Dallas Press over the
weekend the remarks attributed to Special Agent Hosty
by certain officials of the Dallas Police Department
concerning Oswald immediately following the latter's
arrest by the Dallas Police Department on the afternoon
of November 22, 1963, which allegedly were contained in
a memorandum from Lt. Jack Revill of the Dallas Police
Department to Chief Curry, I wanted to bring the following
information to your attention.

      On December 20, 1963 I had lunch with Chief
Curry at the Dallas Athletic Club in connection with some
Citizens Traffic Commission business. Following this
conversation, I told him that I simply could not understand what the basis was for his having remarked on
television the day following the assassination the fact
that the Bureau had not made known to him previously the
presence of Oswald in this area. I suggested to him that
he write a letter of apology to the Director, admitting
that this was a mistake in judgment on his part, that
perhaps he had jumped to erroneous conclusions on the
basis of incomplete information which had been relayed to
him during the height of the action on November 22nd, and
certainly that it had been my experience that where mistakes
in judgment had been made in the past, that the Director
would take cognizance of same and that by his future actions,
he could demonstrate to the Director and the Bureau his
desire to continue the fine relation which has existed
through the years.

105-82555—3814

ENCLOSURE

Letter from retired SAC William A. Murphy to SAC J. Gordon Shanklin regarding the authenticity of Revill's statement. Murphy's claim to have seen the letter
before the last paragraph was added offers the strongest evidence that Revill fal-
sified his testimony to shift the blame for Kennedy's death from the Dallas police
to the FBI. (Document length: 2 pages) FREEDOM OF INFORMATION/PRIVACY ACT

On a date early in January this year, I had occasion to be in the office of Deputy Chief Ray Lunday, Traffic Division, discussing the current plans for the year for the Citizens Traffic Commission. Chief Curry passed by and suggested when I was through with Chief Lunday to stop by in his office. I did so.

Chief Curry then recalled our previous conversation at the Dallas Athletic Club and said, I want to show you something that will explain the remarks that you inquired about that I had made on television. He then pulled from his desk a memorandum which I recalled to be on Police Department memorandum stationary, from Lt. Revill to either Captain Gannaway or to Chief Curry, which read in substance this.

Agent Hosty of the FBI informed me this afternoon that the FBI had interviewed Oswald, that he had been in the Marine Corps, but had been given a dishonorable discharge subsequent to his having gone over to Russia, where he married a Russian girl, later returning to the United States with her, and that she was residing with Mrs. Paine at an address in Irving, Texas. This entire memorandum consisted of approximately three or four brief paragraphs, and positively there was no information set forth in that memorandum indicating that Hosty had in any way represented that Oswald had any dangerous tendencies or that he was in any way considered capable of assassinating the President. There was no statement in the memorandum as to when or where Oswald had been interviewed. I had this memorandum in my own hands, read it carefully, and returned it to Chief Curry. Anyone who says that the original memorandum which Chief Curry made available to me contained the remarks now attributed to Agent Hosty is a liar. To me, information set forth in Revill's memorandum concerning his conversation with Hosty contained nothing more than would have been reasonable for any Agent working on security matters to have furnished at that time. Had I considered the remarks attributed to Hosty to be other than in exact propiety from the Bureau's standpoint, you may be assured I would have brought them to the Bureau's attention forthwith. The original memorandum which I reviewed was not a notarized document, but was simply an inter-department memorandum of the Dallas Police Department.

I resent with all the vehemence I possess this attempt to discredit Agent Hosty and the Bureau.

Sincerely,

WILLIAM A. MURPHY

275

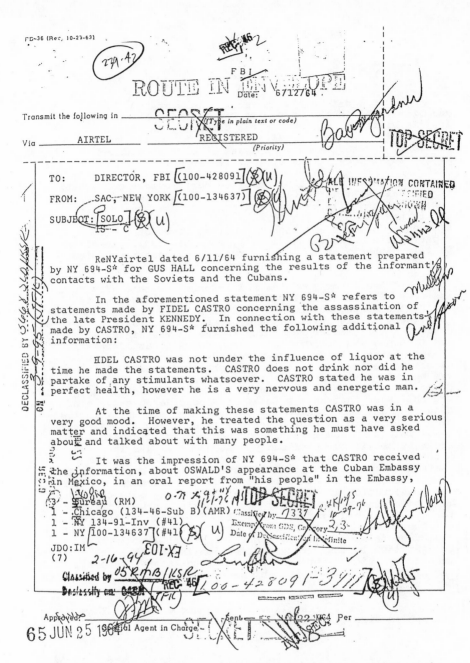

FD-36 (Rev. 10-29-63)

FBI

Date: 6712764

ROUTE IN ENVELOPE

Transmit the following in _____ SECRET _____ *(Type in plain text or code)*

Via _____ AIRTEL _____ REGISTERED
                                (Priority)

TOP SECRET

TO: DIRECTOR, FBI [(100-428091]

FROM: SAC, NEW YORK [(100-134637)]

SUBJECT: [SOLO]
         IS - C

ALL INFORMATION CONTAINED

        ReNYairtel dated 6/11/64 furnishing a statement prepared
by NY 694-S* for GUS HALL concerning the results of the informant's
contacts with the Soviets and the Cubans.

        In the aforementioned statement NY 694-S* refers to
statements made by FIDEL CASTRO concerning the assassination of
the late President KENNEDY. In connection with these statements
made by CASTRO, NY 694-S* furnished the following additional
information:

        FIDEL CASTRO was not under the influence of liquor at the
time he made the statements. CASTRO does not drink nor did he
partake of any stimulants whatsoever. CASTRO stated he was in
perfect health, however he is a very nervous and energetic man.

        At the time of making these statements CASTRO was in a
very good mood. However, he treated the question as a very serious
matter and indicated that this was something he must have asked
about and talked about with many people.

        It was the impression of NY 694-S* that CASTRO received
the information, about OSWALD'S appearance at the Cuban Embassy
in Mexico, in an oral report from "his people" in the Embassy,

3 - Bureau (RM)
1 - Chicago (134-46-Sub B)(AMR)
1 - NY 134-91-Inv (#41)
1 - NY [100-134637] (#41)

JDO:IM
(7)   2-16-94

TOP SECRET

Classified by
Declassify on

REC 46   100-428091-3911

Approved: _____ Sent _____ M _____ Per _____
            Special Agent in Charge

65 JUN 25 1964

Top secret memo to Hoover regarding Fidel Castro's statements about the
Kennedy assassination. This report, which includes Castro relating Oswald's
threat at the Cuban Embassy ("I'm going to kill that bastard. I'm going to kill
Kennedy."), is based on information gathered by SOLO source, historically one
of the FBI's most valuable and dependable informants. However, as each government investigation shied away from Cuban and Soviet issues, this report was
ignored or impugned as untrustworthy. (Document length: 3 pages) NATIONAL
ARCHIVES

because he, CASTRO, was told about it immediately. NY 694-S* does not know the identities of the individuals who told CASTRO. NY 694-S* advised that CASTRO said, "I was told this by my people in the Embassy -- exactly how he (OSWALD) stalked in and walked in and ran out. That in itself was a suspicious movement, because nobody comes to an Embassy for a visa (they go to a Consulate)." The Informant stated that the implication was that OSWALD came running in like a "mad man" demanding a visa and immediately the people in the Embassy suspected something wrong - why go to the Soviet Union through Cuba? An attempt is being made to involve Cuba in this conspiracy from the beginning.

CASTRO did not indicate, at any time, that he had read any books about the assassination but gave NY 694-S* the impression that he based his information upon his actual thinking and experience gained from knowledge of guns/and reports he received from his Embassy people. _Cuba_

The statements made by FIDEL/CASTRO concerning the assassination were accurate. Although CASTRO spoke to NY 694-S* in broken English, without benefit of translation, there is no question as to the accuracy of what he said for the informant indicated he had made notes at the time CASTRO was talking and he had scribbled down what he considered was important. CASTRO stated that when OSWALD was refused his visa at the Cuban Embassy in Mexico City, he acted like a real madman and started yelling and shouting and yelled on his way out, "I'm going to kill that bastard. I'm going to kill Kennedy." NY 694-S* is of the opinion that the Cuban Embassy people must have told OSWALD something to the effect that they were sorry that they did not let Americans into Cuba because the U.S. Government stopped Cuba from letting them in and that is when OSWALD shouted out the statement about killing President KENNEDY. _LEE HARVEY OSWALD_
TEXAS

NY 694-S* stated that he later discussed CASTRO'S statements with BEATRICE JOHNSON, the CPUSA representative in Cuba, and they decided they would never talk about this because it was dynamite. NY 694-S* is of the opinion that in making these statements concerning the assassination, CASTRO was neither engaging in dramatics nor oratory but was speaking on the basis of facts given to him by his Embassy personnel who dealt with OSWALD and apparently had made a full, detailed report to CASTRO after President KENNEDY was assassinated. NY 694-S* is of the opinion that CASTRO was trying to imply that the assassination was a deliberate and conscientious plot to involve Cuba as well as the Soviet Union because no one goes to the Soviet Union by way of Cuba, especially an American. NY 694-S* is of the opinion that CASTRO had nothing to do with the assassination and was concerned mainly with the question of the guilt of OSWALD and that this was a conspiracy not only of OSWALD but of two or three other people involved. The informant stated that CASTRO made no comment as to the fact that he was pleased that President KENNEDY was killed and showed no elation about the matter and discussed it in a very serious manner.

NY 694-S* advised that when CASTRO made the statement that OSWALD himself could not have done this job alone, and could not have fired the rifle three times in succession and hit the same target with that telescopic arrangement but needed the help of at least two other men, that when he made this statement he was basing it on theory as a result of these experiments that he conducted and not on any firsthand information in his possession.

NY 694-S* stated that at the meeting in which he had these discussions with CASTRO, the following persons were present:

FIDEL CASTRO
Dr. RENE VALLEJO, CASTRO'S interpreter
BEATRICE JOHNSON
NY 694-S* (Jack Childs)

NY 694-S* advised that he did not hear or obtain any other information concerning the assassination in Cuba or elsewhere.

NY 694-S* advised that he does not know why CASTRO conducted the experiments with the rifle but he received the impression that CASTRO conducted the experiments to prove to himself that it took more than one man to do it. NY 694-S* stated that CASTRO claims to be a sharpshooter and he prides himself on being the best, that CASTRO did not think it was possible for one man to fire three shots and hit a target under these conditions in the reported amount of time. NY 694-S* stated that conducting the tests was CASTRO'S own personal idea to prove to himself that it could not be done and that when CASTRO and his men could not do it CASTRO concluded OSWALD must have had help.

NY 694-S* advised that he does not know when or where CASTRO conducted these tests nor did CASTRO make any statements concerning the time and place.

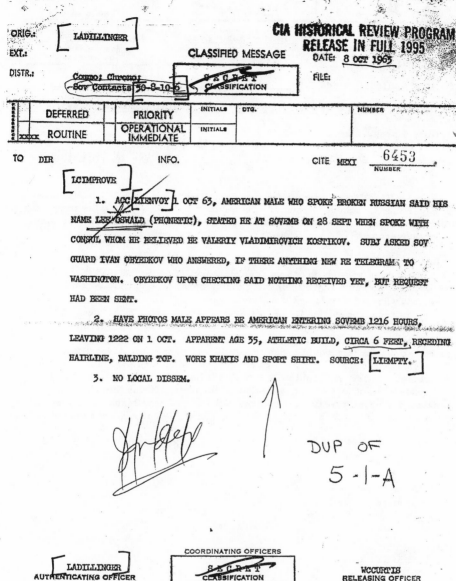

FORM 1364
11-57

(44)

ORIG.: LADILLINGER

EXT.:

CLASSIFIED MESSAGE

DISTR.: Comno; Chrono;
Sov Contacts 50-8-10-6

SECRET
CLASSIFICATION

FILE:

		INITIALS	DTG.		NUMBER
DEFERRED	PRIORITY				
xxxx ROUTINE	OPERATIONAL IMMEDIATE	INITIALS			

TO   DIR   INFO.   CITE MEXI   6453
                                              NUMBER

LCIMPROVE

1. ACC LIENVOY 1 OCT 63, AMERICAN MALE WHO SPOKE BROKEN RUSSIAN SAID HIS NAME LEE OSWALD (PHONETIC), STATED HE AT SOVEMB ON 28 SEPT WHEN SPOKE WITH CONSUL WHOM HE BELIEVED BE VALERIY VLADIMIROVICH KOSTIKOV. SUBJ ASKED SOV GUARD IVAN OBYEDKOV WHO ANSWERED, IF THERE ANYTHING NEW RE TELEGRAM TO WASHINGTON. OBYEDKOV UPON CHECKING SAID NOTHING RECEIVED YET, BUT REQUEST HAD BEEN SENT.

2. HAVE PHOTOS MALE APPEARS BE AMERICAN ENTERING SOVEMB 1216 HOURS, LEAVING 1222 ON 1 OCT. APPARENT AGE 35, ATHLETIC BUILD, CIRCA 6 FEET, RECEDING HAIRLINE, BALDING TOP. WORE KHAKIS AND SPORT SHIRT. SOURCE: LIEMPTY.

3. NO LOCAL DISSEM.

DUP OF
5-1-A

COORDINATING OFFICERS

LADILLINGER
AUTHENTICATING OFFICER

SECRET
CLASSIFICATION

OUTGOING

WCCURTIS
RELEASING OFFICER

CIA message of October 8, 1963, reporting that Oswald spoke with V. V. Kostikov (the "Comrade Kostine" Oswald mentioned in his letter to the Soviet Embassy) on September 28, 1963. V. V. Kostikov, ostensibly a vice consul at the Soviet Embassy, was actually a KGB agent involved with international sabotage, terrorism, and assassinations. The photos mentioned were not of Oswald. NATIONAL ARCHIVES

	CLASSIFICATION	PROCESSING ACTION.
	S-E-C-R-E-T	MARKED FOR INDEXING

TO
Chief, KURIOT   Attn: Photographic Branch   xx   NO INDEXING REQUIRED

INFO.
Chief, WH Division   Nov 12 8 59 AM '63   ONLY QUALIFIED DESK CAN JUDGE INDEXING

FROM
Chief of Station, Mexico City   MICROFILM

SUBJECT
AQUATIC/Use of the VLS-2 Trigger Device at the LIERODE Basehouse

ACTION REQUIRED · REFERENCES

Action: Paragraph 4.

Reference: HMMA-22307, para 5.c.

CIA HISTORICAL REVIEW PROGRAM RELEASE IN FULL 1995

1. The VLS-2 Trigger Device, installed at the LIERODE basehouse to cover the Consulate entrance, is performing well with little false triggering. The 500mm lens on the VLS-2 had to be replaced by the 6 inch lens for wider target coverage.

2. During the first two weeks of operation, the VLS-2 would trigger traffic entering and leaving the target entrance. Concerned with the consumption of film and the necessity of reloading the camera twice daily, L-22 devised a system whereby the VLS-2 would only photograph people leaving but not entering the target building. L-22's system works about 80 percent of the time, cutting film consumption considerably. L-22 had been focusing the VLS-2 on the white framed glass door so that when targets entered or departed this area the targets would cross this field and trigger the device. (See Enclosure A for the VLS-2 area of coverage). Since one side of the door was not closed and targets could walk into this office, the VLS-2 was focused on the shade area of this entrance instead of the door. It was found that since Mexicans generally wear dark colored clothing and have black hair, they can pass into the office without triggering the VLS-2. When a person leaves by

(continued)

Enclosures:
  A. Area Coverage
  B. Results of Testing
  C. Coverage

Distribution:
  2 - KURIOT, w/encls
  1 - WH, w/encls

CROSS REFERENCE TO	DISPATCH SYMBOL AND NUMBER	DATE
	HMMA-22433	7 Nov 1963
	CLASSIFICATION	HQS FILE NUMBER
	S-E-C-R-E-T	50-6-18

An internal CIA dispatch regarding the inadequacies of the surveillance camera stationed outside the Soviet Embassy in Mexico City. This equipment failed to capture Oswald on film at the Soviet Embassy because he entered and exited through a side door. (Document length: 2 pages) NATIONAL ARCHIVES

this entrance, the man's shirt or face will trigger the device photographing
a front or side view depending on how the subject leaves the entrance. This
system does not work when a person enters the building with light clothing.

3. L-22 used the K-100 with a 152mm lens for one day, turning in
10 fee of 16mm film. (See Enclosure B for the results of this testing.)
The Robot Star and the Telyt 400mm lens are now being used with the VLS-2
on this project. (See Enclosure C for this coverage.) The Robot Star
camera which was given to L-22 with the VLS-2 broke down after 4 days of
photographing. PARMUTH replaced this with another Robot. Five days
later the second camera failed to advance properly. In both cases the spring
would not advance the film for more than 15 exposures at a full winding. Both
cameras given to L-22 were 55 shot Robot Stars.

4. It is requested that a substitute camera be shipped to the Station
as soon as possible to replace the Robot Star camera on this project. The
camera should have a motor or sping to advance the film and should be
mounted on the Telyt 400mm lens and supplied with a proper focusing housing
if different from those that are used with the Telyt lens.

Willard C. CURTIS

ORIG : C. BUSTOS pm
UNIT : WH/3/Mexico   □ INDEX   S E C R E T
EXT : 5940   □ NO INDEX
DATE : 10 Oct 1963   □ FILE IN CS FILE NO.

12-62
ROUTING

1		4	
2		5	
3		6	

TO : SEE BELOW   CS COPY

O OCT 63 20   12z

FROM: XXXXXXXX CENTRAL INTELLIGENCE AGENCY

CONF: WH 8

SIG GEN
DEFERRED
R   ROUTINE

INFO : CI, CI/OFS, CI/SI, FI, SR 7, RF, VR
XX

TO   INFO   CITE DIR 74673

DEPARTMENT OF STATE
FEDERAL BUREAU OF INVESTIGATION
XXXXXXXXXXXXXXXXXXXXXXXXX
DEPARTMENT OF THE NAVY

SUBJECT: LEE HENRY OSWALD

CIA HISTORICAL REVIEW PROGRAM
RELEASE IN FULL 1995

1. ON 1 OCTOBER 1963 A RELIABLE AND SENSITIVE SOURCE
IN MEXICO REPORTED THAT AN AMERICAN MALE, WHO IDENTIFIED
HIMSELF AS LEE OSWALD, CONTACTED THE SOVIET EMBASSY IN
MEXICO CITY INQUIRING WHETHER THE EMBASSY HAD RECEIVED
ANY NEWS CONCERNING A TELEGRAM WHICH HAD BEEN SENT TO
WASHINGTON. THE AMERICAN WAS DESCRIBED AS APPROXIMATELY
35 YEARS OLD, WITH AN ATHLETIC BUILD, ABOUT SIX FEET TALL,
WITH A RECEDING HAIRLINE.

2. IT IS BELIEVED THAT OSWALD MAY BE IDENTICAL TO LEE
HENRY OSWALD, BORN ON 18 OCTOBER 1939 IN NEW ORLEANS, LOUISIANA,
A FORMER U.S. MARINE WHO DEFECTED TO THE SOVIET UNION IN
OCTOBER 1959 AND LATER MADE ARRANGEMENTS THROUGH THE UNITED
STATES EMBASSY IN MOSCOW TO RETURN TO THE UNITED STATES WITH
HIS RUSSIAN-BORN WIFE, MARINA NIKOLAEVNA PUSAKOVA, AND THEIR

201-289248
(CONTINUED)
10 Oct 63

Document Number 6-3

for FOIA Review on APR 1976   COORDINATING OFFICERS
RELEASING OFFICER   CS COPY

GROUP 1
Excluded from automatic
downgrading and
declassification

AUTHENTICATING
OFFICER.

S E C R E T

REPRODUCTION BY OTHER THAN THE ISSUING OFFICE IS PROHIBITED.   Copy No.

CIA memo of October 10, 1963, documenting the visits of "Lee Henry Oswald"
to the Soviet Embassy in Mexico City. (Document length: 2 pages) NATIONAL
ARCHIVES

ORIG :
UNIT :
EXT :
DATE :

☐ INDEX
☐ NO. INDEX
☐ FILE IN CS FILE NO.

SECRET

ROUTING

1		4	
2		5	
3		6	

TO :

FROM : DIRECTOR

CONF See Sanitized File
Number
For sterile copy of this document.

INFO :

201-289248

ABSTRACT ☒ INDEX

DATE 10 Oct 63

DEFERRED

ROUTINE

PAGE TWO

TO   INFO   CITE DIR

CHILD.

3.   THE INFORMATION IN PARAGRAPH ONE IS BEING DISSEMINATED

TO YOUR REPRESENTATIVES IN MEXICO CITY.   ANY FURTHER INFORMATION

RECEIVED ON THIS SUBJECT WILL BE FURNISHED YOU. THIS INFORMATION

IS BEING MADE AVAILABLE TO THE IMMIGRATION AND NATURALIZATION
SERVICE.   END OF MESSAGE

INFO BASED ON MEXI 6453 (IN 36017) 201-289248

J. Roman
J. ROMAN
CI/LIAISON
RELEASING OFFICER

CI/SIG/Egerter (in draft)
SR/CI/Roll (in draft)

COORDINATING OFFICERS

SECRET

L. N. GALLARY
C/WH/R
AUTHENTICATING
OFFICER

REPRODUCTION BY OTHER THAN THE ISSUING OFFIC PROHIB, Copy No.

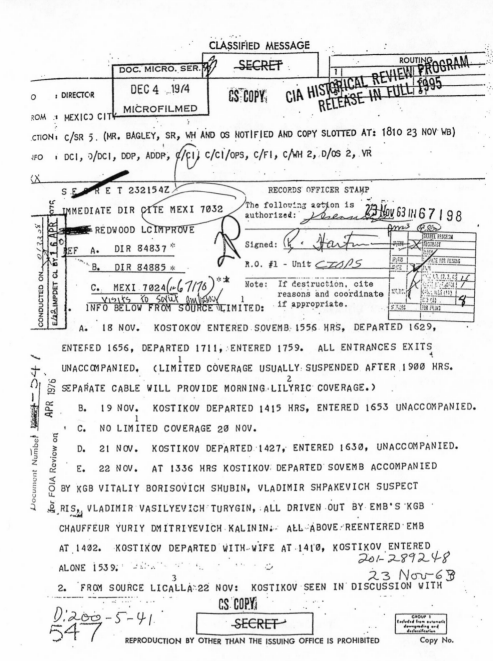

CLASSIFIED MESSAGE

DOC. MICRO. SER. ~~SECRET~~

DEC 4 1974   CS COPY   CIA HISTORICAL REVIEW PROGRAM
MICROFILMED   RELEASE IN FULL 1995

O   : DIRECTOR
ROM : MEXICO CITY

CTION: C/SR 5. (MR. BAGLEY, SR, WH AND OS NOTIFIED AND COPY SLOTTED AT: 1810 23 NOV WB)

IFO : DCI, D/DCI, DDP, ADDP, C/CI, C/CI/OPS, C/FI, C/WH 2, D/OS 2, VR

S E C R E T 232154Z

IMMEDIATE DIR CITE MEXI 7032

REDWOOD LCIMPROVE

REF A.   DIR 84837 *

     B.   DIR 84885 *

     C.   MEXI 7024 (+67176) **
          VISITS TO SOVIET EMBASSY

1. INFO BELOW FROM SOURCE LIMITED:

RECORDS OFFICER STAMP

The following action is authorized: 23 NOV 63 IN 67 198

Signed: R. Hartun

R.O. #1 - Unit CI/OPS

Note: If destruction, cite reasons and coordinate if appropriate.

A.   18 NOV.   KOSTOKOV ENTERED SOVEMB 1556 HRS, DEPARTED 1629,
ENTERED 1656, DEPARTED 1711, ENTERED 1759.   ALL ENTRANCES EXITS
UNACCOMPANIED. (LIMITED COVERAGE USUALLY SUSPENDED AFTER 1900 HRS.
SEPARATE CABLE WILL PROVIDE MORNING LILYRIC COVERAGE.)

B.   19 NOV.   KOSTIKOV DEPARTED 1415 HRS, ENTERED 1653 UNACCOMPANIED.

C.   NO LIMITED COVERAGE 20 NOV.

D.   21 NOV.   KOSTIKOV DEPARTED 1427, ENTERED 1630, UNACCOMPANIED.

E.   22 NOV.   AT 1336 HRS KOSTIKOV DEPARTED SOVEMB ACCOMPANIED
BY KGB VITALIY BORISOVICH SHUBIN, VLADIMIR SHPAKEVICH SUSPECT
RIS, VLADIMIR VASILYEVICH TURYGIN, ALL DRIVEN OUT BY EMB'S KGB
CHAUFFEUR YURIY DMITRIYEVICH KALININ.   ALL ABOVE REENTERED EMB
AT 1402. KOSTIKOV DEPARTED WITH WIFE AT 1410, KOSTIKOV ENTERED
ALONE 1539.   201-289248
                                               23 Nov 63
2.   FROM SOURCE LICALLA 22 NOV: KOSTIKOV SEEN IN DISCUSSION WITH

CS COPY

D:200-5-41
547

~~SECRET~~

REPRODUCTION BY OTHER THAN THE ISSUING OFFICE IS PROHIBITED   Copy No.

GROUP 1
Excluded from automatic downgrading and declassification

CIA message documenting the surveillance of Kostikov on the days leading up to and including November 22, 1963. The CIA considered Kostikov one of the most dangerous Soviet agents in the western hemisphere. (Document length: 2 pages) NATIONAL ARCHIVES

SECRET IN 67198 PAGE 2

SHUBIN AT 1005 HRS. SHORTLY AFTERWARDS WENT TO MAIN GATE AND
DEPARTED (APPARENTLY ALONE) AT 1016 HRS.

3. INFO BELOW FROM SOURCE LIMITED ON ALFERIEV.[1]

   A. 18 NOV. NO RECORD ALFERIEV APPEARANCE. (HOWEVER NOTE REF C
LILYRIC REPORTING[2] WHICH THAT HE ENTERED AT 0857 HRS, NOT SEEN TO
HAVE DEPARTED.)

   B. 19 NOV. ENTERED 1210 HRS ALONE, DEPARTED 1312 WITH KGB
ALEKSEY IVANOVICH GARMASHEV, THEY RETURNED 1352, DEPARTURE
NOT NOTED ENTERED 1533 -LONE.

   C. NO COVERAGE 20 NOV.

   D. 21 NOV. ALFERIEV DEPARTED 1202 ALONE, ENTERED 1346.

   E. 22 NOV. DEPARTED ALONE 1432, ENTERED ALONE 1436, DEPARETD
ALONE 1508, ENTERED ALONE 1517.

4. AWAITING LICALLA[3] 22 NOV COVERAGE ALFERIEV.

5. COMPOSITE REPORTING OF LIMITED[1] AND LICALLA[3] FOR 22 NOV DOES
NOT PRESENT ANY UNUSUAL SOVEMB PERSONNEL ACTIVITY.

S E C R E T

C/S COMMENT: *Requested information on Kostokov and Alferiev.
               **Forwarded information on Kostokov and Alferiev.

SECRET

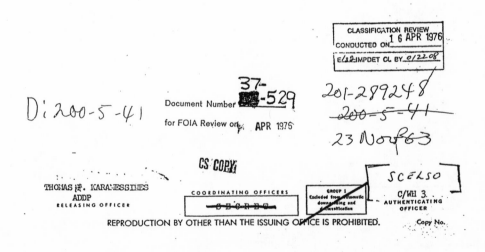

TO : MEXICO CITY

FROM: DIRECTOR

CONF: WH 8

INFO : DCI, D/DCI, DDP, ADDP, CI, CI/OPS, FI, SR 7, SAS 8, OS 2, VR

XXX

TO   FLASH MEXI   INFO   CITE DIR   84916

1. ARREST OF SILIVA DURAN IS EXTREMELY SERIOUS MATTER WHICH COULD PREJUDICE [ODYOKE] FREEDOM OF ACTION ON ENTIRE QUESTION OF [PBRUMEN] RESPONSIBILITY. WITH FULL REGARD FOR MEXICAN INTERESTS, REQUEST YOU ENSURE THAT HER ARREST IS KEPT ABSOLUTELY SECRET, THAT NO INFORMATION FROM HER IS PUBLISHED OR LEAKED, THAT ALL SUCH INFO IS CABLED TO US, AND THAT FACT OF HER ARREST AND HER STATEMENTS ARE NOT SPREAD TO LEFTIST OR DISLOYAL CIRCLES IN THE MEXICAN GOVERNMENT.

2. WE ARE TRYING TO GET MORE INFO ON OSWALD FROM [ODENVY] AND WILL ADVISE DIRECT OR THROUGH [ODENVY] MEXI.

END OF MESSAGE

CLASSIFICATION REVIEW
CONDUCTED ON 1 6 APR 1976
E/12 IMPDET CL BY 012208

D: 200-5-41

Document Number 37-529
for FOIA Review on APR 1976

201-289248
200-5-41
23 Nov 63

CS COPY

THOMAS H. KARAMESSINES
ADDP
RELEASING OFFICER

COORDINATING OFFICERS

SECRET

GROUP 1
Excluded from automatic downgrading and declassification

SCELSO
C/WH 3
AUTHENTICATING OFFICER

REPRODUCTION BY OTHER THAN THE ISSUING OFFICE IS PROHIBITED.   Copy No.

CIA message of November 23, 1963, reporting the arrest of Silvia Duran, the receptionist at the Cuban Consulate, by Mexican authorities. The report emphasizes the importance that her arrest be kept absolutely secret because she was arrested on the basis of secret CIA audio surveillance of the Cuban Embassy. NATIONAL ARCHIVES

SECRET

MEMORANDUM FOR: Chief, CI
                   Chief, SR Division
                   Chief, CI/SI

FROM: [SCELSO]

SUBJECT: Inaccuracies and Errors in Draft of [GFFLOOR] Report

1. I gathered from our conference in Mr. Helms' office on Tuesday 24 December 1963 that inaccuracies and policy errors were found in my draft of an initial report on the [GFFLOOR] case. This does not surprise me. Mr. Helms noted certain items he wanted changed or omitted and also instructed me to recheck the accuracy of the entire paper.

2. It would help me greatly if your would let me know what inaccuracies you found, if any, and what other changes you would recommend. As I understand it, my initial recommendation that the draft be considered nothing more than a working paper for those who prepare the final report was accepted by those present, and that the entire subject matter will be reworked anyway, incorporating the new material received from the FBI and elsewhere.

3. If you find it convenient, please mark your comments on your copy and lend it back to me. I will return it to you.

[SCELSO]
Chief, WH/3

SECRET

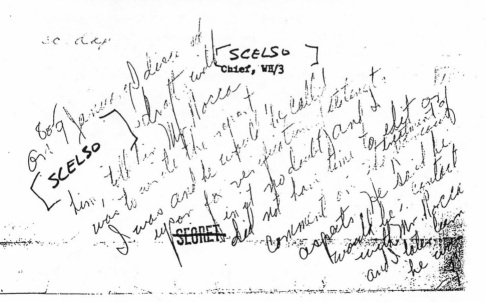

CIA memo regarding the director's mandated changes and omissions in CIA reports on [GFFLOOR], the Oswald case, to outside agencies. NATIONAL ARCHIVES

XAAZ 35907

SUMMARY of Relevant Information on Lee Harvey OSWALD at 0700
24 November 1963.

1. Our first information on OSWALD came from [a technical operation] in Mexico City and was cabled in on 9 October 1963. It revealed that on 1 October 1963 Lee OSWALD had been in touch there with Soviet Consul Valery KOSTIKOV about a telegram which the Soviet Embassy was supposed to send on him to the Soviet Embassy in Washington. The data showed that OSWALD had also been at the Soviet Embassy on 28 September. Traces showed OSWALD was a former U. S. defector to the USSR and on 10 October CIA Headquarters notified the FBI, State and the Navy (OSWALD had been a Marine). Our Mexico Station was told to pass its information on OSWALD to the Mexico City offices of the FBI, the Immigration and Naturalization Service and the Embassy. Since our Agency is not supposed to investigate U. S. citizens abroad without special request, we did nothing further on the case.

2. After the assassination of President Kennedy on 22 November, Mexico Station, which immediately recalled its earlier report on OSWALD and cabled us about it, began researching all its files and records for reports which might relate to him. It turned up pictures of a man believed to be OSWALD entering the Soviet and Cuban Embassies on various days in October, including 1 October, but when some of these pictures were sent to the FBI in Dallas they proved to be someone other

Document Number 130-592
for FOIA Review on APR 1976

CLASSIFICATION REVIEW
CONDUCTED ON 24 MAY 1976
E____IMPDET CL BY 012208

RECORD COPY

26 nov 63.
201-289248

CIA summary report of November 24, 1963. While this report mentions Kostikov by name, it does not indicate anything about his true identity. (Document length: 4 pages) NATIONAL ARCHIVES

288

than OSWALD. Mexico Station has, to date, found no pictures of OSWALD entering the Soviet or Cuban Embassy.

3. The search did reveal more data from technical operations, however. This information, which comes in in great masses, had not been previously associated with OSWALD because his name is not actually mentioned in it, but the subject matter shows it is about him, and our expert monitor says the voice is identical with the voice of 1 October known to be OSWALD's.

4. This further technical information covers a round-robin of telephone calls and visits which OSWALD made to the Soviet and Cuban Embassies in Mexico City between 27 September and 3 October 1963. This has been supplemented by reports on his travel in and out of Mexico obtained by the U. S. Consulate in the border town of Nuevo Laredo from Mexican Immigration Service records.

5. In brief, all this information shows that Lee Harvey OSWALD entered Mexico (apparently by car) at Nuevo Laredo on 26 September 1963, claiming he was a photographer, living in New Orleans and bound for Mexico City. On 27 September he was in Mexico City phoning the Soviet Embassy to ask for a visa so he could go to Odessa, USSR. On 28 September, he was at the Cuban Embassy, and Silvia DURAN, a Mexican Employee of the Cuban Embassy, telephoned the Soviet Embassy about his problem. It seems that OSWALD (whose name is not mentioned) wanted a Cuban transit visa so he could go to Cuba and wait there for a Soviet

visa which would permit him and his wife to go on to the Soviet
Union. Silvia DURAN asked assurance that the Russians would grant
him the visa. A while later a Soviet official calls Silvia DURAN
back and explains that the visa applicant had been dealing with
the Soviet Consulate in Washington about the same matter and that
they could not be sure that he would ever get the Soviet visa.
The Soviet official added that the applicant had a letter showing
he belonged to an organization in favor of Cuba. Silvia DURAN and
the Soviet official agree to table the matter.

6. On 28 September 1963, OSWALD again visits the Cuban Embassy
and talks to Silvia DURAN about the same matter, and she phones the
Soviet Embassy. OSWALD also talks to a Soviet official on her phone
and says he will come to the Soviet Embassy and give him what is
apparently a forwarding address where he can be reached. There is
some hint this address may be in Cuba.

7. On 1 October, OSWALD has his phone conversation with Soviet
Consul KOSTIKOV about his visa, and on the same day, OSWALD phones
the Soviet Military Attache about the same matter. The Military Attache
gives him the number of the Consul. Finally, on 3 October, OSWALD
phoned the Military Attache again and tried to talk about a visa, but
the Military Attache again referred him to the Consul and give him
the right phone number.

8. That same day, 3 October 1963, OSWALD drove back into the
United States at the Nuevo Laredo-Laredo, Texas crossing point. He

had travelled on a Mexican Tourist Card in lieu of passport.

9. On 23 November 1963, Mexican authorities,[

]and who had noticed the name of
Lee OSWALD in it, arrested Silvia DURAN and her husband and interrogated
them. She confirmed the information given above, saying that Lee
OSWALD had professed to be a Communist and an admirer of Castro. She
and her husband are being held incommunicado and their arrest will
not be made known, for the time being.

10. Observation of the Soviet and Cuban Embassies in Mexico
and of their principal intelligence officers, including KOSTIKOV,
since the assassination of President Kennedy, by[both technical and]
physical surveillance, shows nothing unusual.

11. Mexican President Lopez Mateos is aware of this case[

.] He will doubtless support any
further police action which is necessary.

~~SECRET~~

27 November 1963

MEMORANDUM TO: Mr. Clark D. Anderson, Legal Attache

FROM : Winston M. Scott

SUBJECT : Lee Harvey OSWALD with alias

1. Reference is made to our conversation of 26 November 1963 concerning the above-named Subject.

2. Attached are photostatic copies of transcripts of all the conversations from technical operations of this office which are possibly pertinent in this case. They include:

   a. A telephone call to the Soviet Embassy made at 1037 hours on 27 September 1963 by a man outside (Hombre Fuera - "HF" to an Hombre Dentro - "HD"). The man outside said he needed "unas visas" to go to Odessa.

   b. A telephone call to the Soviet Embassy made at 1605 hours on 27 September 1963 by Silvia DURAN of the Cuban Embassy saying there was an American citizen at the Cuban Embassy requesting a Cuban visa in transit to the USSR. She was asked to leave her telephone number (11-28-47).

   c. A telephone call to the Cuban Embassy made at 1626 hours on 27 September 1963 by an unidentified man in the Soviet Embassy asking for Silvia DURAN. They discuss the visa application for the "American" who with his Russian wife wanted to go via Cuba to the USSR. The Soviet says he has had no reply from Washington, etc.

   d. A telephone call to the Soviet Embassy made at 1151 hours on 28 September 1963 by Silvia DURAN of the Cuban Embassy who puts on an unidentified norteamerican man who tells the Soviet that he was just at their Embassy and wants to give them his address. The Soviet tells him to return to the Embassy with the address.

#6973

~~SECRET~~ DUP OF
192-625

CIA memo of November 27, 1963, from Winston M. Scott, CIA Station Chief, Mexico City, to Mr. Clark D. Anderson, legal attaché, concerning information from seven telephone taps. The memo reports Oswald's contacts with the Soviet and Cuban embassies, then requests that the information not be shared with anyone outside the CIA to protect the secrecy of the CIA's audio surveillance. (Document length: 2 pages) NATIONAL ARCHIVES

e. A telephone call to the Soviet Military Attache at 1031 hours on 1 October 1963 by an unidentified man speaking broken Russian who asked about a telegram which they were to send to Washington. Unidentified man said he was at the Soviet Embassy "last Saturday". Soviet told him to call 15-60-55.

f. A telephone call to the Soviet Embassy at 1035 hours on 1 October 1963 by the same man who called previously (28 September 63) and spoke broken Russian. He said his name was Lee OSWALD and wanted to know if they had heard anything. Soviet said no.

g. A telephone call to the Soviet Embassy (Military Attache) at 1539 hours on 3 October 1963 by an unidentified man requesting a visa. (By the context of other conversations by OSWALD and the fact that this caller spoke in broken Spanish and English rather than Russian which he used previously, it is probable that this caller is not OSWALD.)

3. It is requested that, due to the sensitivity of the source of the attached, this information be strictly controlled and not be disseminated to anyone outside the organization to which the addressee belongs without prior and complete clearance and authorization of my organization.

Attachments (7)

Distribution:
Orig w/atts: Addressee
        1: 50 [ ] CIA File # ·
        (: P-8593)

11 December 1963

MEMORANDUM FOR: Deputy Director (Plans)

SUBJECT: Plans for the [GPFLOOR] Investigation

Not sent. Questions put orally to Mr. Helms. 11 Nov. 63

1. Here are several recommendations for the further handling of the [GPFLOOR] case:

a. It looks like the FBI report may even be released to the public. This would compromise our [telephone tap] operations in Mexico, because the Soviets would see that the FBI had advance information on the reason for Oswald's visit to the Soviet Embassy. Our clearing the FBI report was not for its publication, but only for its passage to the Warren Commission. I recommend that you call this to the attention of the Director and ask that page 39 and part of page 40 be revised before release.

Mr. Helms phoned Mr. Angleton this morning.

b. CIA should get four copies of the report right away, to be used as follows:

    1. DCI and DDCI
    2. DDP and then CI Staff
    3. SR
    4. WH Branch 3

ask C/CI to handle

Copying an FBI original would be costly and the exhibits, which are vitally important, could hardly be read in some cases. I think the DCI should ask for these copies.

c. SR should assign someone to concentrate on processing, tracing, and analyzing the information on Oswald's activities in the Soviet Union. This person could work under me, or under the CI Staff, as you choose.

OK

d. If you wish we can write up for the Warren Commission a summary of all the information we have produced on the case to date, [with verbatim transcripts of the telephone calls as]

Should already be doing this.

RECORD COPY

Document Number 377-731

for FOIA Review on MAY 1976

11 DEC 63

CIA message of December 11, 1963 regarding what information should be released to the public and to the Warren Commission. (Document length: 2 pages) NATIONAL ARCHIVES

-2-

attachments. I can do this myself, but I will need a permanent assistant. I will nominate one as soon as I find someone suitable.

e. I am presuming that you want me to stay with this project. If I do, I will have to ask relief from my present job as Chief, WH/3. I cannot handle [GPFLOOR] and at the same time run my Branch which has [about 45 people in headquarters and well over 100 in seven Central American countries.]

2. If you will just indicate your decisions on this page, I will take those actions which are in my province.

O.K., love.

$$\boxed{\begin{array}{c} SCELSO \\ C/WH/3 \end{array}}$$

We Discover Lee OSWALD in Mexico City

CIA did produce one very significant piece of information on Lee OSWALD before he shot President Kennedy. On 1 October 1963, [our Mexico City Station intercepted] a telephone call Lee OSWALD made from someplace in Mexico City to the Soviet Embassy there, using his own name. Speaking broken Russian and using his true name, OSWALD was talking to the Embassy guard, OBYEDKOV, who often answers the phone. OSWALD said he had visited the Embassy the previous Saturday (28 September 1963) and spoken to a consul whose name he had forgotten, and who had promised to send a telegram for him to Washington. He wanted to know if there were "anything new." The guard said if the consul was dark it was (Valeriy Vladmirovich) KOSTIKOV. The guard checked with someone else and said that the message had gone out but no answer had been received. He then hung up.

This piece of information was produced from [

] It

CIA summary report of December 13, 1963. Unlike the earlier summary, this more complete report indicates a "particularly sinister aspect of Oswald's dealings with the Soviets in Mexico City" due to his meeting with Kostikov. Agent Hosty never received the information in this report regarding Kostikov's role in the KGB. (Document length: 22 pages) NATIONAL ARCHIVES is highly secret [

] which are transcribed and reviewed by our

small staff in Mexico City. By 9 October, the OSWALD telephone conversa-

tion of 1 October had been [transcribed and a summary of it] cabled to

Washington. The name Lee OSWALD meant nothing special to our Mexico

City Station, but in their report they did judge him to be an American

male.

The cabled report was received in Washington on 9 October and checked

in our files, where it was immediately noted that the Lee OSWALD phoning

the Soviet Embassy in Mexico City was probably the Lee OSWALD who had

defected to the Soviet Union in 1959 and returned to the USA in 1962. On

10 October 1963, the day after the report from Mexico City, CIA Headquarters

sent out a cabled report about Lee OSWALD's phone call to the Soviet

Embassy; the report went to the FBI, the Department of State (because

OSWALD was a US citizen), and to the Navy Department (because he was a

former Marine.) The cabled report to these agencies highlighted the liklihood that the Lee OSWALD mentioned was probably the former defector.

A copy of this same cable was delivered by hand to the Immigration and

Naturalization Service, with which we have no cable link. The same day

a long cable went out to Mexico City informing our Station of the back-

ground of defector Lee OSWALD and asking for more information. Our Station

was instructed to pass its information on the phone call to the Mexico

City offices of the FBI, the Embassy, the Naval Attache, and the Immigra-

tion and Naturalization Service. This was done.

In its original report of 9 October, Mexico City had said it had a

photograph of an apparent American male leaving the Soviet Embassy on

1 October 1963, the day OSWALD phone there. [A very sensitive operation

in Mexico City provides us with secretly taken photographs of many but not

all visitors to the Soviet Embassy there, taken with telephoto lenses.]

Accordingly, we cabled the Navy Department on 24 October 1963 asking for

a photograph of Lee OSWALD from his Marine Corps days so we could compare

photos. We had not received this photograph by 22 November 1963, but in

any event, it turned out that the man photographed outside the Soviet

Embassy was not OSWALD anyway. As chance would have it, none of our

several photo observation points in Mexico City had ever taken an identi-

fiable picture of Lee OSWALD.

Our Mexico City Station very often produces information like this

on US citizens contacting Soviet bloc embassies in Mexico City. Frequently

the information we get is extremely incriminating, and on one or two

occasions we have even been able to apprehend and return to the USA

American military personnel who are attempting to defect. In all such

cases, our Headquarters desk requests and obtains the special permission of

the Deputy Director for Plans to pass the derogatory information on a US

citizen to other government agencies. Derogatory information on Americans

is not treated routinely; in each case the DDP or his Assistant personally

scrutinize the information, make sure it is credible, and decide whether and

to whom it will be passed. Only in absolute emergencies is the Mexico City

Station authorized to pass such information directly to the FBI office in

the U.S. Embassy.

At this writing (13 December 1963) we do not know what action the FBI

SECRET

and other agencies may have taken based on our report. We surmise that the

FBI may have made local checks through Mexican authorities to see if

Lee OSWALD was actually in Mexico City on 1 October. Indeed, later in-

vestigation has confirmed all the details of his trip, where he stayed,

and what he did. To avoid crossing lines with the FBI, our Mexico Station

undertook no local investigation of its own. As we now know, OSWALD left

Mexico on 3 October and was no longer there when our report was put out.

22 November 1963

When word of the shooting of President Kennedy reached the offices

of our operating divisions and staffs on the afternoon of Friday 22 Novem-

ber 1963, transistor radios were turned on everywhere to follow the

tragedy. When the name of Lee OSWALD was heard, the effect was electric.

A phone message from the FBI came at about the same time, naming OSWALD as the possible assassin and asking for traces. The message was passed

on at once by the Chief CI, Mr. Angleton, to Mr. Birch O'Neal of his

Special Investigations Unit. [Mrs. Betty Egeter] of this Unit immediately

recognized the name of Lee OSWALD and went for his file. At the same

time, [Mrs. Bustos] of the Mexico Desk, who had written our first report on

OSWALD on 10 October recognized the name from radio reports and went

after the same file. [Mr. Reichhardt,] Mexico Desk Chief, who was home on

leave, heard the news and phoned in a reminder that we had something on

OSWALD. While we were preparing a cable to Mexico City asking them for

more information on OSWALD, Mexico City itself heard OSWALD's name on the

Voice of America broadcast and cabled to us a reminder of the information

the Station had sent in on him.

For the next week, a dozen people in the Agency were continuously

engaged in handling incoming messages on the case, writing reports to be

cabled out, tracing the names mentioned, and researching files. Within a

week, 27 cabled reports had gone out to the White House, the State Depart-

ment, and the FBI. Many cables of guidance and inquiry had been sent to

our overseas stations, and many pieces of information on OSWALD and his
wife had been received back. The Mexico City Station researched [its
telephone taps] very thoroughly and came up with several more conversations
probably involving OSWALD, but not actually mentioning this name; these
connected him also to the Cuban Consulate in Mexico City. Several Mexicans
were arrested and questioned about his activities, giving a good picture
of what he was really up to. Many conferences were held with the FBI
liaison officer who asked us for certain actions and passed us information
from the FBI investigation. On the minus side, a host of fabricators,
some anonymous, bombarded overseas embassies with spurious tips on the case,
most of which we investigated. All of these are soon discredited, but they
are still coming in.

During this phase of our work, we served primarily in support of the
FBI, which was entrusted by the President with the major responsibility for
the investigation. The FBI was too busy to supply us with much of its
own information, but answers were given to specific questions we posed to
assist our investigation. The Department of State did photograph its entire

file on OSWALD and pass them to us, and the FBI gave us a copy of the

Soviet Consular file on OSWALD which had been publicly given by the Soviet

Ambassador to the Secretary of State. On Friday 6 December 1963, Deputy

Attorney General Katzenbach invited us to review the FBI's comprehensive

report on the case to make sure our sources were not jeopardized and that

our information was correctly quoted. We found the report highly

interesting and no threat to our security, as long as it was read only

by the authorized investigative bodies.

After the first few days, the CIA investigation of the case was

handled at Headquarters by a small staff usually charged with investigation

and analysis of the most important security cases, and by a few officers

and analysts of our Western Hemisphere Division.

Reports From Mexico

As soon as our Mexico City Station realized that Lee OSWALD was the

prime suspect, it began re-screening all [the written telephone transcripts]

in its files covering the Soviet Embassy for the pertinent period. [The

actual tapes were also reviewed, but many of them had been erased after the normal two weeks wait.] Several calls believed to involve OSWALD were

discovered and their contents cabled to Washington, where they were

disseminated to the White House, the State Department, the Federal

Bureau of Investigation.

OSWALD's name was not actually mentioned in these additional calls,

but similarity of speech and various plain points of content link them

to him. These calls are summarized below in chronological order.

They cover the period from 27 September 1963 to 3 October 1963, the whole

span of OSWALD's visit to Mexico City as later learned from travel records.

27 September - A man phones the Soviet Military Attache and

says he needs a visa to go to Odessa. Man answering says he should call

15-60-55 and ask for the Consul. Caller asks for the address, and it is

given to him. (There is no special reason for linking this call to OSWALD.)

27 September, 4:05 PM - The Cuban Consulate phoned the Soviet

Consulate. Silvia Duran, Mexican national clerk of the Cuban Consulate

talked to a Soviet official, saying that a male American citizen was at the

Cuban Consulate asking for a transit visa to pass through Cuba on his way to the Soviet Union. She wants to know to whom he talked in the Soviet

Consulate and who told him he would have no problem about it. If a Soviet

visa is assured, the Cuban Consulate can grant him a transit visa and

simply notify Cuban immigration authorities. The Soviet first asks her

to wait, and then she has to explain the whole thing over again to another

Soviet official, who takes her telephone number and promises to call her

back. Silvia DURAN concludes this call by telling the Soviet she herself

has moved and gives her new address for the Soviet Embassy bulletin. He

asks her to phone (Sergey Semenovich) KUKHARENKO (Second Secretary who puts

out the Bulletin) to give him the new address and he asks who the Cuban

Cultural Attache is. Silvia DURAN gives the Attache's name as Teresa

PROENZA and adds her telephone number.

27 September, 4:26 PM - A Soviet official calls Silvia DURAN

back and tells her that the "American" had been to see the Soviet's and

shown them a letter from the Soviet Consulate in Washington indicating that

he had been waiting for visas for himself and his wife to go to the Soviet

Union for a long time, but that no answer had come from Washington, adding that the wait was sometimes four or five months. The "American" had

shown the Soviets a letter showing he was a member of an organization in

favor of Cuba and had claimed that the Cubans could not give him a visa

without a Russian visa. Silvia DURAN rejoins that they have the same

problem; the "American" is still at the Consulate; they cannot give him a

transit visa unless he is assured of a Soviet visa, even though he just

wants to go to Cuba to wait there for his Soviet visa to be granted. He

does not know anyone in Cuba. They end the conversation on this note.

Silvia DURAN says that she will note this on his "card," and the Soviet

concludes by saying, "Besides he is not known." He excuses himself for the

inconvenience he has caused and Silvia DURAN says it is all right.

28 September - Silvia DURAN calls the Soviet Embassy from the

Cuban Consulate. She says that she has the American with her again. The

Soviet answering asks her to wait. When another Soviet takes up the phone,

Silvia puts the American on. The American tries to talk Russian to the

Soviet who answers in English. The American asks him to speak Russian. The

American says that he had been in the Soviet Embassy and spoken with the

Consul, and that they had taken his address. The Soviet replies that he knows that. The American then says, somewhat enigmatically: "I did not know it then. I went to the Cuban Embassy to ask them for my address because they have it." The Soviet invites him to stop by again and give them the address, and the American agrees to do so. (In this conversation, the American was speaking hardly recognizable Russian.) ·

As far as our records show, OSWALD did not phone the Soviet or Cuban Embassies again until Tuesday 1 October 1963. The intervening days were a Sunday and a Monday. The contents of his later calls seem to show he did not contact the Soviets on those days.

1 October, 10:31 AM - A man calls the Soviet Military Attache in broken Russian and says he had been at their place the previous Saturday (28 September) and talked to their Consul. They had said they would send a telegram to Washington, and he wanted to know if there were anything new. The Soviets ask him to call another phone number and gives him 15-60-55, saying to ask for a Consul.

1 October 10:45 AM - (This is the phone call in which OSWALD

307

used his true name and which was therefore cabled to Washington on 9

October 1963.) Lee OSWALD called the Soviet Embassy and announced his

own name, saying he had visited them the previous Saturday and spoken

with a Consul. They had said they would send a telegram to Washington,

and he wanted to know if there were anything new. He did not remember

the name of the Consul. The Soviet, who was Embassy guard OBYEDKOV

replied: "KOSTIKOV; he is dark." OSWALD replied: "Yes, my name is

OSWALD." The Soviet excused himself for a minute and then said they

hadn't received anything yet. OSWALD asked if they hadn't done anything

and the guard replied they had sent a request but that nothing had been

received as yet." OSWALD started to say: "And what...", but the Soviet

hung up.

    3 October 1963 - A man speaking broken Spanish at first and then

English phoned the Soviet Military Attache and asked about a visa. The

Atteche's office referred him to the consulate, giving the number 15-60-55.

The caller wrote it down. The attache official shrugged off another question about whether the caller could get a visa, and the conversation

ended. (There is no special reason to tie this in with OSWALD, who is now

known to have re-entered the US at Laredo the same day.)

the information on Lee OSWALD also came to the attention of

President LOPEZ Mateos after 22 November. The next day, 23 November, he

called it to the attention of our Chief of Station, who was already

working feverishly on the case. Similarly, the Mexicans noticed the

involvement of Cuban Consular employee Silvia DURAN, a Mexican national.

Our Station suggested that she be arrested and interrogated about OSWALD.

The Mexican authorities had the same idea and she and her husband were

arrested on 23 November 1963, in the midst of a party at their home. All

the guests were soon released but Silvia and her husband were questioned

and released on 25 November 1963.

Silvia's husband, Horacio DURAN Navarro, an industrial designer,

said under police interrogation that when OSWALD was named as the assassin of President Kennedy, his wife had recognized the name and recalled she had waited on OSWALD when he came to apply for a Cuban transit visa; he remembered she had said she dealt with the Soviet Consulate as well to find out whether he had a Soviet visa. Horacio DURAN recalled his wife had said OSWALD became angry and she had to call out the Cuban Consul, Eusebio AZCUE, to quiet him.

Silvia DURAN told the same story. She was a leftist sympathizer with Cuba and had worked for the Mexican-Cuban Institute of Cultural Relations. She recalled OSWALD well, described him accurately, related how he had wanted a Cuban visa but could not get one without the assurance of a Soviet visa, and remembered his tiff with the Consul. She admitted she had phoned the Soviet Embassy about him.

The sum total of the statements of Silvia DURAN and her husband was to confirm that OSWALD was in Mexico to get a Cuban visa so he could wait in Cuba for his Soviet visa. The Soviet Consular file passed to the State Department in Washington by the Soviet Embassy confirms a long exchange between first, Mrs. Marina OSWALD, and later her husband, and the Soviet

Consulate in Washington about their requests for permission to return to the Soviet Union. OSWALD was still writing to the Soviets in Washington about this as late as 9 November 1963.

Silvia DURAN was arrested again on 27 November and held until 29 November. She told essentially the same story over again.

Well-placed sources [within the Cuban Embassy] in Mexico City stated that when Silvia DURAN was released from police arrest the first time on 25 November, she was quite pleased with herself. She told her colleagues the same story set out above, adding only that the Mexican police had threatened to extradite her to the United States to confront Lee Harvey OSWALD. The reaction within the Cuban Embassy to the news of President Kennedy's death was sombre. To date, there is no credible information in CIA files which would appear to link Lee OSWALD with the Cuban government or the Cuban intelligence service.

The whole question of whether Lee OSWALD had any secret connection with the Soviets or Cubans in Mexico cannot yet be answered, but certain parts of the evidence indicate to the contrary. Silvia DURAN and the

Soviet Consular officials spoke of him as a man with "no friends in Cuba" on the one hand, and as a man not "known" in the Soviet Embassy, on the other. The very openness of his visits and the phone calls speak against any secret role. His trip to Mexico was not itself a secret act; he traveled under his real name or a close variant of it, lived openly in Mexican hotels, and corresponded with the Soviets through the open mails about it when he got back to the US. His trip to Mexico was apparently made necessary because it was the nearest Cuban diplomatic installation where he could apply for a visa.

A perplexing aspect of OSWALD's trafficking with the Cubans and Soviets in Mexico City is his assertion in his call of 28 September that he did not know his address when he was at the Soviet Consulate and came to the Cuban Consulate because they had it. It is hard to explain just what he meant, but it should be remembered that he was talking in Russian, a language he could not manage, and that when he came to Mexico he was in the process of moving from New Orleans to Texas. He may not have memorized his new address in Texas, whatever it was, and may not have been able to ley hands on it when he was in the Soviet Consulate that day. Perhaps

he had earlier given the address to Silvia DURAN and wanted to look it

up on her card.

A particularly sinister aspect of OSWALD's dealings with the Soviets

in Mexico City arises from the liklihood that he met with Soviet Consul

Valeriy Vladimirovich KOSTIKOV. In his 1 October phone call to the

Soviet Embassy, the guard OBYEDKOV suggests that the Consul OSWALD had

talked to was KOSTIKOV if he was dark. OSWALD seems to agree with this,

but the identification is very casual. In his 9 November letter to the

Soviet Consulate in Washington, OSWALD gives the name of the man he dealt

with as "KOSTIN," but there is no person of that exact name in the Soviet

Embassy in Mexico City. KOSTIKOV is accredited as a Consular Attache and

does actually do a lot of consular work; but he is believed to be a

Soviet KGB officer, and it is believed that he works for Department 13 of

the KGB, the Department charged with sabotage and assassinations. The

suspicion that KOSTIKOV is a KGB officer arose from his work habits, and

his association with other KGB officers. It was hardened when it was found that he handled a Soviet agent who was trained to do sabotage work and that he turned this agent over to another KGB officer who is definitely known to work for the 13th Department. It is generally true in KGB work that sabotage agents are handled only by 13th Department officers.

Embassy guard Ivan Ivanovich OBYEDKOV is himself believed to be a KGB man from previous assignments as a bodyguard and surveillant. But unless some direct evidence of Soviet complicity is discovered, it is most likely that OSWALD's dealing with KGB men OBYEDKOV and KOSTIKOV was nothing more than a grim coincidence, a coincidence due in part to the Soviet habit of placing intelligence men in the Embassies in positions where they receive a large portion of the visitors and phone calls. All of the five consular officers in the Soviet Embassy are known or suspected intelligence officers. Certainly if OSWALD had been a Soviet agent in training for an assassination assignment or even for sabotage work, the Soviets would have stopped him from making open visits and phone calls to the Soviet Embassy in Mexico after he tried it a couple of times. Our experience in Mexico, studying the Soviet intelligence service at close range, indicates that they do make some mistakes and are sometimes insecure in their methods, but that they do not persist in such glaring errors.

Some insight on the Cuban attitude toward the arrest of Silvia DURAN and the involvement of the Cuban Consulate in the OSWALD case can be gained from two [intercepted phone] calls made between Cuban President Osvaldo DORTICOS and Cuban Ambassador to Mexico Joaquin HERNANDEZ Armas on 26 November 1963, the day after Silvia DURAN was released from her first arrest. At 09:40 AM that morning, President DORTICOS phoned the Ambassador from Havana and asked him several questions about a report which the Ambassador had sent in on the arrest of Silvia DURAN and the Lee OSWALD case. The whole conversation is consistent with the theory that OSWALD merely wanted a visa. The Ambassador did mention the altercation which OSWALD had with Consul AZCUE, and he says that Mexican police bruised Silvia DURAN's arms a little shaking her to impress her with the importance of their questions. They had asked her if she had been intimate with OSWALD and she had denied it. President DORTICOS twice asked Ambassador

HERNANDEZ whether the Mexican police had asked Silvia DURAN questions

about "money," and the President apparently wanted to know whether the

Mexicans thought the Cubans had paid OSWALD money. HERNANDEZ insisted

the Mexicans had not offered Silvia DURAN money, and DORTICOS gave

up trying to put across his point. President DORTICOS instructed

HERNANDEZ to keep on questioning Silvia DURAN and to phone him back.

At 7:39 PM that evening Ambassador HERNANDEZ did call President

DORTICOS back, saying he had questioned "that person" again and she has

nothing new to add. President DORTICOS returns to the issue of whether

"they had threatened her so that she would make a statement that the

Consulate had given money to the man""that American." But Ambassador

HERNANDEZ persists in misunderstanding DORTICOS, answers in the negative,

and says: "Absolutely nothing was given to her." DORTICOS seems to give

up, and the conversation dies out after a few more general remarks.

We do not know for sure what made President DORTICOS press for inform

tion about Cuban money passed to OSWALD, but rumors were current in Mexico

and even, we understand, in the USA, that OSWALD had returned from Mexico

City with about $5,000. Perhaps DORTICOS was trying to learn whether

the Mexican police believed that the Cubans had financed OSWALD. In any

event, the Cuban Government sent the Mexicans a stiff note of protest

over the arrest and detention of Silvia DURAN, but the Mexicans

rejected the note.

[S'CELSO]

ORIG :

UNIT : WH 3 ☐ INDEX

EXT : 5613 ☐ NO INDEX

DATE : 20 DECEMBER 1963 ☐ FILE IN CS FILE NO.

TO : MEXICO CITY

FROM: DIRECTOR

CONF: C/WH 2

INFO : DCI, D/DCI, DDP, C/CI, C/CI/SI, VR

20 Dec 63 18 13z

SIG CEN

DEFERRED

R ROUTINE

The ... us action is au... ...: *Keremity*

Signed: G. Hartman

TO MEXI INFO R.O... ... CIOPS CITE DIR 90466

[GPFLOOR]

REF MEXI 7115 (IN 69636) *

Note: If ... ... cite reasons and coordinate if appropriate.

1. OUR PRESENT PLAN IN PASSING INFO TO WARREN COMMISSION IS TO ELIMINATE MENTION OF [TELEPHONE TAPS,] IN ORDER PROTECT [YOUR] CONTINUING OPS. WILL RELY INSTEAD ON STATEMENTS OF SILVIA DURAN AND ON CONTENTS OF SOVIET CONSULAR FILE WHICH SOVIETS GAVE [ODACID] HERE. FILE SHOWS BOTH OSWALD AND WIFE WERE DICKERING WITH SOVIETS IN WASHINGTON BY MAIL TO GET PERMISSION TO RETURN TO RUSSIA.

2. EXACT DETAILED INFO FROM [LICRYP75] ON JUST WHAT SILVIA DURAN AND OTHER OFFICIALS SAID ABOUT OSWALD'S VISITS AND HIS DEALINGS WOULD BE VALUABLE AND USABLE CORROBORATIVE EVIDENCE. REQUEST YOU REQUESTION THEM CAREFULLY ON THESE POINTS, ATTEMPTING GET AS MUCH AUTHENTIC DATA AS POSSIBLE, WITHOUT MIXING IN WHAT THEY KNOW FROM NEWSPAPERS. PLS CABLE SUMMARIES AND POUCH DETAILED STATEMENTS.

CLASSIFICATION REVIEW 25 MAY 1976

CONDUCTED ON _____

END OF MESSAGE ____ JMPDET CL BY 012208

C/S Comment:*Re interrogation of Silvia Duran.

DOC. MICRO. SER.

DEC 4 1974

MICROFILMED

[SCELSO]

by authority of RICHARD HELMS DDP

RELEASING OFFICER D 200-5-41

201-289248

Document Number 420-75

for FOIA Review on MAY 1976

COORDINATING OFFICERS

GROUP 1 Excluded from automatic downgrading and declassification

AUTHENTICATING OFFICER

Copy No.

REPRODUCTION BY OTHER THAN THE ISSUING OFFICE IS PROHIBITED.

201-289248

CIA message of December 20, 1963, indicating that all mention of phone taps will be eliminated from information passed to the Warren Commission. NATIONAL ARCHIVES

Index

#32465057